MW01675970

The Book of Knots and Ropework

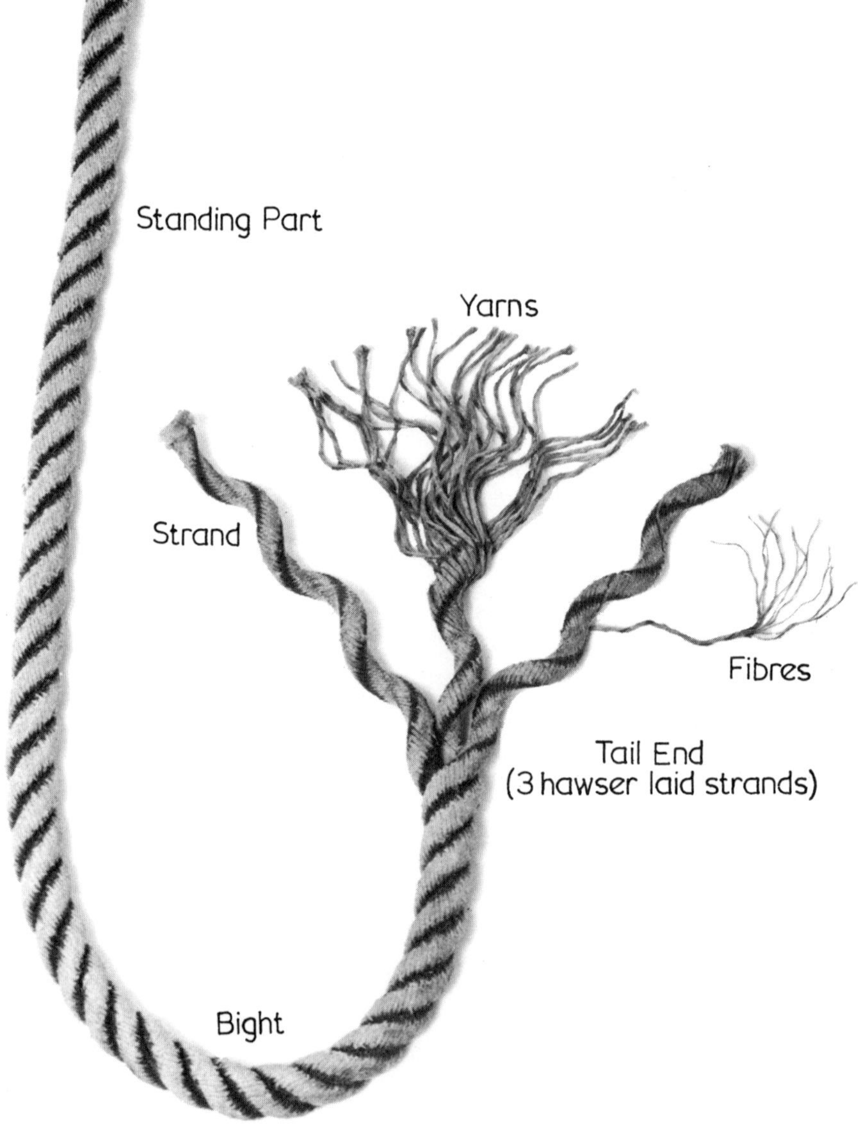
Standing Part
Yarns
Strand
Fibres
Tail End
(3 hawser laid strands)
Bight

The Book of Knots and Ropework

(Practical and Decorative)

Eric C. Fry

Photographs by Peter Wilson

CROWN PUBLISHERS, INC.
NEW YORK

Copyright © 1977, 1978, 1981 by Eric Fry and Peter Wilson
All rights reserved. No part of this book may be reproduced or transmitted in any form or by any means, electronic or mechanical, including photocopying, recording, or by any information storage and retrieval system, without permission in writing from the publisher.
First American edition published 1982 by Crown Publishers, Inc., One Park Avenue, New York, New York 10016, and simultaneously in Canada by General Publishing Company Limited
Manufactured in the United States of America

Originally published in Great Britain in 1977 as *The Shell Book of Knots and Ropework* and in 1978 as *The Shell Book of Practical and Decorative Ropework* by David & Charles (Publishers) Limited.

ISBN: 0-517-54885-2 (cloth)
0-517-54886-0 (paper)
10 9 8 7 6 5 4 3 2 1

First American Edition

Contents

PART TWO

Decorative Knots

Plaits

Sennits

Mats

Other knots and two toggles

Introduction

We are naturally gratified that the success of our two books of *Knots and Ropework* and *Practical and Decorative Ropework* has been such that this combined volume is called for. A few basic knots were necessarily duplicated in the separate books and these duplications have of course been removed. Otherwise text and photographs are unchanged. Unlike boat design, there have been no sensational developments in ropework but presentation can be improved and our style seems to be popular.

Part One comprises the basic knots and splices with a few of the decorative type thrown in for good measure. Part Two is devoted principally to the decorative work practised by the old sailing-ship seamen whose craftsmanship approached art. Certainly it is on the level of macramé. Much of it is indeed macramé.

The difficulty of teaching knotting without the pupil viewing the work 'backwards' or the tutor becoming a contortionist is obvious and many books have been produced illustrating the art with sketches, diagrams and written instructions which can be equally confusing.

This book invites the pupil to learn from that which he sees, regarding the hands as his, or her, own as the case may be.

In fact there are very few *true* knots, only four according to some schools of thought, the great majority of so called knots being either bends or hitches. Nevertheless all are formed from a series of bights and tucks in association with the all-important twisting of the rope to maintain the lay and ensure no unwanted turns in unexpected places.

'To go against the grain' is essentially a carpenters' expression, subsequently associated with human nature. So it is with rope. Although rope does not have a grain, it most certainly has its equivalent in its *lay*, which if mishandled will become more cantankerous than any grain – timber or human. Some understanding of this *lay* – this *life* which is born into every rope, during its manufacture in the rope-walk is necessary.

With the exception of braided, or plaited rope, all ropes consist of *fibres, yarns* and *strands.* During manufacture, *fibres* are twisted to form *yarns, yarns* twisted to form *strands;* and *strands* twisted to form the finished rope, the whole operation being carried out simultaneously and progressively, under tension. It is therefore in the nature of the rope to permit itself to be further twisted in the direction in which it was made, but to rebel against being twisted in the opposite direction, ie against its lay.

Anyone attempting to coil a right-hand laid rope left-handed will soon discover this, whereas, when not only coiled 'with the lay' but also with an additional twist for every turn of the coil the rope will be most obedient, and almost coil itself.

Similarly, when tying a knot it is sometimes necessary to deliberately put a turn into the rope, or more often take out an unwanted turn. The bowline (Knot 15) is an ideal example of this and if the rope is not twisted as shown, an unsightly turn will be found in the finished bight. When working with unlaid strands, as in splicing, it is obvious that each strand must be twisted as it is drawn tight, to maintain the lay and there are occasions when the rope is deliberately forced against its lay to advantage as in the 'eye splice in the middle of a rope' (Knot 36).

Different ropes, dependent on whether they are hard or soft and pliable, will react in varying degrees and it is only with practice that it becomes possible to 'get the feel' of any rope.

The majority of rope in common use, whether it be of vegetable or man-made fibre is the three-strand, right-hand, hawser-laid rope, which is used throughout Part One of the book.

Some knowledge of the terms employed is also necessary and the frontispiece plate, apart from showing the construction of the rope, also indicates the *standing part*, the *bight* and the *tail* or *tail end*.

Whippings, the use of sail twine (or similar) to secure a rope's end from fraying are not shown in detail; suffice to say that there are three main types, *Common, West Country* and *Sailmakers'* (or *palm and needle*).

A whipping should always be applied to the individual strands when working with an unlaid end of rope, but as this is a temporary measure, a few turns of sail twine finished in a reef knot is all that is needed. The application of a lighted match will effectively seal the ends of any man-made fibre and wire will not unstrand if cut with an oxy-acetylene torch instead of with a hammer and chisel.

Other types of rope comprise the four-strand shroud-laid rope with a central core also laid right-handed and the nine-strand cable-laid, the latter being three complete three-strand, hawser-laid ropes, laid up together left-handed, thus forming a nine-strand rope. The comparatively new braided (or plaited) rope is being increasingly used, particularly by the yachting fraternity.

No matter how utilitarian a knot or piece of ropework may be, by long maritime tradition it has to be seen to be good as well as being efficient. Hence the familiar Turk's head that enhances the appearance of a tiller *and* gives the helmsman a firmer grip. There has, though, never been any question of decoration for its own sake because, whether it was an elaborate working knot or plaited cordage, each had its purpose and place in the overall scheme from tack knot and highly ornate sea-chest handles to tiddly mat.

The majority of the knots in Part Two are of the 'tiddly' kind. *Tit-ley* was the original word but, by the early 1900s, 'tiddly' had become the accepted seafaring expression for practically anything and everything which was 'fancy', 'out of the ordinary' or, by dictionary definition, 'simple perfection'. Whatever interpretation was given and in whatever context the really old-time sailorman used the original word may be left to the imagination but his son's best going-ashore clothes became his 'tiddly gear', he was said to look 'tiddly' when so dressed and even the pride of the Royal Navy, the *Royal Sovereign,* became the *Tiddly Quid.* (For the benefit of younger readers, a 'quid' was a colloquial term for a sovereign which was twenty shillings in old currency.)

As before, each knot is illustrated step by step including photographs of the hands manipulating the rope, thus the reader should have no difficulty in following any sequence.

Four individual strands have been used, even for knots which can be and very often are made on the three strands of an unlaid rope. To avoid repetition such knots and/or plaits are indicated throughout with an asterisk. Others, such as the tack knot, which would be made only on stranded rope, are shown accordingly.

In case the whole may appear awesome, two things may be said. Firstly, an understanding of Knots 7, 53 and 55 is all that is needed to complete the bell toggle (Knot 94). Secondly, however complicated any piece may appear to be it is in fact only a multiplicity of simple twists (turns) and bends (bights) locked into position. The star knot is an ideal example as it looks difficult, yet there are only six basic movements, repeated on each of as many strands as are employed.

As far as usage is concerned one does not have to be a seaman or yacht owner to appreciate the application of 'tiddly' ropework, even in the home. Try covering a queer-shaped bottle to make a standard lamp, for instance. Naturally it has more applications, certainly too numerous to specify, aboard even the smallest of boats. The onus must be left to the imagination of the owner, but to say the least, any metal handle provides a more secure and warmer grip if covered, particularly if it is a question of hanging on to it hour after hour in heavy weather, whilst hand grips on shrouds, rails etc can be very useful—so why not make them 'tiddly'?

PART ONE

1 Overhand or Thumb Knot Half-Hitch, Round Turn and Two Half-Hitches

The overhand or thumb knot (Figs 1 and 2) is not particularly useful in itself, other than for tying up parcels or a most un-seamanlike stopper knot.
The slightest re-arrangement however (Fig 3) gives it the appearance of a *half-hitch*, the basis of many other knots.
Fig 4, the *round turn*, followed by Figs 5 to 8 completes the *round turn and two half-hitches*, an accepted method of making any rope's end fast.

1

2

3

4

5

6

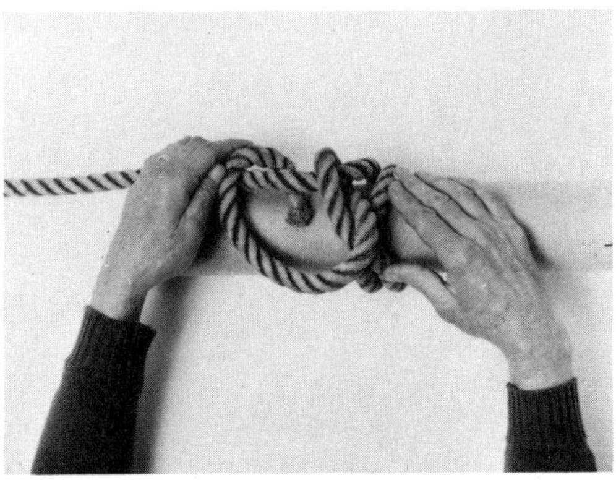
7

8

2
Double Thumb Knot

A decorative, but not particularly stable method of joining two ropes of equal size. It would mainly be used on small cordage, fishing tackle and the like.

1

2

3

4

5

6

3
Figure of Eight

When deliberately arranged as in Fig 4, it forms a quick, non-decorative and somewhat un-seamanlike stopper knot.
More generally, it was used, in series, at given centres throughout the length of the lifelines, hanging from the wire connecting the heads of the lifeboat davits to the waterline.

1

2

3

4

4
Continuous Figures of Eight

Figures of eight knots are made at given centres, usually about three feet apart, for the full length of the lifelines, which hang from the lifeboat davits to the waterline, obviously to facilitate climbing down.
The job of forming each knot separately and hauling through, perhaps sixty feet or more of standing part, each time may well be imagined and the illustrations show the method of forming this series of knots in one movement.
The distance between each knot is governed by the length of the lower bights shown in Fig 4. For the purpose of photography, only three emerging knots are shown, but the principle holds good and any number of knots may be made, dependent on the length of the rope.
See Knot 3 for the formation of the initial figure of eight knot.

1

2

3

4

5

6

7

8

5
Reef Knot

By far the most well known of knots, it is useful to finish off two ends, but should not be used to join two ropes, if such ropes are to be subjected to strain, as it will undoubtedly jam solid.
It is invariably associated with the useless granny knot (a reef knot 'gone wrong' which will never hold).
The hallmark of the reef knot is the standing part and the tail of both ends laying together as they emerge from opposite sides of the knot. Best remembered by the mnemonic 'left over right, right over left', or vice versa.

1

2

3

4

6 Carrick Bend

There are two methods of forming the Carrick bend and the first,. Figs 1 to 3, is in many ways similar to the reef knot, even to the extent that a minor error will result in a granny knot. It is a useful knot for joining two ends, particularly of large ropes and will not jam.

The tails should be seized to their respective standing parts and, although the knot has been shown flat for photographic clarity, the two bights will take up positions at right angles to each other, when under load.

Figs 4 to 6 show the alternative Carrick bend, which being a 'flat' knot by its nature, will not take up the right-angular position, and is used as the basis for the Carrick mat, when it is doubled and followed around as many times as required.

It is also the basis for the decorative *diamond knot* shown in Knot 7.

1

2

3

4

5

6

7 Diamond Knot

This is a purely decorative knot and would be used to form the eye of a lanyard or perhaps the commencement of a bell rope.
It is a natural progression from the second type of Carrick bend, made in the centre of a line with a small bight, which eventually forms the eye.
The two ends are 'followed around' and brought up through the centre of the original Carrick bend, after which the knot is worked towards the eye and all parts are drawn tight. See also Knot 54.

1

2

3

4

5

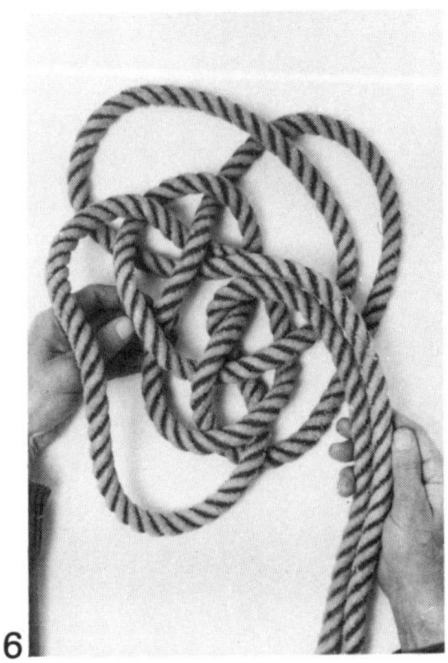
6

7

8

9

8 Sheet Bend, Double Sheet Bend

The most commonly accepted knot for joining two ropes together and probably the best, particularly if the ropes are of different sizes, when the larger rope provides the bight and the smaller, the *bends* or turns.

The only difference between the sheet bend and the double sheet bend is that two turns are taken around the bight of the main rope for the latter, whilst the former has only one turn. Figs 1 to 5 illustrate the sheet bend and 6 to 8 the double sheet bend.

This knot is even more efficient if both ropes are of the same size.

1

2

3

4

5

6

7

8

9
Binder Turn

One of the lesser known knots and a variation of the sheet bend, it is used for the same purpose and the same rule applies for ropes of different sizes.

The fact that both tails emerge on the same side and lay together with the one standing part, makes it suitable for working close up to a block, or even for passing over a large sheave when hauled in the one direction, ie, with the lay of the tails.

1

2

3

4

5

10
Tom Fool's Knot

Not particularly useful in itself, a trick knot, as the name implies, it does form the basis for other, more practical knots (Knots 11 and 12).

It is undoubtedly the best knot to illustrate the essential hands/rope relationship. It should be tied with one continuous, sweeping movement of the hands, meeting and parting, thus emphasising the understanding of 'the lay', use of the fingertips, and the sensitivity of the hands necessary to all successful knotting.

1

2

3

4

5

6

11 Man Harness from Fool's Knot

The fool's knot (Knot 10) with two half-hitches, combine to form the harness, sometimes known as a *chair knot*, suitable for lowering a casualty over a ship's side or down the face of a building.

The fool's knot is made at the centre of a rope which must be at least twice as long as the descent with the bights adjusted so that one is twice the size of the other; their sizes also being governed by the size of the casualty, eg a child or an adult.

For photographic purposes the bights have been formed in miniature and would be considerably larger than illustrated, even for a child.

A half-hitch is turned and cast on from both ends to complete the harness, which is then arranged on the casualty with the smaller bight around the chest and under the armpits, the larger bight under the thighs, and the knot itself in front of the casualty, just above chest level. One half of the rope is retained for lowering and the other end thrown down to an assistant. The casualty is lowered in a sitting position with the weight of the body taken on the thighs. The assistant below hauls off with his standing part, keeping the casualty clear of the ship's side.

1

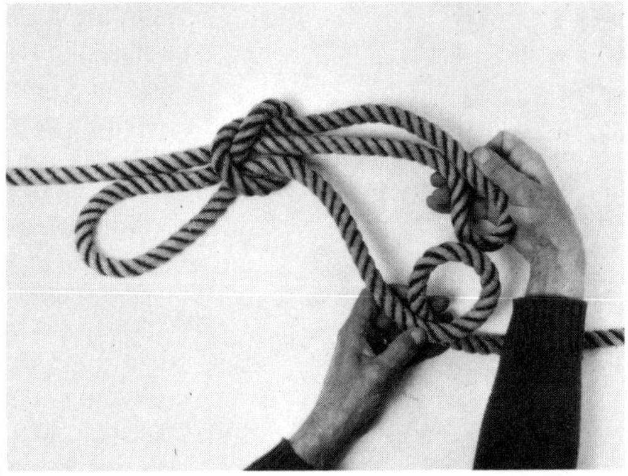
2

3

4

5

6

12 Sheep Shank from Fool's Knot, Pinned Sheep Shank

There are several ways of making a *sheep shank* but the purpose of all of them is to shorten the rope without cutting it. In this instance, the fool's knot neither adds to nor detracts from the efficiency of the completed knot, but, at best, in a long shank, does hold the three parts together at the centre, the fool's knot itself not being under load.

As illustrated, the knot is completed by turning and casting a half-hitch over the bights at the extreme ends of the fool's knot, on both sides of the centre.

In the pinned version, Figs 6 to 8, further bights of the standing parts are raised at both ends, through the existing end bights of the knot and secured by the insertion of marlin spikes or similar pins. The pins must be secured in position with a lashing (not shown) and the whole has no especial purpose or use, other than as an elaborate means of ensuring that the end hitches do not work their way off, particularly if the rope is subjected to a fluctuating tension.

Under these conditions it would suffice to seize the end bights to the standing parts *after the initial load has been applied.*

1

2

3

4

5

6

7

8

13 Sheep Shank

The common sheep shank is simply two opposite bights, their length being the amount by which the rope is required to be shortened, laid parallel and half-hitches, turned and cast over both ends.
The finished knot should be held in position until the rope has taken the strain, whilst if subjected to fluctuating loads, the protruding bights should be seized to their standing parts, after the knot has been first stretched to its limit.
The strength of the rope is obviously increased between the hitches, but this is of no value as the standing parts are the governing factor.

1

2

3

4

14 Shamrock Knot

This almost comes under the heading of a decorative knot and is of the same family as the jury masthead knot. Its practical use is limited, but with the tails joined with a short splice and the bights lengthened and adjusted, it could provide an ideal sling for a spherical object.

1

2

3

4

5

6

15 Bowline

This knot can be tied by forming the loop shown in Fig 4 separately and poking the tail end up through afterwards, but it is more professional to reach the stage shown in Fig 4 with one continuous movement. The tail is held across the standing part, Fig 1, and the right hand rotated clockwise, through almost 180°, whilst the left hand lifts the bight over the tail end, Figs 2 and 3, resulting in the loop being formed with the tail automatically 'up through' all as Fig 4. This will put a turn in the bight which is allowed to escape by a twist of the fingers of the right hand.

The knot is completed by passing the tail around the back of the standing part and returning it down through the loop, Figs 5 to 7.

Running Bowline

The *running bowline* is simply a bowline, tied as above but around its own standing part, thus forming a noose as in Fig 8.

1

2

3

4

5

6

7

8

16 Bowline on a Bight

The initial movements to form this knot are as for the bowline (Knot 15, Figs 1 to 4), except that a bight of the rope is used (Fig 1).

The variation occurs from this point onwards, sufficient of the bight being drawn up through the loop, before being passed down over the two main bights and returned up the back of the knot to its position around the standing parts and/or tail end. This knot can be used as a man harness similar to that shown in Knot 11, by making it in the centre of a long rope, with two standing parts and the sizes of the bights adjusted as previously described.

If the initial bight of Fig 1 is passed around the standing part and back down through the loop (as with the tail of a bowline), the knot becomes a double bowline (not illustrated).

1

2

3

4

5

6

17
Clove Hitch [cast] Clove Hitch [turned]

A clove hitch is *turned* when it is tied around an endless object, eg a rail or mooring ring, Figs 1 to 4. It is *cast* when the two bights are formed in the hands and the knot dropped over a post or the like, Figs 5 to 7. Proceeding from Fig 5, the right hand bight is placed over the left hand bight to arrive at the virtually completed knot shown in Fig 6.

If subjected to continuous tugging this knot tends to work loose and if made fast around an object which can revolve, it may wind itself off. It should therefore, always be finished off with at least one half-hitch.

1

2

3

4

5

6

7

18 Rolling Hitch

This is simply a clove hitch with two (or more) initial turns instead of one, laid back towards the standing part and over its own initial turn(s), thus jamming it, Figs 1 to 4. In the illustrations the tail end has been deliberately kept short to clearly show the lay of these initial turns, particularly in Fig 4, but in practice a longer tail end would be employed and indeed would be essential to complete the knot as may be seen in Fig 6.

As with the clove hitch this knot should be finished off with at least one half-hitch. It will withstand being hauled at right angles to its turns without sliding along the object to which it is tied, however smooth that object may be, provided it is hauled against the initial two or more turns. In Fig 6, it will only hold if hauled to the right.

When a rope or wire is hauled tight over a winch drum or capstan it is necessary to temporarily secure it whilst the end is removed from the drum and made fast permanently to bollards or the like. A short length of rope or light chain, called a stopper is used, one end being made fast to a deck fitting or even around the bollard itself and the other end made fast to the rope or wire in question. The wire is then slackened back until the load is taken by the stopper, when the wire is said to be stoppered off. A rolling hitch would be used to make the stopper fast, in such a case, whilst other uses of course depend on circumstances.

1

2

3

4

5

6

19 Fisherman's Bend or Bucket Hitch

The fisherman's bend is the correct name for this knot, but it is more commonly known as a bucket hitch and as the name implies, it is ideal for making a lanyard fast to the handle of a bucket, or for any similar purpose.

1

2

3

4

20 Timber Hitch

A quick and easily made temporary hitch, recommended for dragging a plank or spar rather than lifting it, for, although it will not slip, provided a steady strain is maintained, there are other, more secure knots if the load is to be raised to any height.

1

2

3

4

21 Cat's Paw

The most efficient method of attaching the bight of a rope, or a sling to a hook, provided that both standing parts are under load. It will prevent the hook sliding along the rope and thus ensures that the load, eg, a spar, will be lifted horizontally. Conversely, by careful selection of the position of the cat's paw in relation to the length of the sling, the load may be lifted at any required angle.

1

2

3

4

22 Backwall Hitch

A quick and efficient method of attaching the tail end of a rope to a hook, provided a constant strain is maintained; the knot being held in position during the initial application of the load, Figs 1 and 2.

Midshipman's Hitch

This is a variation of the Backwall hitch, used for the same purpose, and somewhat more secure, particularly when working with a slippery rope, Figs 3 and 4.

1

2

3

4

23 Thief Knot or Draw Hitch

This is an acknowledged and perfectly efficient knot, but it can be dangerous when used by amateurs as a lifeline. The purpose of the knot is to provide a quick release by simply tugging the tail end, whilst the standing part is capable of supporting a load.

It can be used, with a short tail, whenever it is necessary to slip a load. But it is more often associated with the fire service where its purpose is to provide the means of escape, as a lifeline, coupled with the advantage that the rope is retrievable. Should the building be higher than half the length of the rope, the procedure is repeated from one convenient level to the next, until the operator reaches the ground. In this event, the hitch is formed with the bight at the centre of the rope, and both ends hanging down. The operator, having shinned down the standing part retrieves his rope by tugging the other fall, hence the alternative name of *thief knot.*

It is apparent from the illustrations that one fall of the rope will support a load (the left fall in Fig 6) whilst the other will not and as the two falls lay side by side, confusion between them, whilst understandable, could prove fatal.

Note

The danger of confusing the two falls cannot be too highly stressed, even to professionals much less to amateurs. It was not long ago that such a confusion resulted in a highly trained and competent man falling to his death, with his rope on top of him.

1

2

3

4

5

6

24 Jury Masthead Knot

As the name implies, this knot is used as a temporary measure in the emergency rigging of a jury mast. The centre of the knot is placed over the top of the mast and the twin standing parts form the backstay. Forestay and shrouds are made fast to the remaining three bights and the greater the strain set up in the rigging, the tighter the knot will grip the mast.

It is made at the centre of a rope long enough to provide the backstay(s) and it is usually more convenient to make the second bight slightly larger than the first and third bights. Particular attention must be paid to the relative positions of the three bights when they are interwoven, after which the knot becomes almost automatic.

1

2

3

4

5

6

7

8

25 Rope Ladder Knot

The rope ladder 'knot' is actually the rung of a true rope ladder as distinct from a pilot ladder which has rope sides and timber rungs. It is efficient and most useful aboard small boats as it needs so little stowage space.

It can be made with twin tails at the top for making it fast, or as illustrated, made on the bight of a rope with an eye, seized in position.

The illustrations commence with the top of the ladder and the first rung completed, and proceed to show the formation of the second rung. This is repeated for as many rungs as required, the 'S' formation being made in alternate side ropes to keep the finished ladder symmetrical.

The length of the rung and the number of turns employed is a matter of choice and also depends on the size of the rope being used. It is advisable to make the rungs only slightly wider than the human foot. If the ladder is wider than is strictly necessary there may be excessive sag in the rungs.

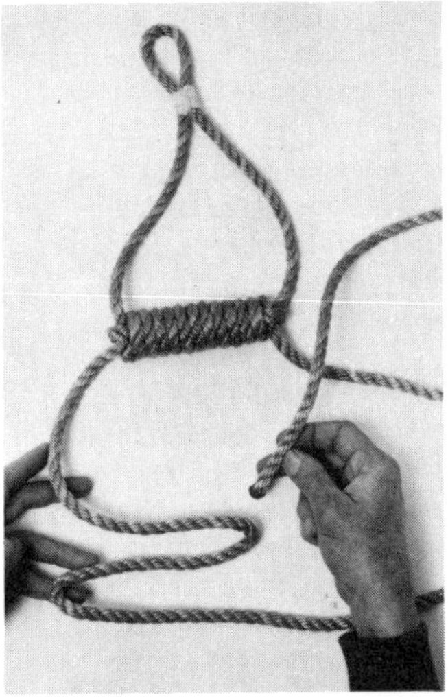

1

2

3

4

5

6

7

8

26 Stage or Scaffold Hitch

The sole purpose of this knot, made at both ends of a plank of wood is to support the plank, or stage as it is called when used in this manner, not only horizontally, but also in such a manner that it will not twist or cant.

The horn is the smaller piece of timber, nailed at right angles to the stage, on the underside. Its purpose is twofold. Firstly, to prevent the whole knot from slipping off the end of the stage and secondly, the one side being longer than the other, to provide room for a person's legs, when sitting on the stage, working against a ship's side.

The knot may be formed without the horns, but when used, as illustrated, the first complete turn is taken on the inside of the horn and the second on the outside, the rope crossing the horn on the underside. The first turn is then not only lifted over the second, but its bight is also passed around the long end of the horn, resulting in two parts of rope crossing the underside of the horn diagonally.

The original second turn is then lifted completely over the first and third turns and this bight placed downwards over the end of the stage, the resulting bights formed at each edge of the stage being suitably adjusted. In this manner, the horn is effectively secured to the stage without having to rely on nails.

The whole may be formed on the end of a rope with a sufficiently long tail to make fast in a bowline, to the standing part some distance above the stage, as illustrated. Otherwise and preferably, the knot is made on the bight of a rope, giving two standing parts, each of which can be individually adjusted to keep the stage level, when made fast overhead.

The photographs have been taken using a miniature stage and a small rope for the sake of convenience, but in practice the size of the stage would be in keeping with its load and span.

1

2

3

4

5

6

7

8

27 Lighterman's Hitch

This is another quick and simple method of forming a temporary eye in the end of a rope, perfectly stable when under constant strain, but otherwise suspect.

The instability could be overcome by seizing the tail to the standing part, but this would defeat the object of ease and speed.

It is most easily made by forming the initial movements of a bowline and repeating the procedure further along the standing part.

For bowline see Knot 15

1

2

3

4

28 Square Knot

There is little that can be said about this knot, its uses are limited, unless as a sling or the like, but it does produce four standing parts, neither of which will render on the other.

1

2

3

4

29
Bargee's Eye Splice

With apologies to all bargees, a rough and ready, rather un-seamanlike but otherwise effective way of making an eye in the end of a rope.

1

2

3

4

30 Monkey's Fist

Made in the end of a heaving line, with a metal ball or similar weight, inserted into the weave, its purpose is to give carrying quality to the line.

Measure off nine hand turns of line and work from this point back towards the tail end, inserting the weight before completing the last three turns. Work the knot tight and to shape, cutting off and burying the tail end.

As heaving line is a comparatively expendable item a separate fist can be made of a better quality cordage, with a protruding eye, to which the heaving line is made fast. By this method the fist can be re-used when it becomes necessary to replace the line. To do this an eye splice is first formed in the end of the line and the splice buried in the first turns.

1

2

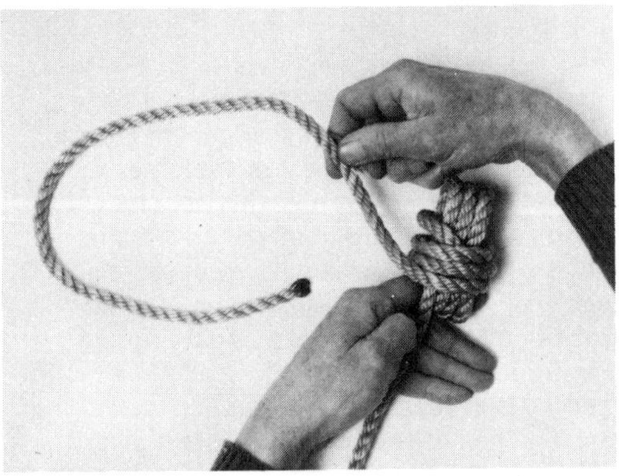
3

4

5

6

7

8

31 Eye Splice

With strands whipped and unlaid for the required distance, it is essential to carefully arrange them as in Fig 1, with the central strand on top, the left hand strand emerging from below the rope, and the remaining strand laying to the right of centre.
This central strand (subsequently referred to as B) is always tucked first, being tucked against the lay under any strand of the standing part, the required size of the eye being the only governing factor, Fig 1.
The left-hand strand (A) is always tucked next, being passed to the left of B, over the strand under which B has been tucked and under the next, Fig 2, the whole being hauled tight as in Fig 3.
The work is now turned over; the back of the splice appears as Fig 4 and the remaining strand C is found, laying on the left.
It is essential that strand C be brought over to the right before being tucked towards the left under the one remaining strand of the standing part as in Fig 5.
When hauled tight the back of the splice appears as Fig 6 which also completes the first full tuck, when one tail should emerge from between each pair of strands. Tucking over one/under one, against the lay is continued until three full tucks have been made, Fig 7. At this stage the splice is virtually completed and the tails may be cut off, allowing a small amount to offset the tendency of the splice to 'draw'. Alternatively the tails may be cut slightly longer, halved and each half of the one strand whipped to the corresponding half of the neighbouring strand, as a safeguard against the splice drawing.
By far the neatest method is to taper the splice as illustrated. The strands are halved and one half of each strand is cut off fairly close to the third tuck, after which the remaining half strands are tucked in the usual manner for a further three full tucks, and the finished splice appears as in Fig 8.

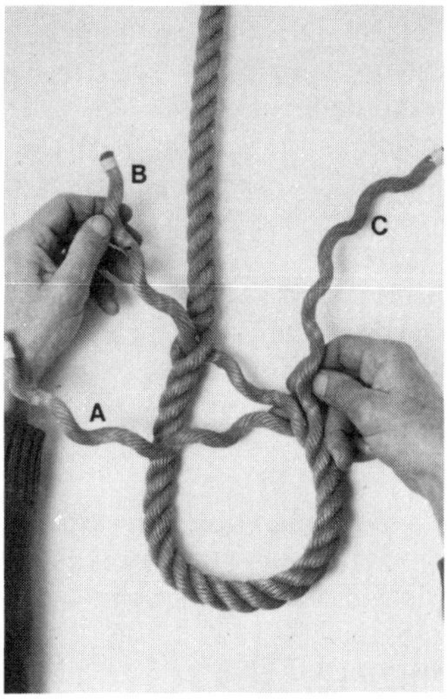

1

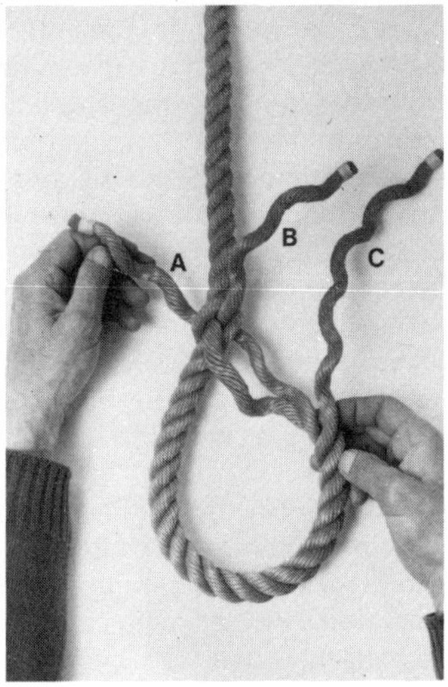

2

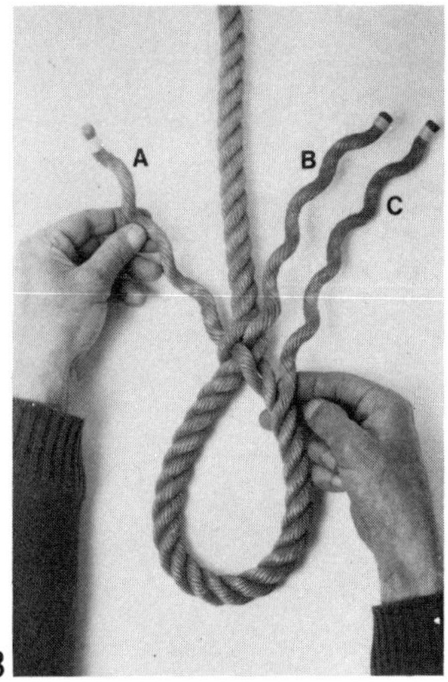

3

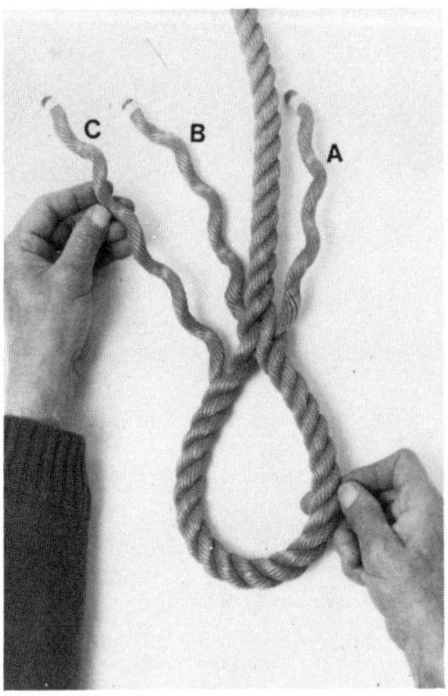

4

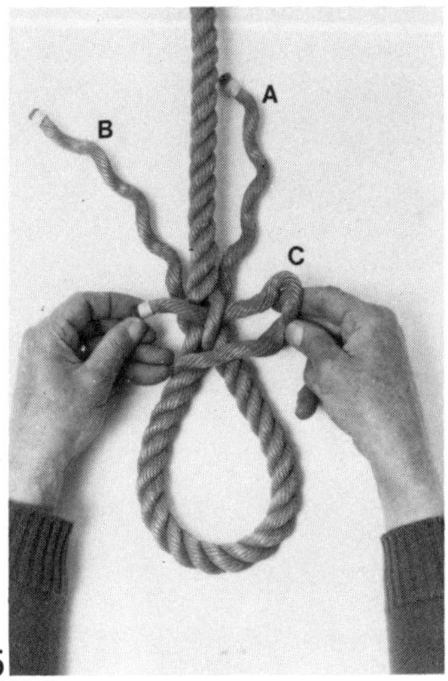

5

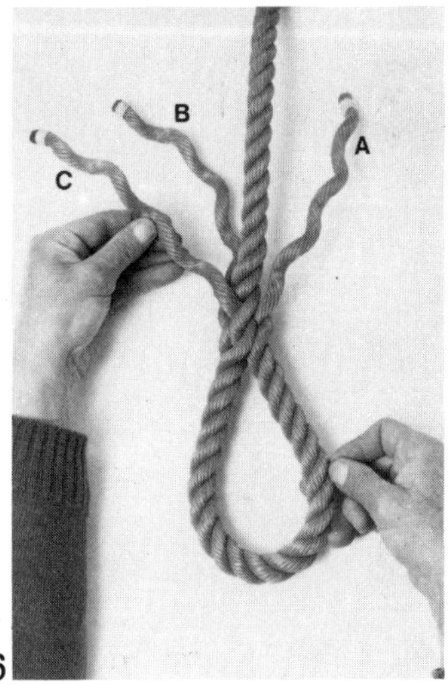

6

7

8

32 Short Splice

This is a method for permanently joining two ropes provided the splice does not have to work over a sheave.

Sufficient length of strands to provide three full tucks (approximately four times the circumference) are unlaid from the ends of both ropes and a whipping put on each. These are interwoven as in Fig 1 and brought tightly together, Fig 2, which point becomes the centre of the splice.

The ends of the right-hand rope are best temporarily whipped to the left-hand standing part and the three remaining strands are tucked in turn, over one/under one against the lay, into the standing part of the right-hand rope, the first full tuck appearing as Fig 3. This is continued until three full tucks have been made, Fig 4.

The whipping is now removed and the whole operation repeated to the left of centre, three full tucks being made with the ends of the right-hand rope into the standing part of the left, when the completed splice appears as Fig 5.

The ends have been left long in the illustration to show their relative positions, but these are now either cut off (allowing a little for the splice to draw) or finished off as described for the eye splice, ie halved and whipped or tapered.

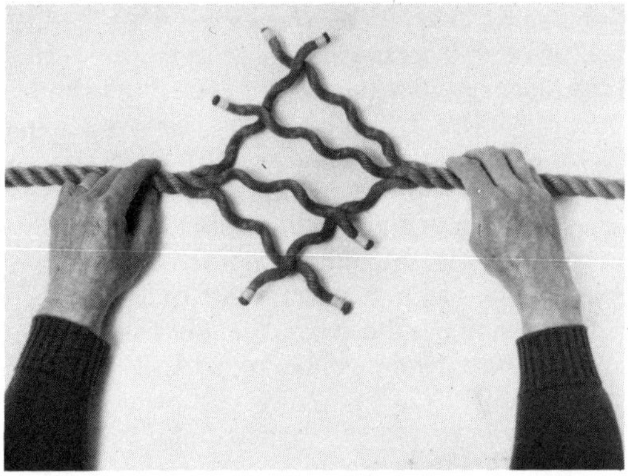
1

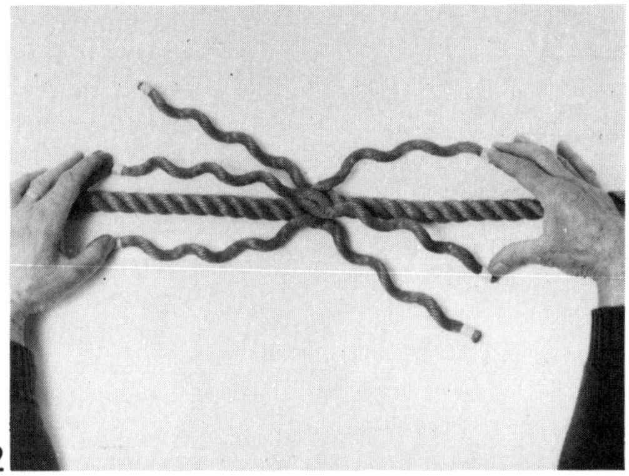
2

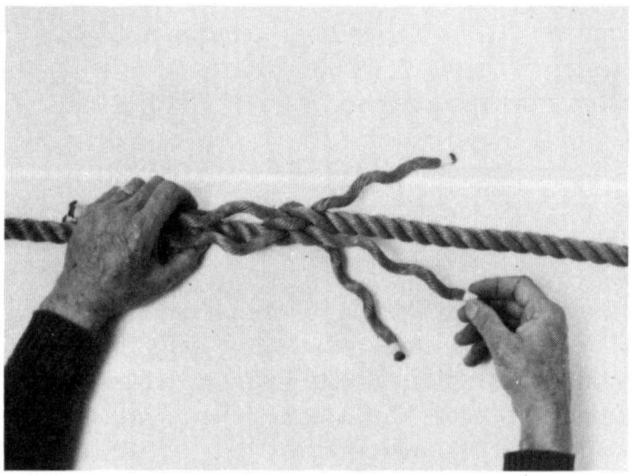
3

4

5

33 Long Splice

The purpose of the long splice is to join two ropes in such a manner that there is little or no increase in the size of the rope, at the junction, whilst the finished work, having the appearance and lay of the original rope, is suitable for working over a sheave.
The splice relies solely on friction for its stability and so is of considerable length, but for the purpose of photography, it has had to be made much shorter than it would be in practise.
Whilst the lengths referred to later are important, there are varying opinions regarding the recommended length of a long splice, suffice to say that the longer the splice, the more secure it will be. Twenty times the circumference of the rope has been adopted in this case.
The unlaid tails are interwoven as if to commence a Short Splice (Knot 32), except that their length is twenty-five times that of the circumference of the rope, Fig 1.
One strand of the right-hand rope is unlaid away to the right for a distance of twenty times the circumference, Fig 2, and its immediate counterpart, from the left-hand rope is laid back in its place, Figs 3 and 4.
At the point where the replacement and unlaid strands meet, the tail of the replacement strand should be approximately five times the circumference in length and the previously unlaid strand is cut to this same length.
The process is repeated on the left-hand side, one strand of the right-hand rope replacing its counterpart in the left-hand rope, Fig 6, and the end of the unlaid strand being cut to length as before.
This leaves two untouched strands at the centre, Fig 6, which are cut to the same length as the other two pairs of tails. When laying up the replacement strands it is essential to twist the strand with every turn of the lay.
The splice is now put under load and well stretched, prior to tucking away the three pairs of tails. This has not been illustrated as there are several methods which can be used:
Each strand is separated into thirds, an overhand knot made with each counterpart third and the whole beaten down into the lay, before tucking each set of three ends under one strand only of the standing part.

or

The thirds may be tucked with the lay around the three corresponding standing part strands, tapering as the work proceeds.

or

The overhand knot is made with the full strands, which are tapered and tucked with the lay around their counterpart strands.

or

The overhand knot is made with the full strands, which are then halved and tucked with the lay around the two adjacent strands of the standing part, tapering as before.

or

The overhand knot may be dispensed with in the last two variations.

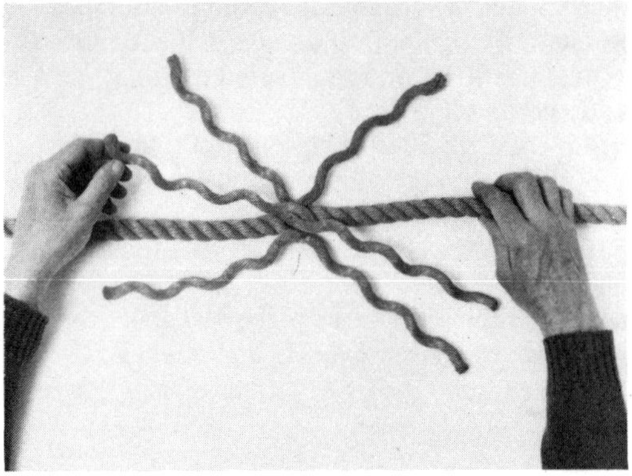
1

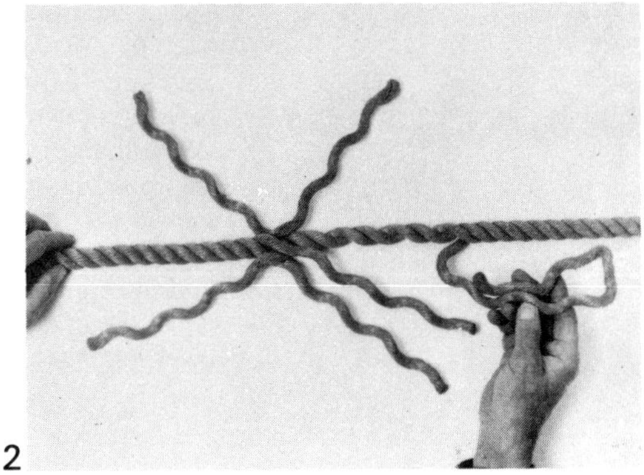
2

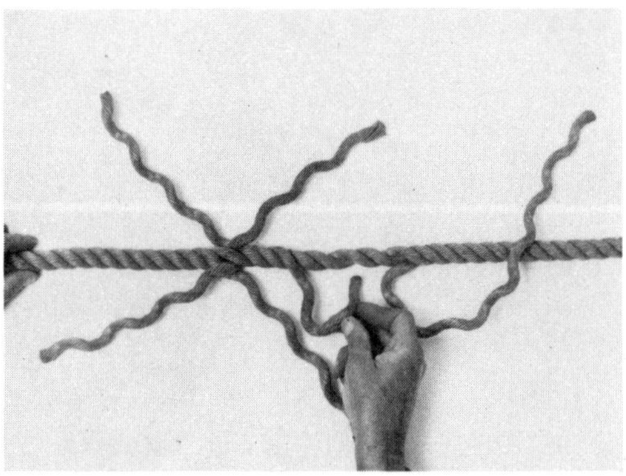
3

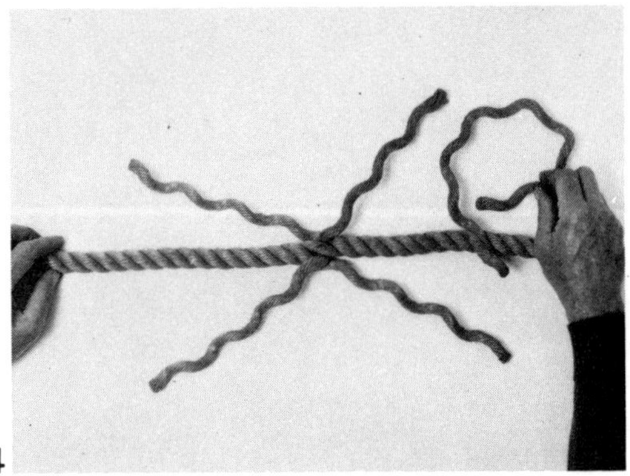
4

5

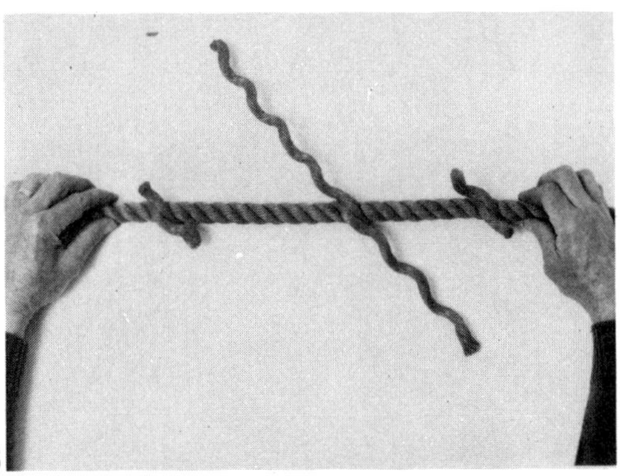
6

34 Back Splice

The sole purpose of this splice is to prevent the end of the rope becoming frayed. Efficient, though not very elegant, it can replace the neater whipping. It is useful in ropes subjected to rough usage, as whippings do come off in time.

With strands unlaid and ends whipped, a crown knot (Plate 43) is formed in the end of the rope, Fig 1. Each strand in turn is tucked over one/under one against the lay, the first full tuck appearing as Fig 5, after which two more full tucks are inserted and the ends trimmed short.

It can be tapered by halving the strands, as in the eye splice, and inserting three more tucks, which improves its appearance.

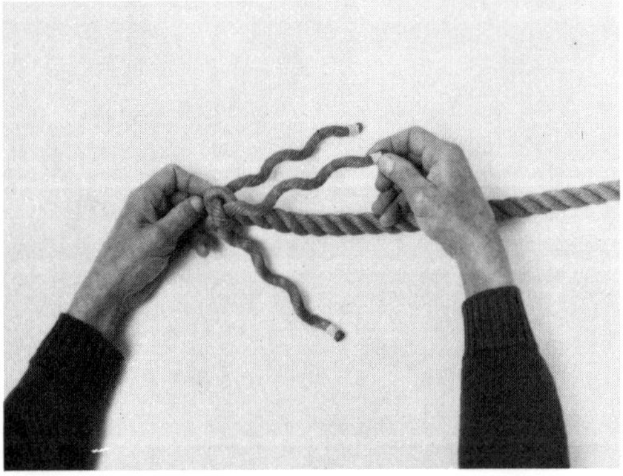

1

2

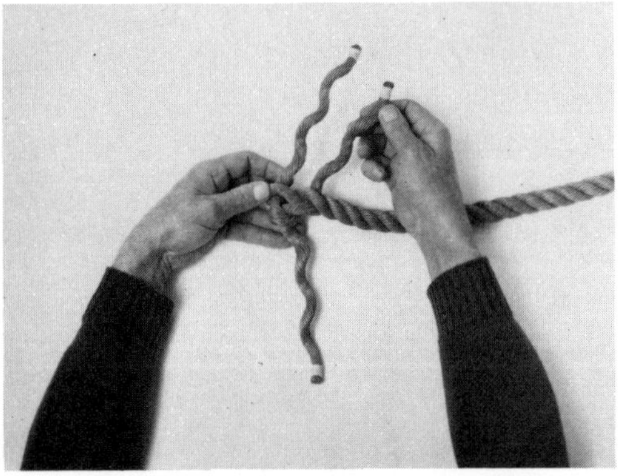

3

4

5

6

35
Cut Splice

This is essentially two eye splices, made by the ends of two ropes into the corresponding standing part of the other, the distance between the splices governing the length of the cut.

With strands unlaid and whipped, the two ends are offered up as Fig 1 and the required length of the cut is established.

The tucking required is identical to that of the eye splice (Plate 31) and the first full tuck of the left-hand end into the right-hand standing part is shown in Fig 2 after which two more full tucks are made and the right-hand splice finished as Fig 3. The process is repeated, the right-hand end being eye spliced into the left-hand standing part when the finished work appears as Fig 4.

The ends have deliberately been left long in Fig 4, to show their respective positions and to illustrate that they may now be finished off in one of the three ways described for the eye splice.

1

2

3

4

36 Eye Splice in Middle of Rope

This is an instance when the rope is deliberately forced against its lay by twisting it in opposite directions. Once the disturbed lay has accepted its position, Fig 1, it will be found to run quite easily, forming three, two-stranded laid bights, Fig 2.

A bight is made in the standing part to the size of the required eye, Fig 3 and the laid bights used as tails to make a normal eye splice (Plate 31), the first full tuck of which is shown in Fig 4.

At least two more full tucks are inserted in the normal over one/under one, against the lay manner and the completed splice appears as Fig 5.

It may be noted that the two-strand laid bights conjoin perfectly with the single strands under which they are tucked, when any three assume the lay of the original rope, whilst the completed splice has the appearance of a nine-strand cable-laid rope.

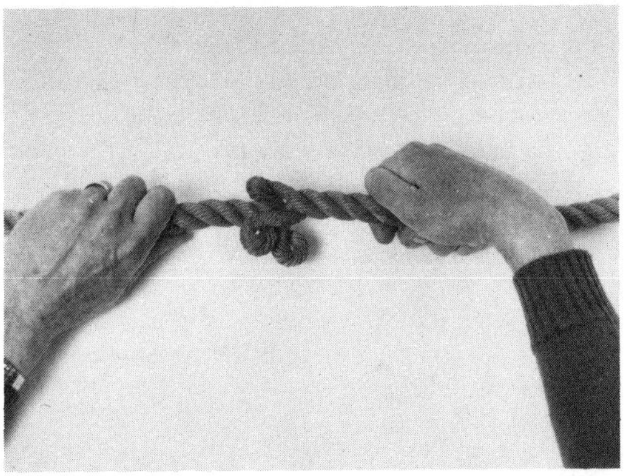
1

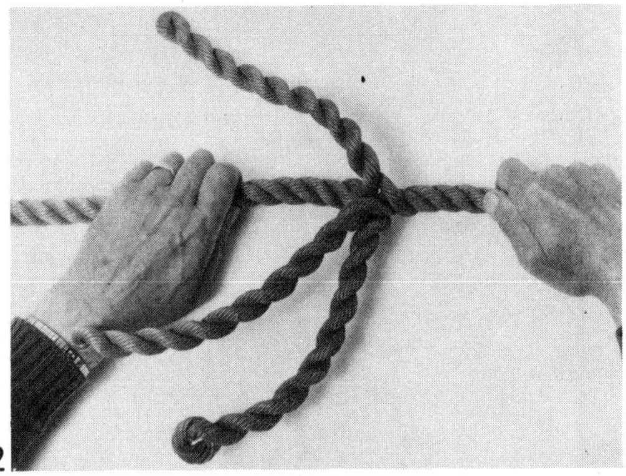
2

3

4

5

37
Flemish Eye

One strand is carefully unlaid and the whole offered up, with the strands crossing at the extremity of the required eye, Fig 1. Care must be taken to ensure that the single strand marries into the vacant lay of the other two, after which it is continuously passed down through the eye filling the vacant lay until it reaches the throat of the eye, Figs 2 and 3. Similarly the double strand is continuously passed up through the eye, being wrapped around the single strand, again filling the vacant lay, until it also reaches the throat of the eye, Fig 4.
The three strands having again met, the single strand is laid back in its original position, to form the tail end (Figs 5 and 6), which is then firmly seized to the standing part.

1

2

3

4

5

6

38 Single Tuck Eye Splice with Wall Knot Finish

This is essentially a decorative eye splice but it can also be useful if the eye is expected to work close up to a sheave.
The first full tuck only of an ordinary eye splice is made, (Plate 31, Figs 1 to 6) as Fig 1. A wall knot (Plate 42) is now formed around the standing part, above the tuck, and hauled tight, Fig 2. This is followed around once more, hauled tight and the tails cut off close to the finished knot, Fig 3.

1

2

3

39 Chain Splice

The purpose of the chain splice is to join a rope pennant to a normal small link of a chain in such a manner that rope and chain will pass freely through a fair-lead. The eye of the splice is its weakest part, its strength being less than that of the standing part and undoubtedly less than that of the chain to which it is attached. It is most often used in conjunction with a mooring chain, when the pennant is only called upon to lift the slack of the chain inboard.

The principle of both the normal method of tucking (over one/under one) and that of the long splice (the laying up of one strand to replace another) are conjoined in its formation.

For the purpose of photography it has been necessary to make the splice much shorter than would be the case in practise and therefore the lengths, referred to below are important.

Unlay one strand only (marked A) for a distance of twenty-five times the circumference of the rope and set aside, reeving the remaining two strands (B and C), still laid together, through the end link of the chain, Fig 1. Haul B and C through the link, back to the standing part and separate them, leaving only sufficient laid rope (two strands) to pass through the link and form the actual eye, Fig 2.

Unlay strand A for a further distance of twenty times the circumference of the rope, Fig 3, replacing it with strand B, laid into the vacated lay in the same way as described for the long splice, until B and A meet as in Fig 4, when the tail of B should be approximately five times the circumference of the rope. Cut A, leaving a tail the same length as that of B.

These tails are now tucked away using any of the methods described for the long splice (Knot 33) to completion as shown in Fig 5 which also shows the remaining unused tail C. This strand is cut to a length suitable for four or five tucks, which are inserted over one/under one against the lay, working around the rope. The finished splice appears as Fig 6.

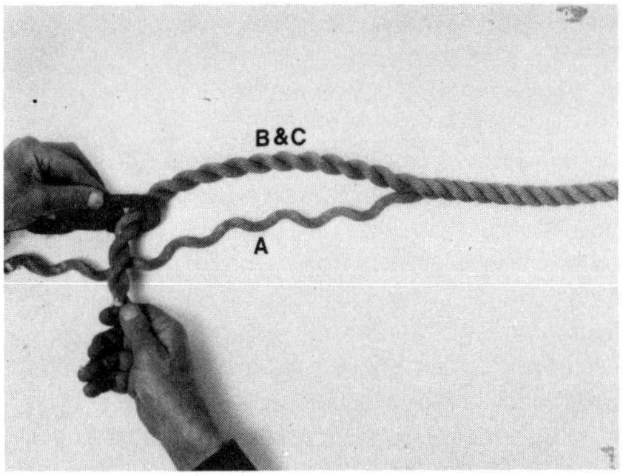

1

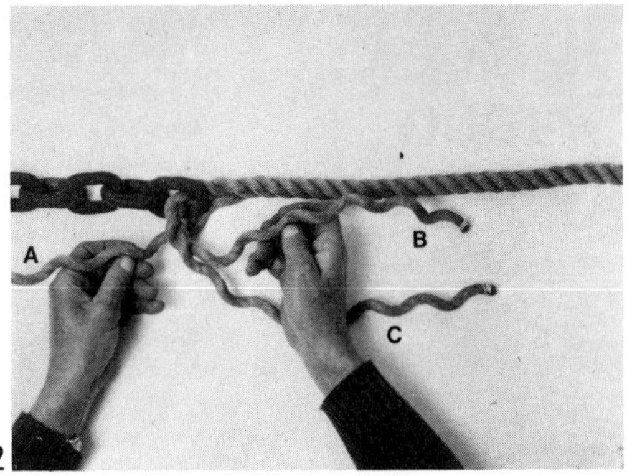

2

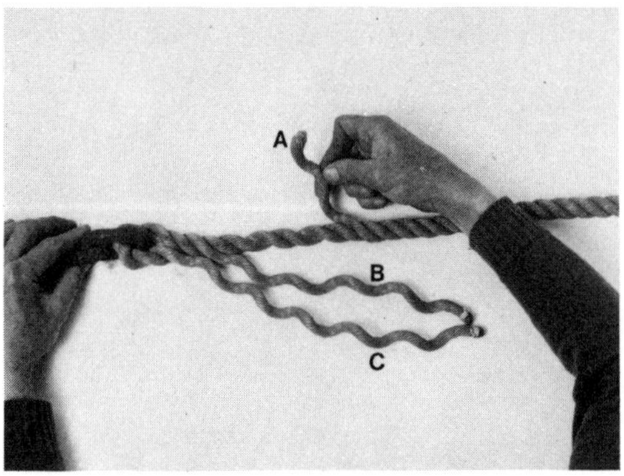

3

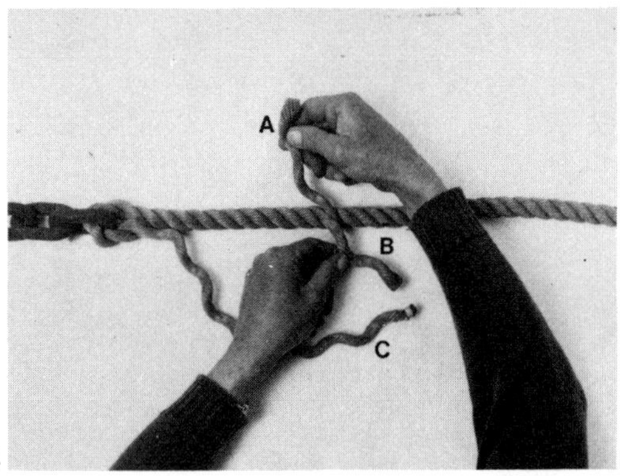

4

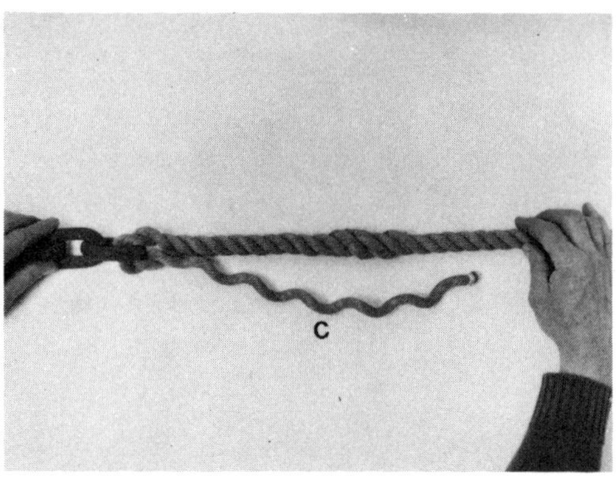

5

6

40 Shroud Knot

This is essentially a decorative method of joining two ropes although it is said to have been the accepted way of repairing shrouds in the olden days, which may well be true in view of its name.

It is certainly nicer looking than a short splice for such a purpose and although it does not require as much material it does not have the strength of a short splice.

The ends of both ropes are unlaid and interwoven as in the commencement of a short splice (Knot 32, Figs 1 and 2). A wall knot (Knot 42), is formed around the standing part of the upper rope with the strands of the lower, above the junction, but against the lay, Fig 1. The procedure is repeated below the junction, with the strands of the upper rope forming a second wall knot also against the lay, Fig 2. All ends are unravelled, thinned out to tapers, and firmly secured at intervals with sail twine, Fig 3, before being served to produce the finished knot shown in Fig 4.

1

2

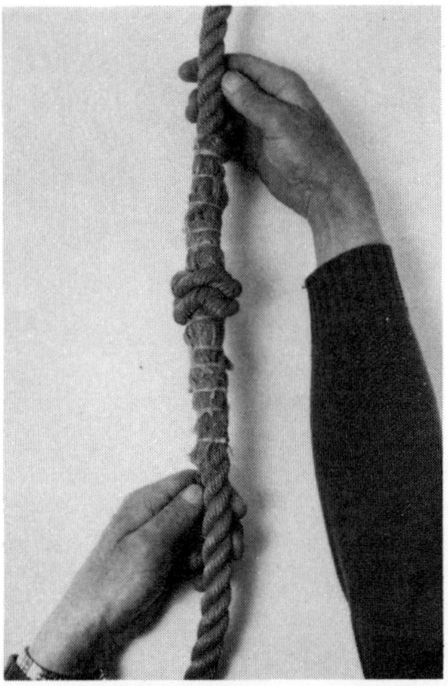

3

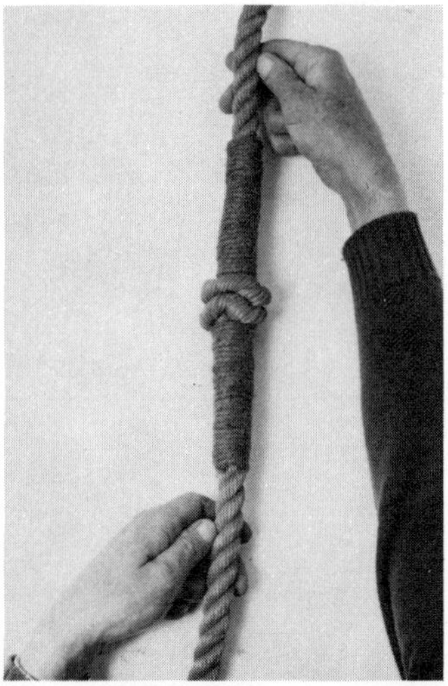

4

41
The Untiable Knot

This consists of a bowline on a bight (Knot 16) with one short standing part spliced around one of the eyes. The other standing part is made fast and the challenge is, to untie the bowline on a bight, without hauling the standing part through or releasing the splice. It is not impossible and a clue to the method used is given in the introduction.

Method
There are no set movements to be made. The knot is kept loose and with the standing part taut, the whole is tumbled over and over towards the end of the rope. In this manner the turns of which the original knot was composed are transferred to the standing part and the last turn, into the eye of the splice itself.

1

42
Wall Knot

More often simply referred to as 'a wall', this knot is formed by passing each strand in turn around and under its neighbour, with the lay, the end of the third strand being passed upwards through the bight formed by the first, Fig 4. It is hauled tight and if made correctly, all three strands emerge from the top of the knot as Fig 5.

The ends have been left long in Fig 5, firstly, to clearly indicate these points of emergence; secondly for comparison with the emergence of the tails of a crown (Knot 43); and thirdly to symbolise that a wall is seldom if ever, used on its own and in practice these tails would continue to be used.

Even in the case of the single tuck eye splice with wall knot finish, Knot 38, where it is built around a standing part, it is followed around.

It is usually associated with the crown knot (Knot 43) whilst the combined wall and crown is in turn, the basis of the man-rope knot (Knot 44).

A slight variation of the wall itself, passing each strand around two neighbouring strands instead of one and it becomes a Matthew Walker (Knot 59).

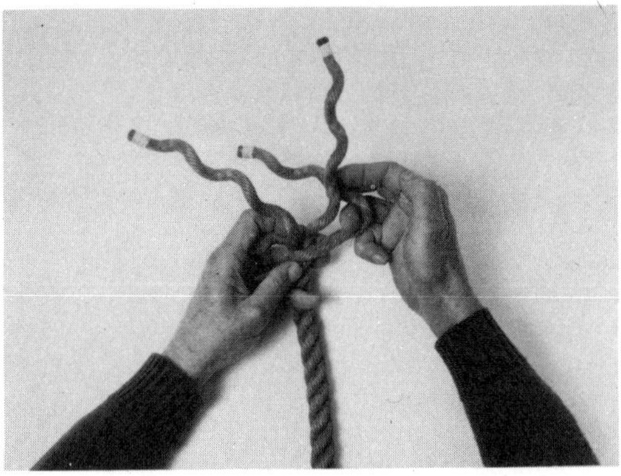

1

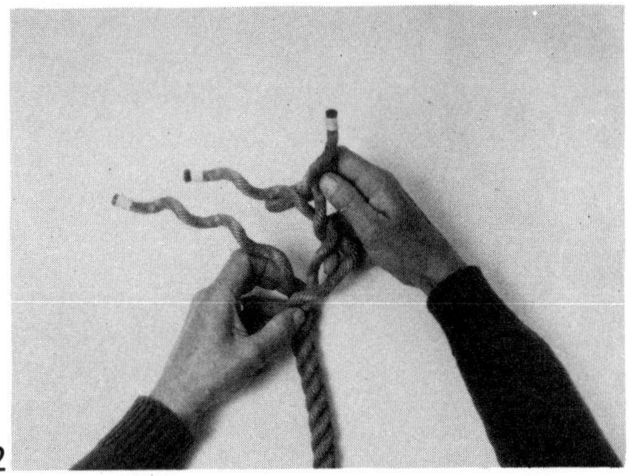

2

3

4

5

43 Crown Knot

The *crown* is very similar to the wall except that each strand in turn, is passed around and over its neighbour, the third strand being passed downwards through the bight formed by the first, Fig 3. As distinct from the wall, the three strands emerge from the bottom of the knot, Fig 4. In keeping with the wall, the crown is seldom if ever used on its own and the ends in Fig 4 have been left long for the same reason as described for the wall. In this case the crown, being the commencement of the back splice, would probably have its ends tucked away accordingly (Knot 34). It is more usually associated with the wall. To form a *stopper knot* the wall is first formed as in Knot 42, after which it is 'crowned' as shown, thus forming the *wall and crown.* This is shown in greater detail in the commencement of the *man-rope knot*, Plate 44, where Fig 1 shows the completed wall and crown, prior to being followed around.

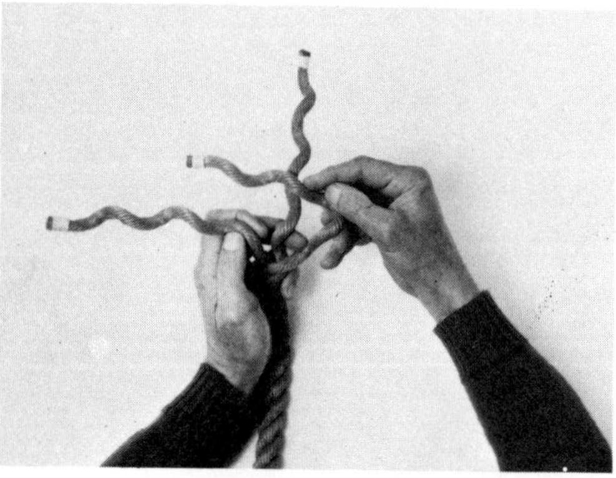

1

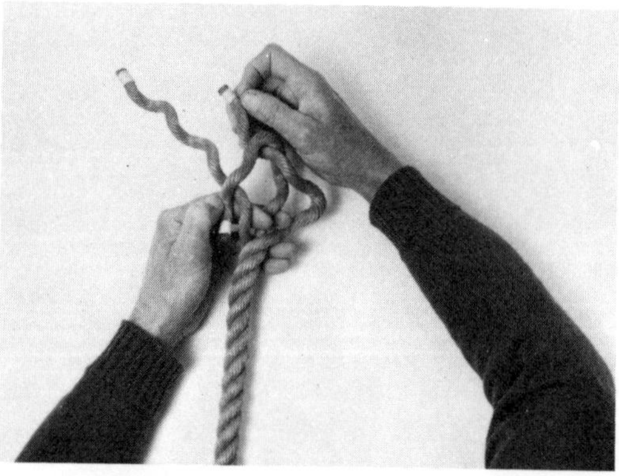

2

3

4

44 Man Rope Knot

This is simply a wall (Knot 42) with a crown (Knot 43) formed on the top, Fig 1, making the wall and crown previously referred to. It will be found that the tails emerging downwards from the crown, lay neatly alongside the strands of the wall below and these strands are followed around with the working tails, Fig 2. Now the tails emerging upwards from the doubled wall re-align with the strands of the original crown and these are also followed around completing the man-rope knot as Fig 3.
As may be expected with any crown the tails emerge in a downwards direction and they have been left long in Fig 3 to illustrate this point. In practice they would, of course, be cut off close to the knot.

1

2

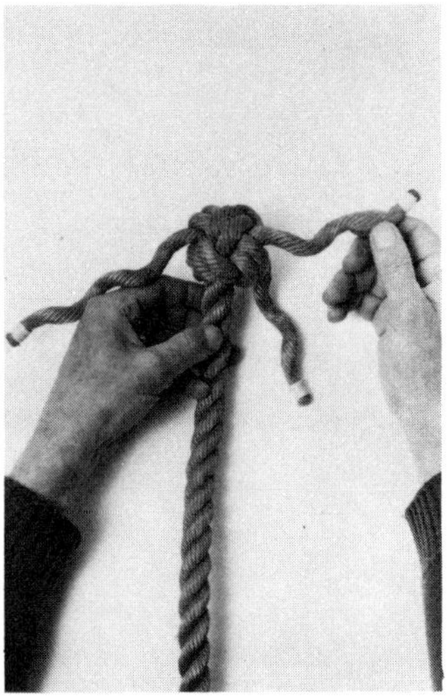
3

45
Turk's Head

The Turk's head is a purely decorative piece of ropework, invariably made around an object such as a guard rail.
It has been commenced on the hand, only to show what happens at the back of the work, as illustrated by the rotation of the hand. In practice, it would be made direct onto the chosen object. Similarly, for photographic purposes and clarity, the working end has been kept short and again, in practice, sufficient length of end would be employed, to complete the work without rendering around.
The rope is arranged as Fig 1 and the working end tucked as Fig 2, thus forming the first cross over, at which time the turns at the back of the hand are laying parallel, Fig 3.
These are now crossed over each other, Fig 4, and the working end tucked between them from right to left, Fig 5. One opening will be found to remain, Fig 6, into which the working end is passed from left to right. On viewing the work from the other side, Fig 7, the working end will be found to have returned to the point of origin, laying alongside the other end and leading in the same direction. (The work was, at this point placed over a cylindrical object, as the remainder is automatic and there is no reason to view the reverse side.)
The working end is now passed over and under around the knot for a second time following exactly the course of the first turns, on the completion of which it will return to the point of origin in its correct lay and pointing in the right direction for a further follow around, Fig 8. The procedure is repeated and the completed work appears as Fig 9, after which the ends are cut short and buried under the turns at the point of origin.
The illustrations show the most simple of Turk's head. More elaborate versions are possible by increasing the parts and turns, whilst the number of times the knot is followed around is a matter of choice.

1

2

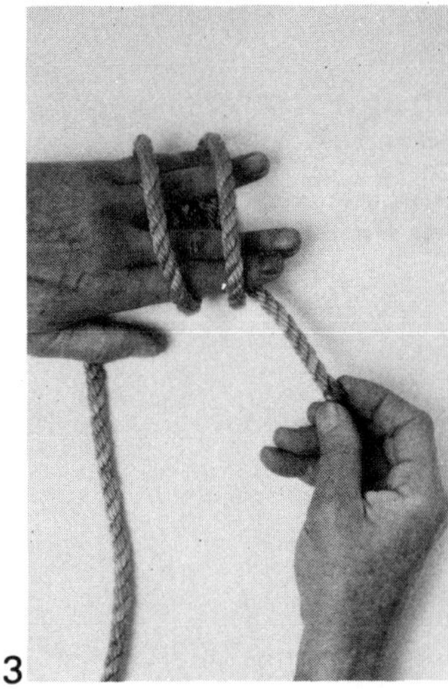
3

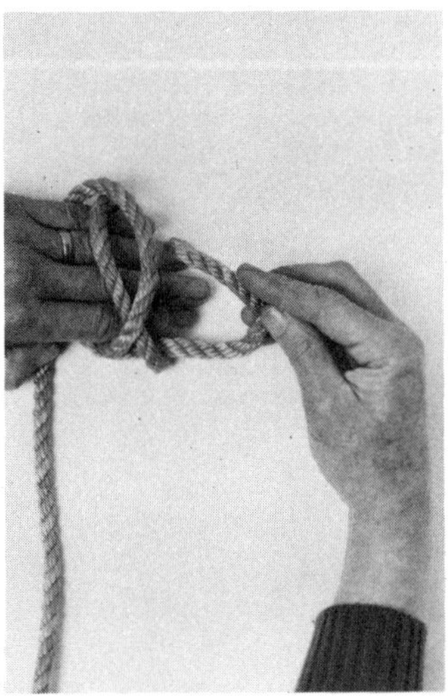
4

5

6

7

8

9

46 Ocean Plait and/or Mat

A considerable length of cordage is required to form this plait and the rope which, from time to time disappears out of the picture and returns, is in fact the bight of a long rope.

The rope is laid up as Fig 1, after which the part in the left hand of this figure is brought over the other tail and up under the one bight as shown in Fig 2. The part now held in the left hand in Fig 2 is the one end which remains in this position and is not used again.

The other end is worked over one/under one as shown in Figs 3 and 4, the first full circuit of the plait being completed as Fig 5, the working end meeting the other at the point of origin, laying alongside it and pointing in the correct direction to continue with the first follow around.

This is completed as Fig 6, when once again the working end returns to the point of origin, ready to commence the third circuit, after which the whole is worked tight and to shape, the ends cut off and buried under the mat. The completed work appears as shown in Fig 7.

The mat may be followed around more than three times, if required, but then the whole tends to become unwieldy and the strands begin to ride up over each other.

It is usually used as the centre piece of a larger mat, perhaps being surrounded by several turns of simple plaiting, before the introduction of a circle of other, smaller mats of a different design, the whole being sewn together with sail twine.

1

2

3

4

5

6

7

47 Admiralty Eye Splice

The regulations governing the use of wire eye splices in industry are necessarily strict and whilst the following eye splices, Admiralty and Liverpool (Knot 48) are considered to be adequate for normal usage, the reader, if considering either splice from the point of view of insurance and/or the regulations must refer back to the regulations, in force at the time.

The main feature of the Admiralty eye splice is, that after the first tuck, all strands are tucked away *over one/under one, against the lay of the standing part.*

There are also, at least three methods of completing the first full tuck, the one illustrated being the 1-6-2-3-5-4 order of tucking. The required size of the eye is established and a seizing put on accordingly, after which all strands are unlaid, ensuring that they are in their right order, the heart being always associated with the first tucking strand, Fig 1. Diagram A shows the relative positions of the tucking strands to the standing part and strand No 1, together with the heart is the first to be tucked, from left to right, Fig 2, and hauled tight, Fig 3.

The heart is now cut out and Diagram B shows the sequence of the next tuck, when strand 6 is tucked, also from left to right as Fig 4, before being hauled tight.

In accordance with the sequence and Diagram C, strand 2 is the next to be tucked from right to left, around the same strand of the standing part as strand 6, but in the opposite direction, providing the locking tuck, as shown in Fig 5, after which it is hauled tight. Strand No 3, as shown by Diagram D and Fig 6 follows suit and as previously, this shows the point of entry and direction of the strand. It is of course, as with previous strands, hauled tight, but is not shown as such, since this would make the illustrations unintelligible.

Strand 5, Diagram E is the next to be tucked and it must be noted that whilst all previous strands have been tucked under one this strand is tucked under two. Diagram E also shows strand 5 being tucked from left to right, whereas Fig 7 in association with this diagram appears to contradict the fact. The reason for this is that Fig 7 (for the first time) is a view of the back of the splice. (Note the reversal of the long leg of the seizing.)

Still viewing the back of the splice, strand 4 (Diagram F) is tucked between the same two strands of the standing part as strand 5, but under one strand only, all as Fig 8.

The completed first tuck appears as Fig 9 and has been deliberately left slack for clarity. In practice each strand is hammered down with a mallet as it is tucked. All strands are now tucked over one/under one, against the lay, each being hammered down in turn, when the finished work appears as Fig 10, which shows five full tucks.

If the splice is to be served, it is necessary to taper it and this is done by halving all strands and inserting three further tucks with the halved strands, similar to that shown for the eye splice in rope (Knot 31).

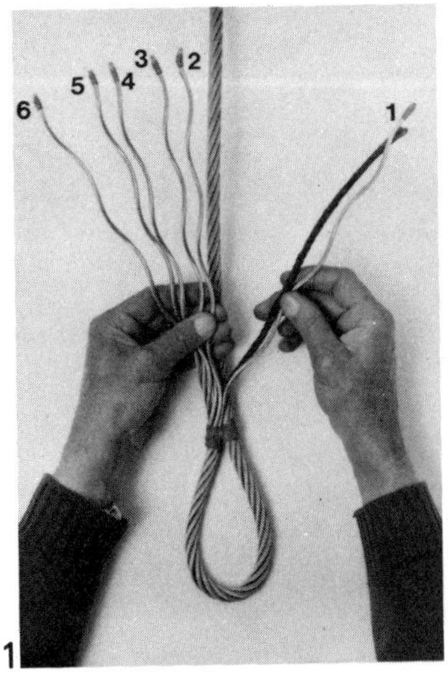

1

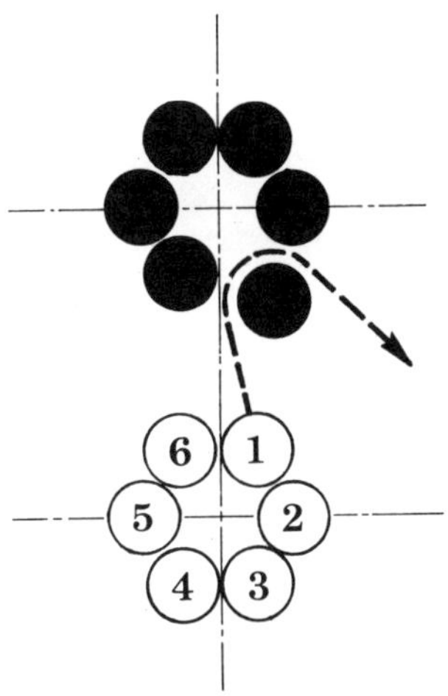

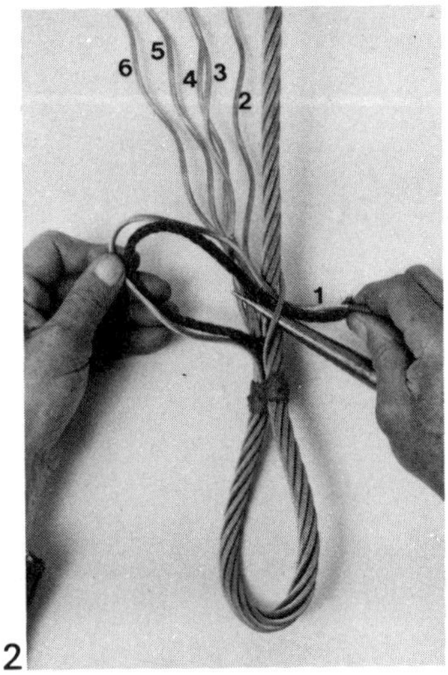

A 2

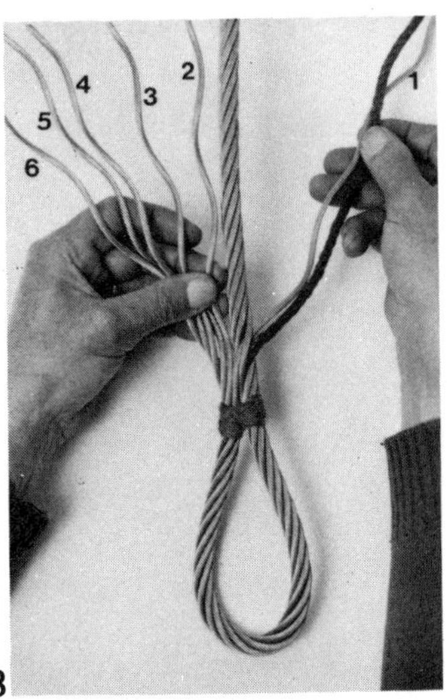

3

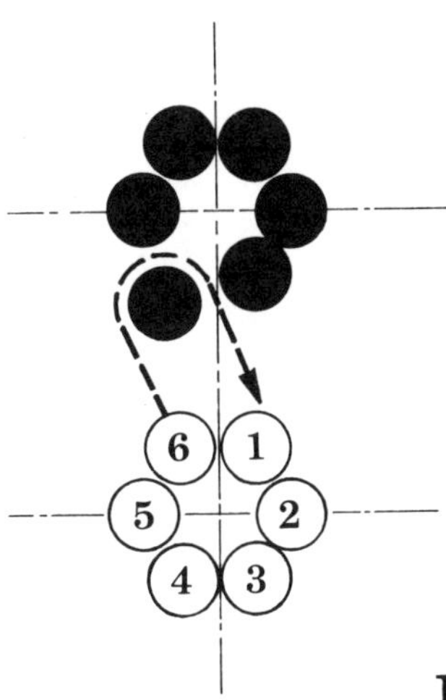

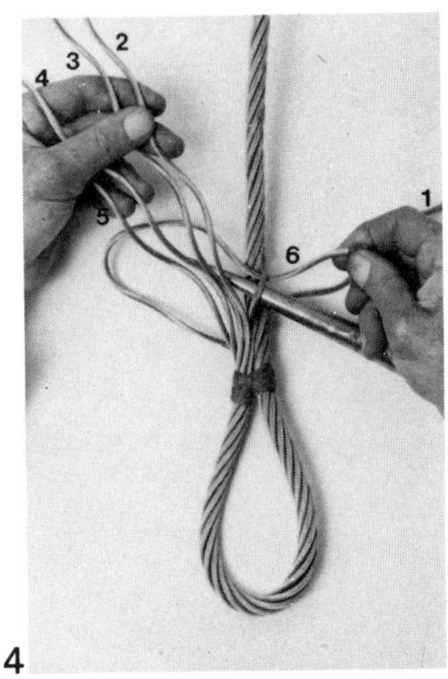

B 4

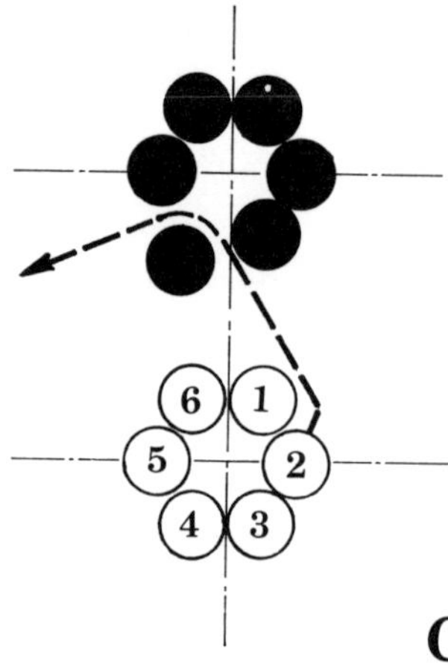

C

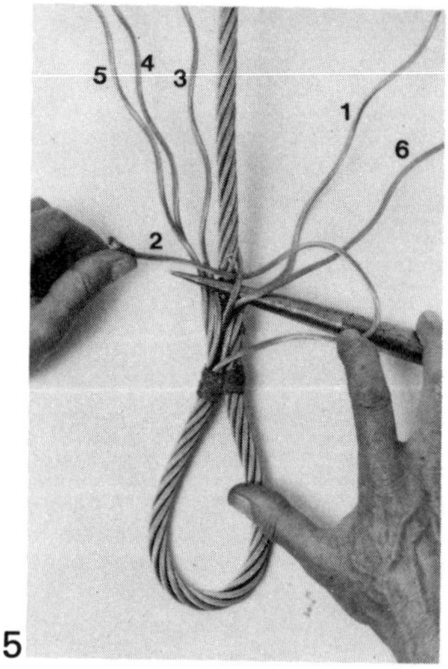

5

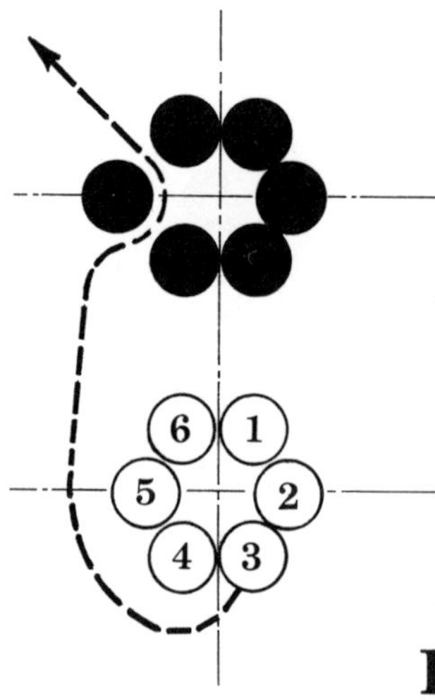

D

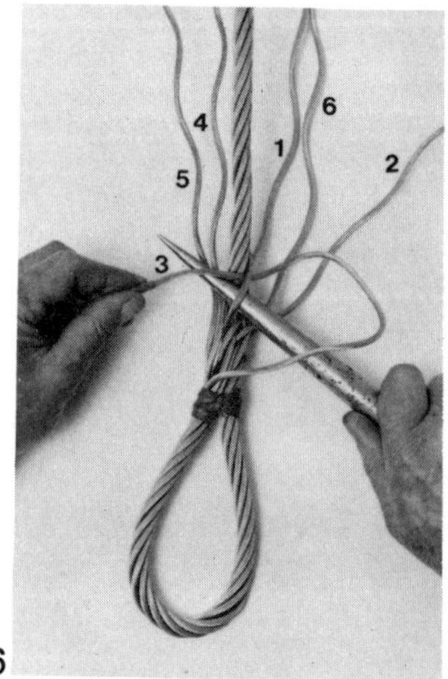

6

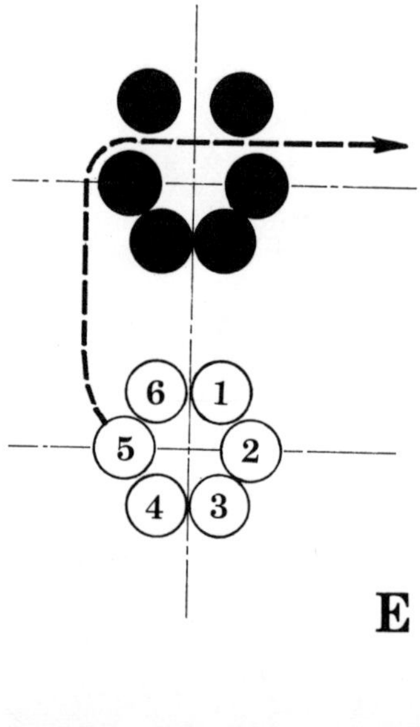

E

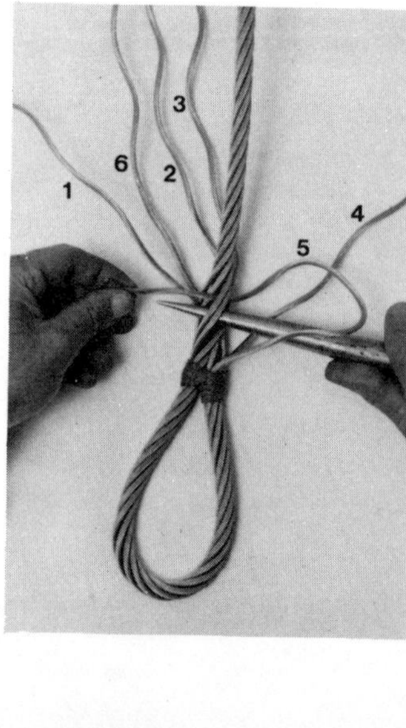

7

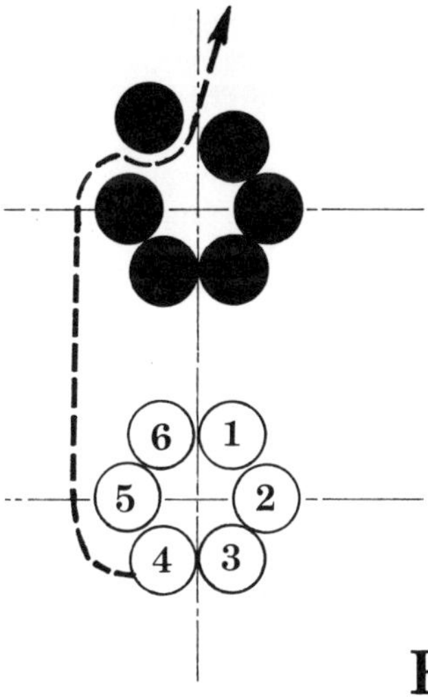

F

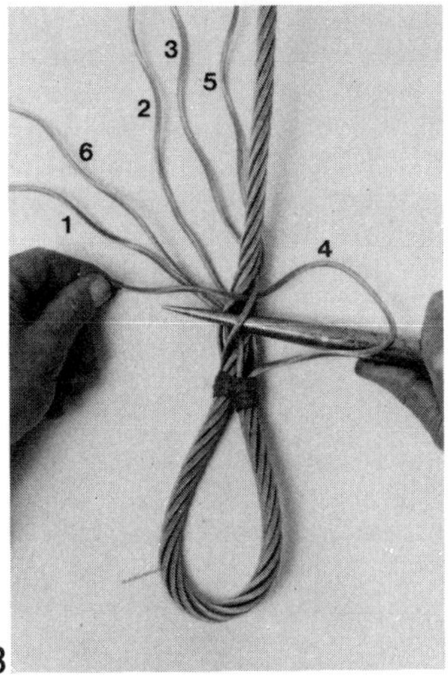

8

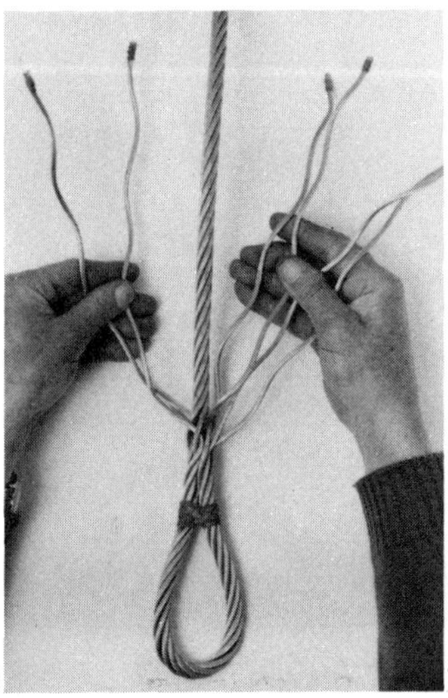

9

10

48 Liverpool Eye Splice

The 1-6-2-3-5-4 method (Knot 47) of inserting the first tuck can be used in this splice, but an alternative is illustrated, in which five of the six strands enter the standing part between the same two strands and the sixth forms the locking tuck.

The Liverpool splice is not as efficient as the Admiralty and should definitely not be used when the wire into which it is formed is likely to revolve under load.

All strands are unlaid, care being taken to maintain them in their correct order, 1 to 6, which is the order of tucking and strand 1 is established (Fig 1) whilst Diagram G indicates its tucked direction and position. The spike is inserted between the appropriate strands of the standing part, lifting one strand only, under which strand 1, together with the heart, is tucked from right to left, Fig 2, and hauled tight as Fig 3, after which the heart is cut off. The spike is partially withdrawn and re-inserted under two strands, Diagram H and strand 2 is tucked as Fig 4.

As it is almost a question of repetition, strands 3, 4 and 5 are tucked by again partially withdrawing the spike and re-inserting under three strands, Diagram J, to receive strand 3; four strands, Diagram K to receive strand 4; five strands, Diagram L to receive strand 5.

At this stage, strand 6 is the only one remaining untucked and the front of the splice appears as Fig 5, with the back as Fig 6, strand 6 being on the right.

This is now tucked under the same strand of the standing part as strand 1, but in the opposite direction, Diagram M and Fig 7. On completion, the finished first full tuck appears as Fig 8.

All strands should be hammered down with a mallet as they are tucked, but all have been left loose so that the illustration is as clear as possible. From this point onwards, the weakness of the Liverpool splice becomes apparent.

The spike is inserted under any one strand, above the first full tuck and the corresponding tail, in professional jargon is continually tucked under this strand, with the lay; more simply, the tail is wound around and around this one strand. Once inserted, the spike is twisted around the wire ahead of the tail end. The first tail, completely tucked is shown in Fig 9. The process is repeated with each tail in turn being wound around its appropriate strand of the standing part to completion as in Fig 10.

The heart must not be disturbed when tucking strands 4 and 5, which are laid on the opposite side of the heart to the first three, and maintain the position of the heart in the middle of the wire.

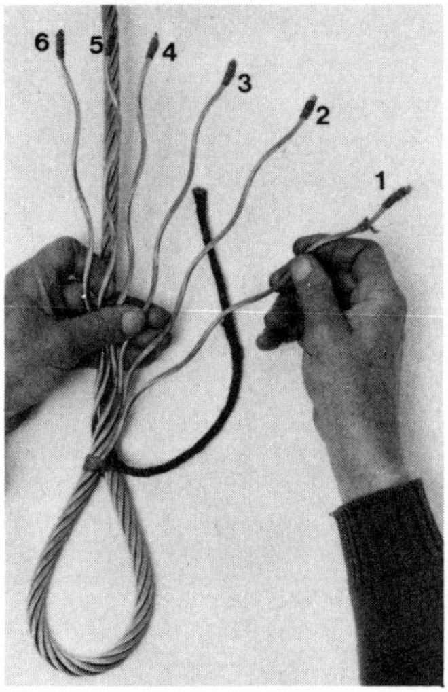
6
5
4
3
2
1

1

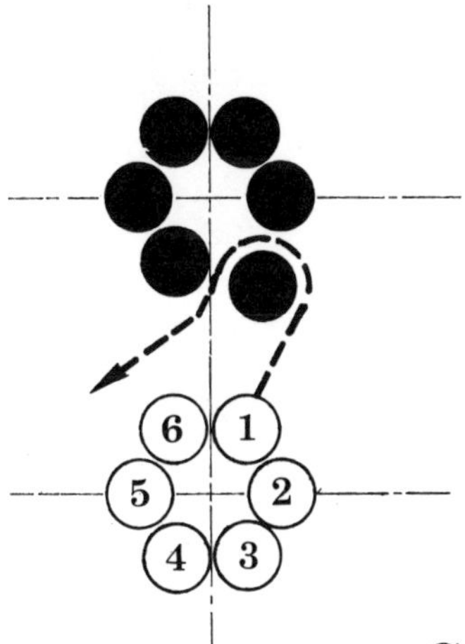
6
1
5
2
4
3

G

5
6
4
3
2
1

2

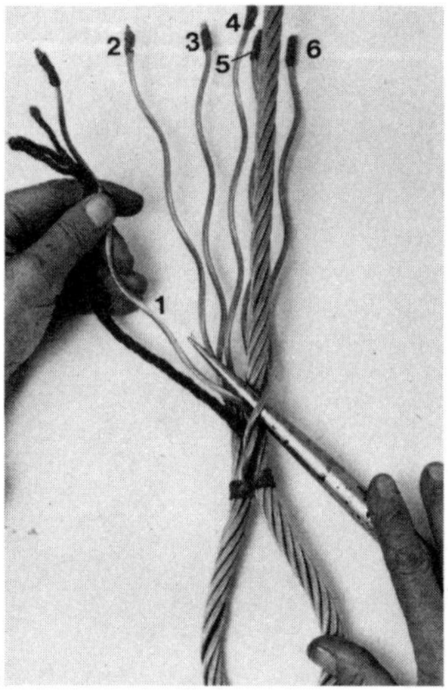
2
3
4
5
6
1

3

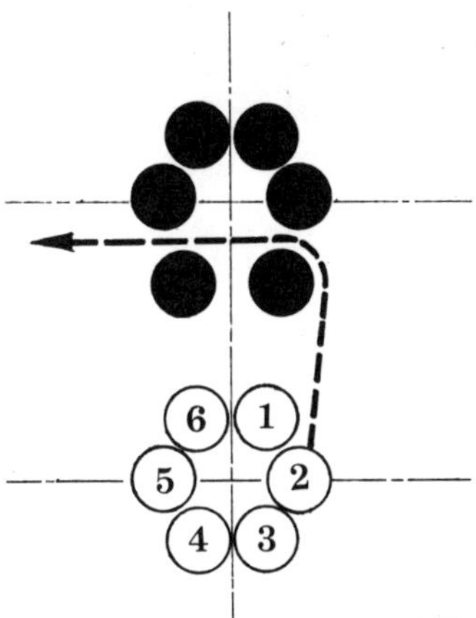
6
1
5
2
4
3

H

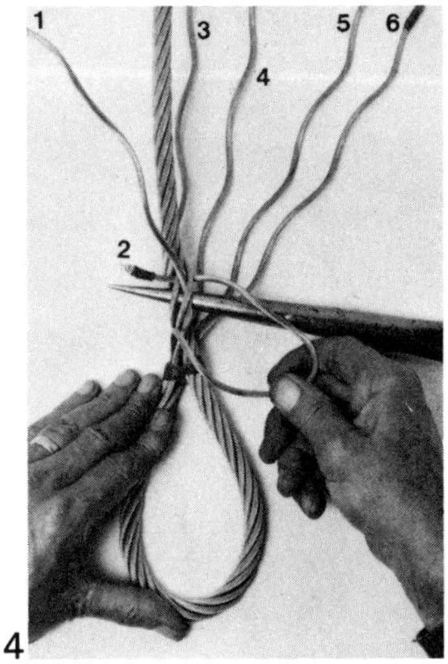
1
3
4
5
6
2

4

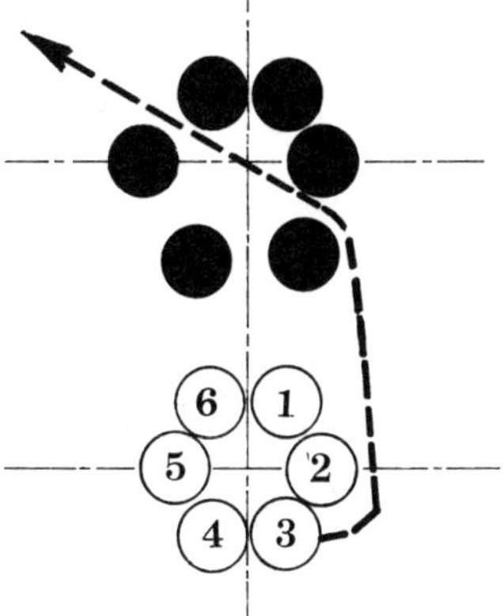
6
1
5
2
4
3

J

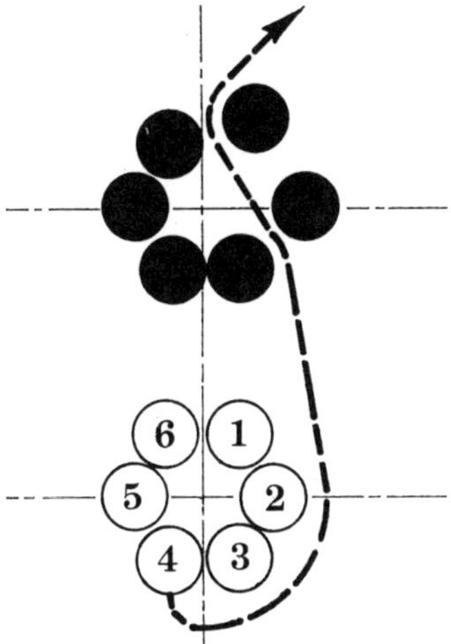
6
1
5
2
4
3

K

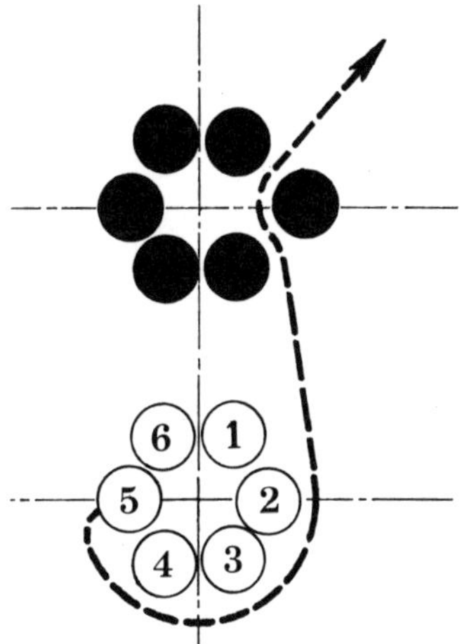
6
1
5
2
4
3

L

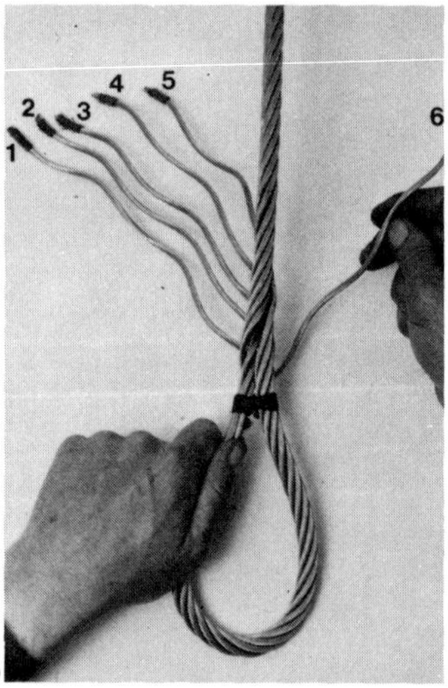

5

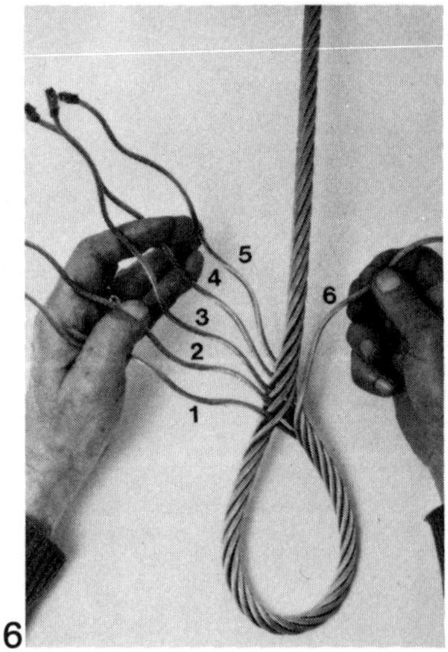

6

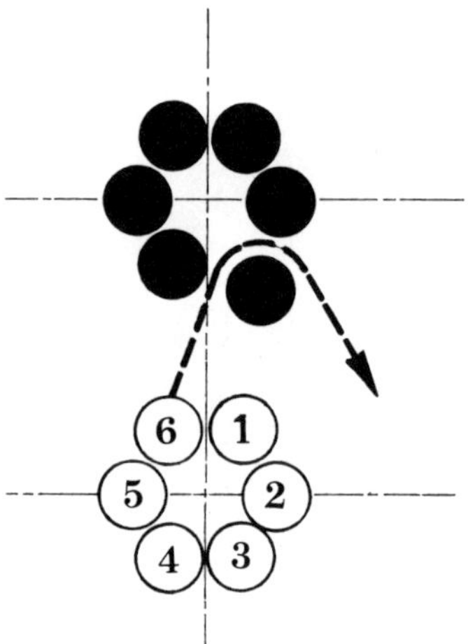

M

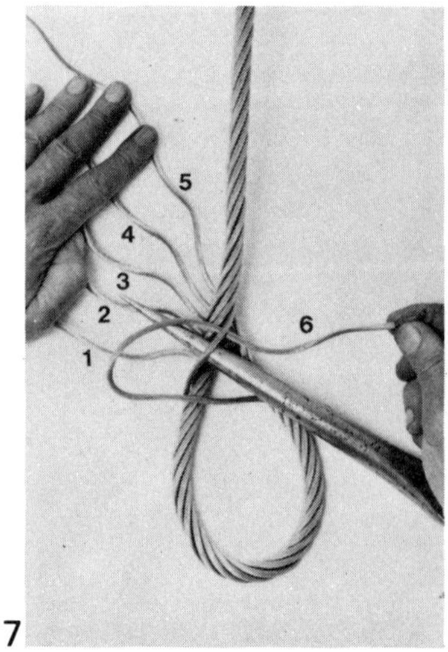

7

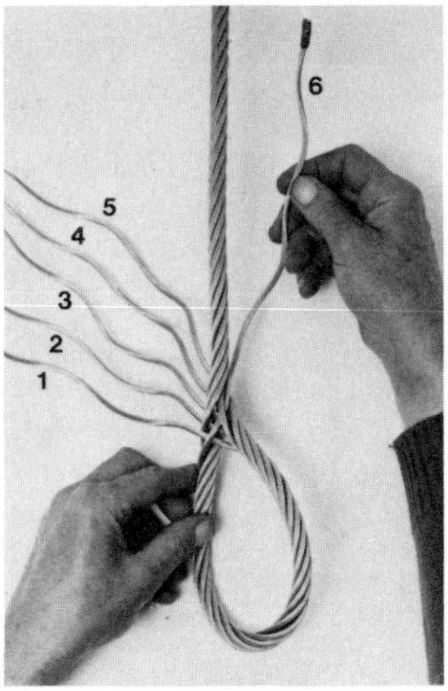

8

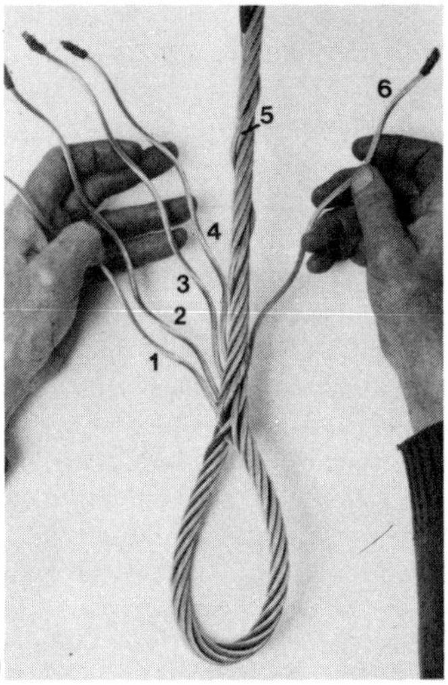

9

10

49 Flemish Eye Splice

This is an easy method of producing a long eye in the end of a wire for general purpose work, as no tools are required. It is not as efficient as a normal eye splice and therefore should not be loaded to the same degree.

The wire is carefully halved, with the heart remaining laid with the three strands on the one side, for a length of approximately two and a half times that of the required eye.

The two sets of strands are crossed at the extremity of the eye, Fig 1, ensuring that the one set fits snugly into the vacant lay of the other and both are married by tucking the left-hand set under and up through the eye and the right hand set over and down, Figs 2 to 5.

This tucking is continued, re-establishing the original six-strand lay until the two sets of strands meet at the throat of the eye, Fig 6. These strands are now re-laid together to form a single six-strand tail, Figs 7 and 8, which is firmly seized to the standing part. The use of a bulldog grip instead of a seizing obviously increases the strength of the eye.

1
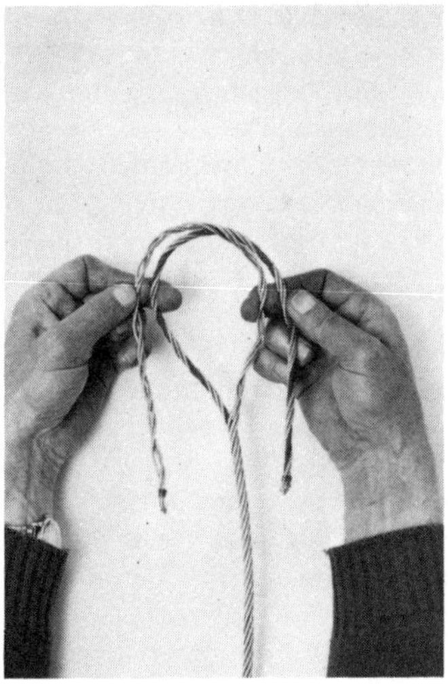

2
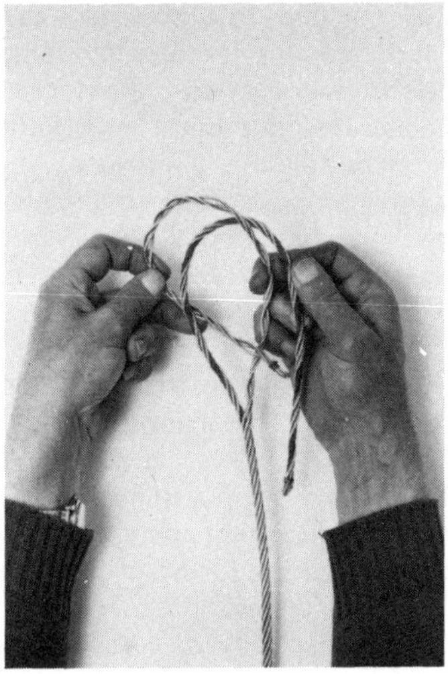

3
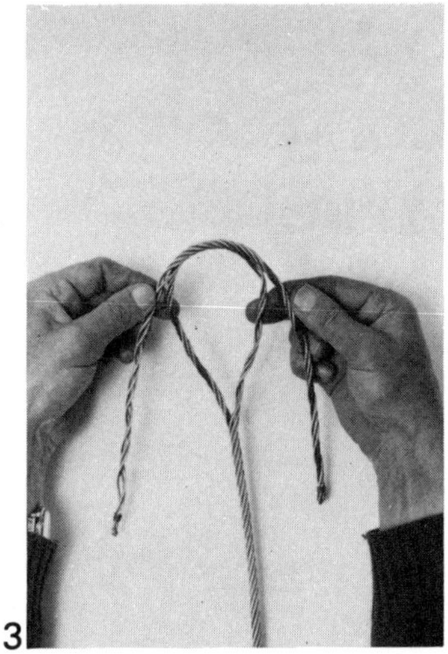

4
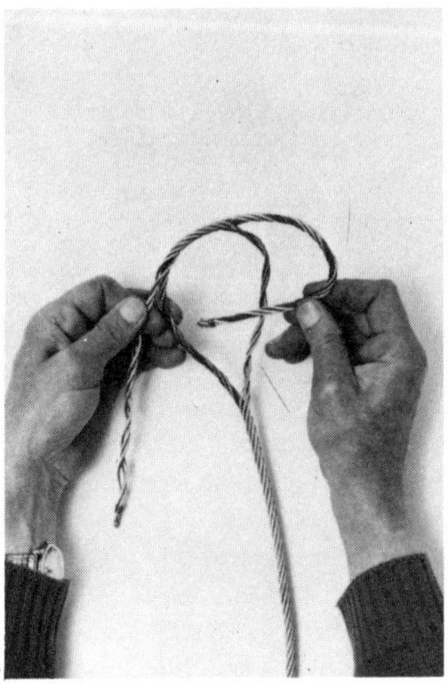

5
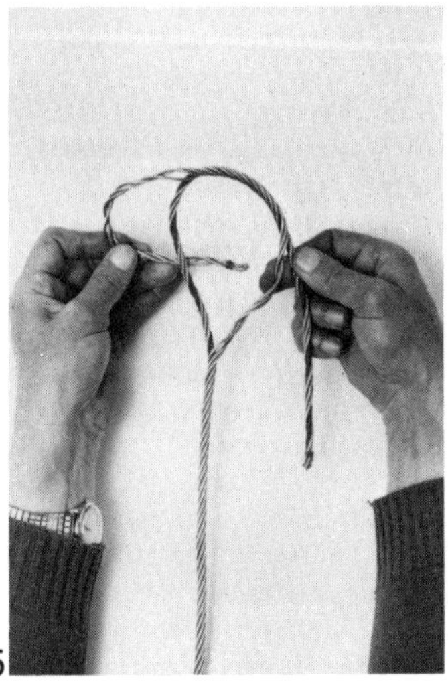

6
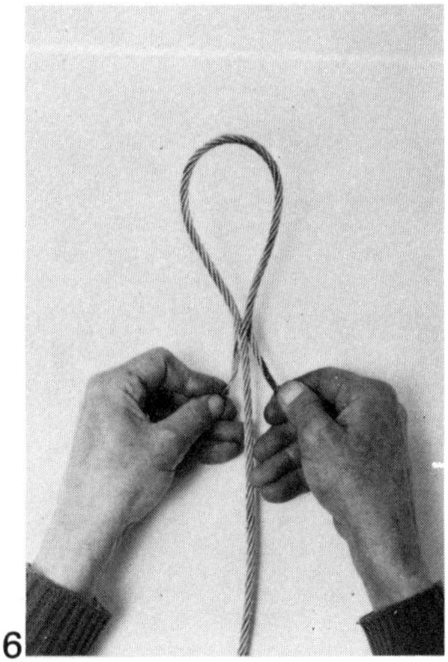

7
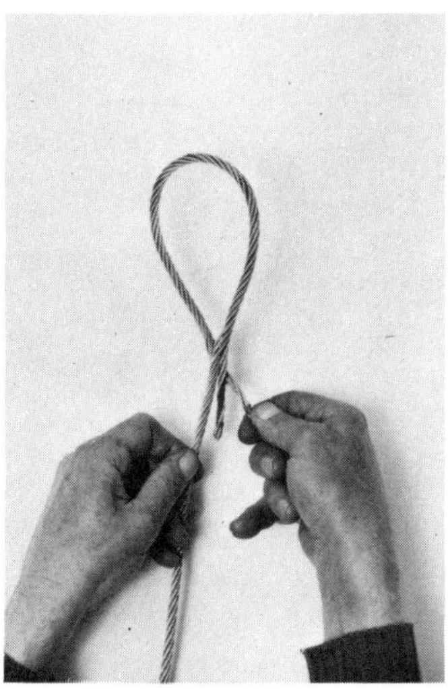

8

50 Long Splice (Wire)

The long splice in wire is made on the same basic principle as that of rope and for the same reason, namely to join two ends in such manner that the diameter of the wire is not increased at the join and it is thus suitable for working over a sheave.
It may be said that it consists of two stages: the unlaying and replacement of corresponding strands, which is comparatively simple, once the principle is understood; and the tucking away of the tail ends, which is the secret of good long-splicing. The former is shown in Figs 1 to 6 and the latter (which also applies to the grommet, Knot 51), in Figs 7 to 14.
Again, as with rope, the splice depends solely on friction for its stability, but a much longer splice is required when working with wire.
The accepted standard for the total length of the splice is 10ft for every one eighth of an inch of the diameter. This does not provide for the tail ends, for which a further 6in per one eighth of diameter is allowed.
It is assumed that the wire illustrated is one inch diameter, in which case the total length of the splice would be 88ft and as it is impossible to photograph such lengths without a complete loss of detail, the splice has been done in miniature and the reader must envisage the true lengths involved.
A temporary whipping is put on each of the two wires 44ft from their respective ends, all strands are unlaid back to these points and the hearts cut out, Fig 1.
The strands are interwoven on the same principle as those of rope in the short splice (Knot 32, Fig 1), until all are meshing alternately, when the two wires are brought together until the ends of the hearts meet and the six pairs of strands are married, Fig 2, when the whipping is removed.
As with the long splice in rope (Knot 33), one corresponding pair of wires is selected, that of the right hand wire unlaid for a distance of 40ft and that of the left, carefully laid back in its place, when 4ft of its length remains at the 40ft mark.
The unlaid right-hand strand is cut to the same length and the first pair of tails, each 4ft long, established 40ft away from the point of marry (the centre of the splice) as Fig 3. The next adjacent, corresponding pair of strands are now worked in the same manner and the second pair of ends, both cut to 4ft long, established 28ft from the marrying point, Fig 4. The process is repeated with the third pair of strands, resulting in the third pair of tails, cut to length as before, 16ft from the centre, Fig 5.
The whole process is repeated to the left of centre resulting in a further three pairs of tails being established and the whole appears as Fig 6, with six pairs of tails, each 4ft long and the distances between them being 12, 12, 32, 12, and 12ft respectively. This completes the basic splice and it only remains to tuck away the tail ends.
Each tail is served for its full length with marline or soft wire to increase the diameter of the strand to approximately that of the heart, Fig 7.
Again for photographic purposes the tails are shown in miniature and the reader is reminded that they are in fact 4ft long.
The heart is exposed and lifted, Fig 8, cut at the crossing point and worked out through the lay for a distance exactly equal to the length of the tail which will eventually replace it, Fig 9, where it is cut off.
There are special tools, designed for tucking the tails namely a

tee needle and tucker, but it can be done with a pair of small spikes or the like. The standing part is opened and working around the wire, with the lay, the tail is gradually worked into the centre of the wire, replacing the heart, Figs 10 to 13. The remaining tail is tucked in a similar manner when the finished work appears as Fig 14 and the whole is repeated for the remaining five pairs of tails.
It is important that there is no gap between the end of the buried tail and the continuation of the heart.

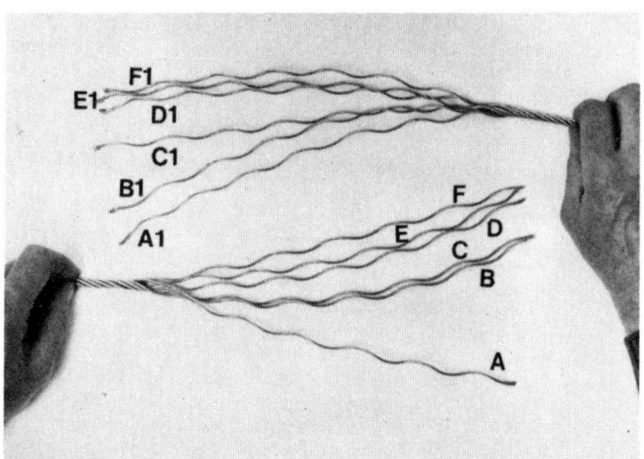

1

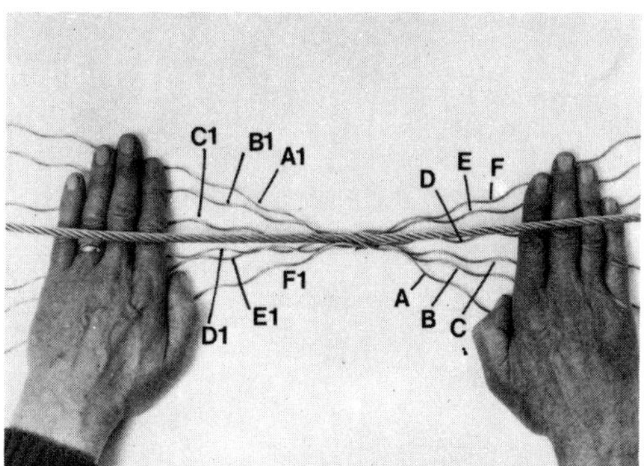

2

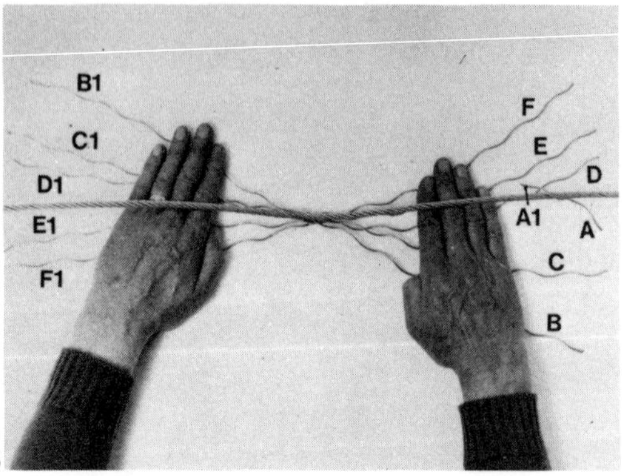
B1
C1
D1
E1
F1
F
E
D
A1
A
C
B
3

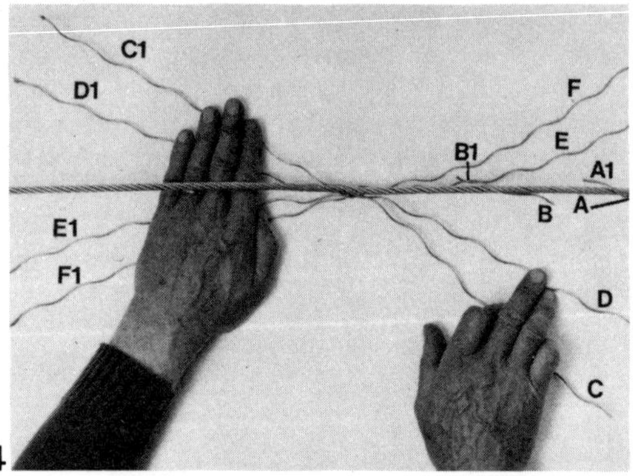
C1
D1
F
E
B1
A1
B
A
E1
F1
D
C
4

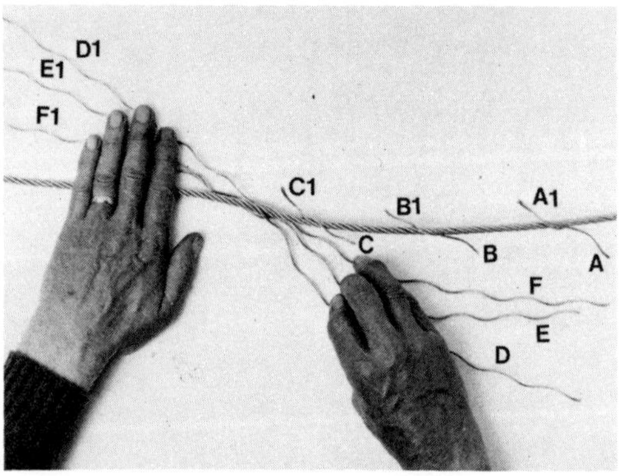
D1
E1
F1
C1
B1
A1
C
B
A
F
E
D
5

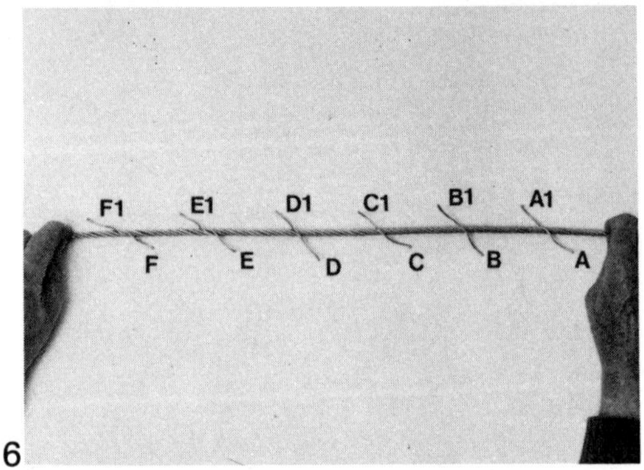
F1
E1
D1
C1
B1
A1
F
E
D
C
B
A
6

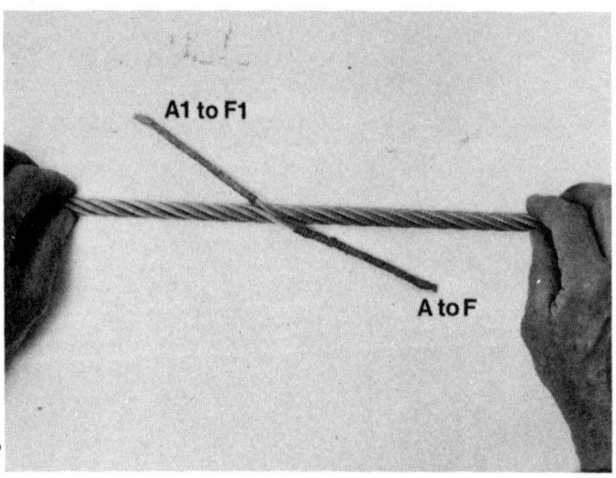
A1 to F1
A to F
7

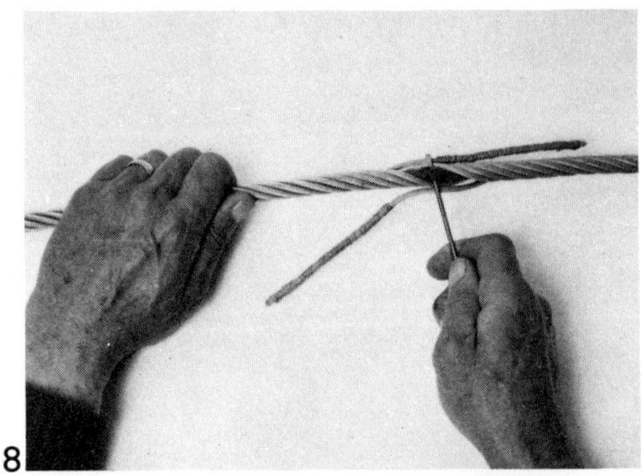
8

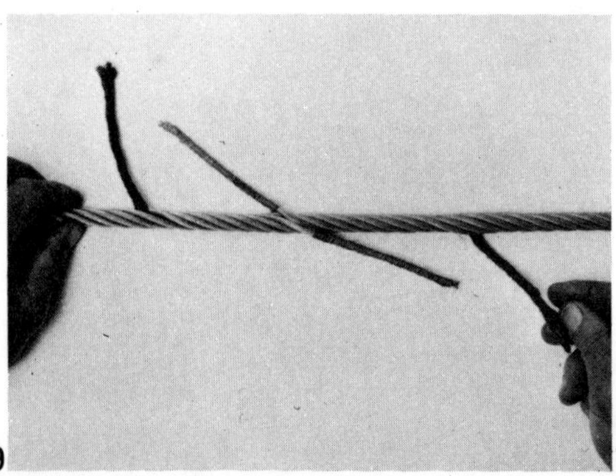
9

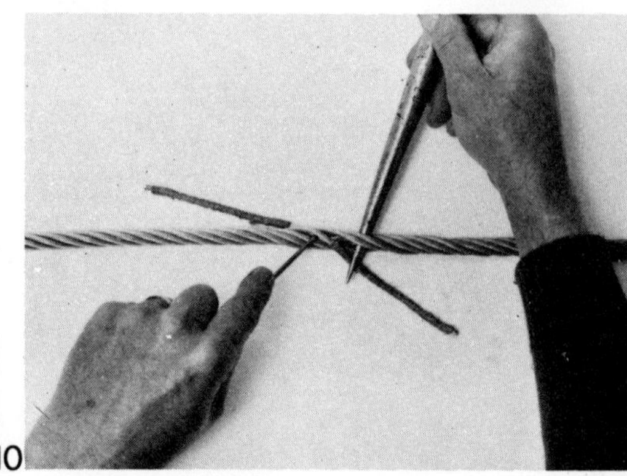
10

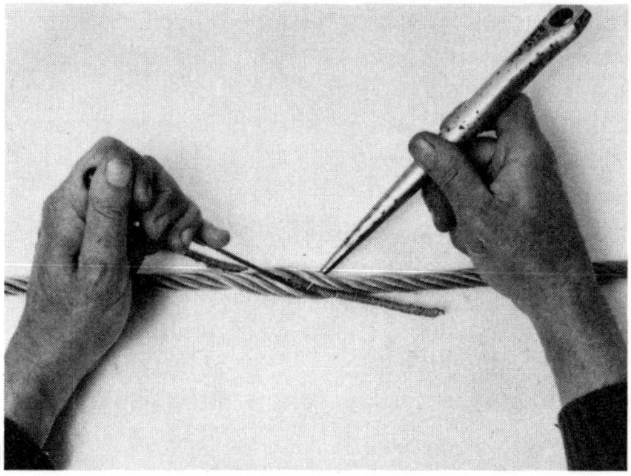
11

12

13

14

51 Grommet [Wire]

In making a grommet the principles of the Flemish eye (counter laying three strands with three corresponding strands and a heart) and the long splice are combined and when the circle of the grommet itself is completed sufficient length of tails must remain to proceed with the long splice, Fig 4.

A length of wire, approximately nine times the diameter of the required grommet is needed and three adjacent strands are carefully unlaid, leaving the heart intact with the remaining three strands.

The unlaid strands are discarded and the heart is removed for equal distances from both ends, leaving a length of heart equal to the circumference of the grommet in the centre of the working strands.

The circle is formed and the two sets of three strands married at the point where the two ends of the heart meet, Fig 1. The right-hand ends are brought under and up and the left-hand ends over and down through the circle, re-forming the six-strand lay as Figs 2 and 3 and continued until the ends meet and the basic grommet is completed Fig 4.

The tails are now unlaid, Fig 5 and as illustrated in Knot 50, a long splice is formed with the three pairs of strands, which are then cut to the required length, Fig 6. It only remains to tuck away the ends as shown in Knot 50, Figs 7 to 14, and the completed grommet appears as Fig 7.

1

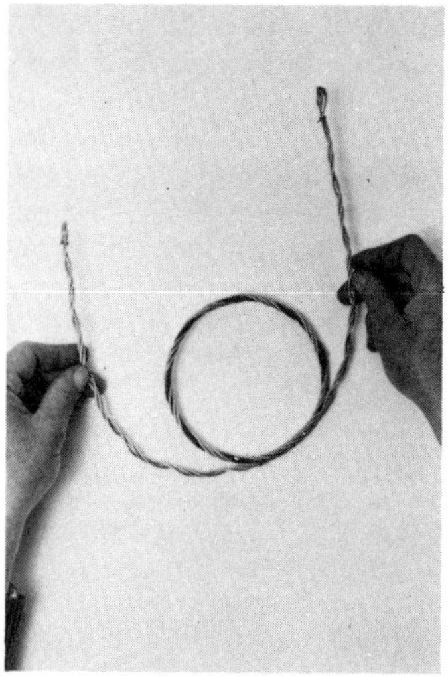
2

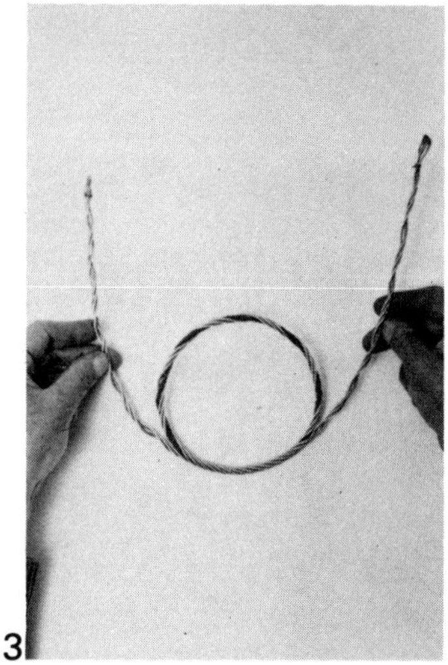
3

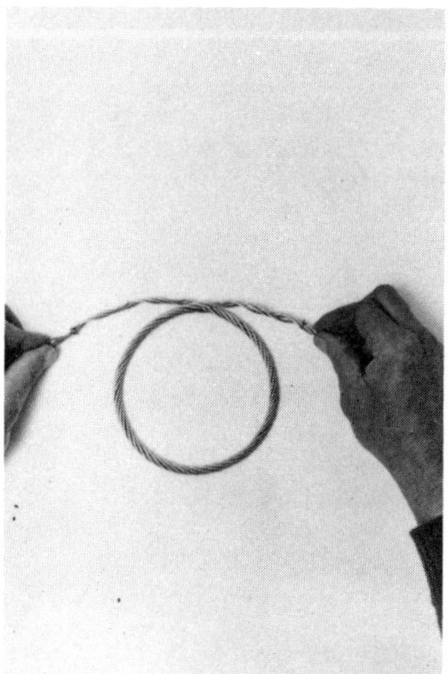
4

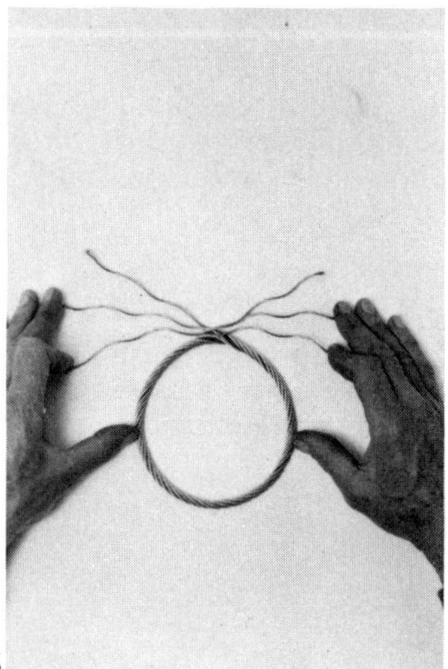
5

6

7

PART TWO

52 To Wall Any Number of Strands

Pass each strand around under its neighbour, working anti-clockwise, Fig 1, and pass the last strand up through the bight of the first (held on the thumb), Fig 2. In a correct wall all strands emerge separately from the top, pointing upwards. Any number of strands may be used and it can be made backwards (ie clockwise).

Double Wall*
The emerging strands, Fig 3, lay alongside previous bights which are 'followed around' until all again emerge separately from the top, pointing upwards as in Fig 4. The knot has been shown 'flat' but when hauled tight it assumes a vertical form, the 'followed around' strands resting on the *wall* below.

Continuous Walling
Suitable only for covering any cylindrical object due to the hollow centre which develops. Strands are whipped to the object and walls made one on top of another, Fig 5A.

Wall Plait*
A reasonably tight plait can be made by continuous walling without a central heart provided not more than four strands are used, Fig 5B.

*Indicates throughout knots using four individual strands that can be made on three strands of an unlaid rope (see Introduction).

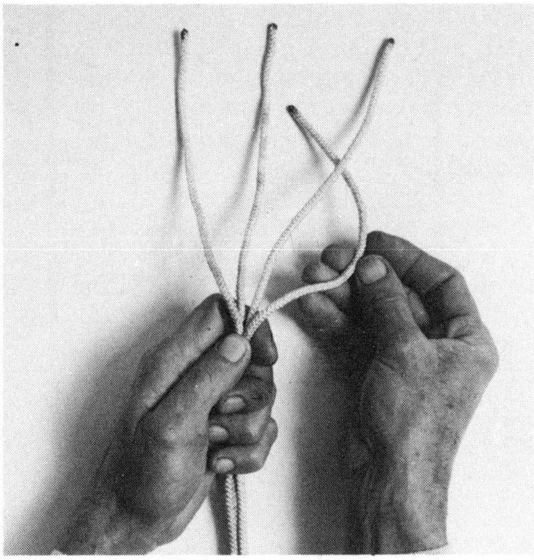

1

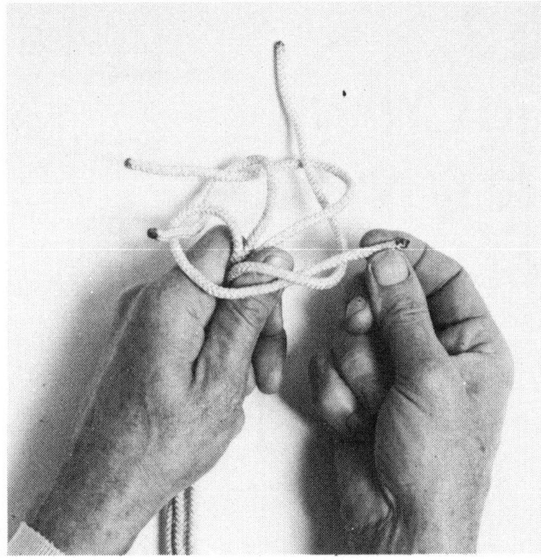

2

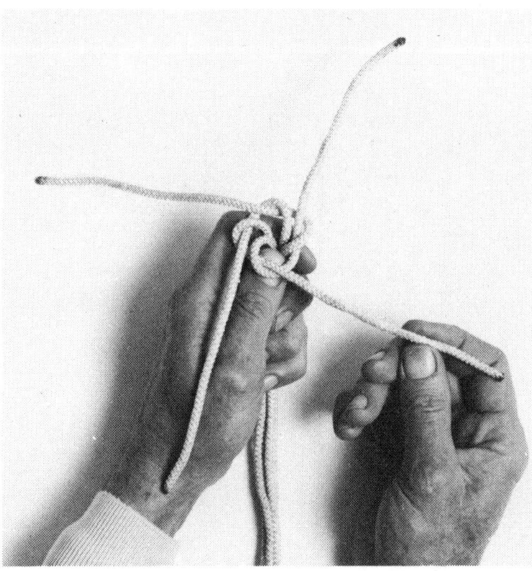

3

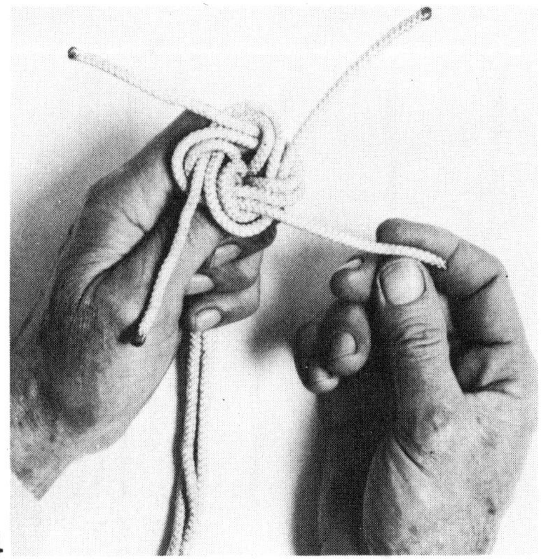

4

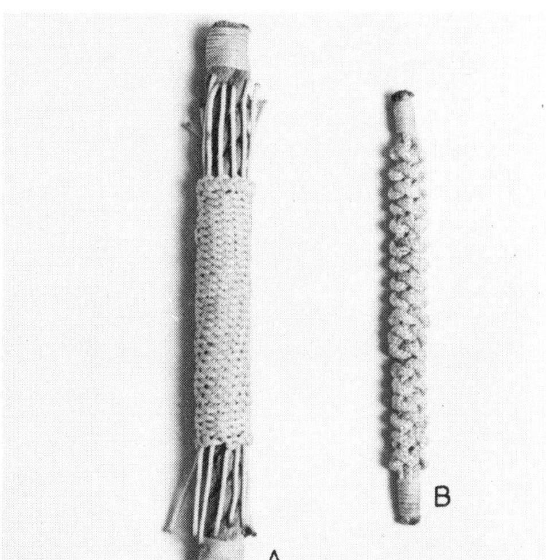

5

53 To Crown Any Number of Strands

Pass each strand around over its neighbour working anti-clockwise, Fig 1, and the last strand down through the bight of the first, Fig 2. All strands should emerge separately from the bottom, pointing downwards, Fig 3. It can also be made backwards (clockwise) and any number of strands used.

Double Crown*
Form the crown as shown in Fig 3, pull back any one strand and make a clockwise turn around the strand it has passed over, returning it to its original position, Fig 4. Repeat with the other three strands, the last passing through the double bight of the first, Fig 5.

Continuous Crowning
This is another method of covering any cylindrical object, by forming one crown on top of another, Fig 6A.

Crown Plait, Spiral*
This is made by continuous crowning, anti-clockwise, without a central heart, not more than four strands being used, when a spiral effect will result, Fig 6B.

Crown Plait, Straight*
A straight, chain-like pattern will result if the crowns are made alternately anti-clockwise and clockwise, Fig 6C.

Wall and Crown Plait*
This is made by forming alternate walls and crowns, using not more than four strands, Fig 6D.

Note
Four strands when crowned also produce a square knot.

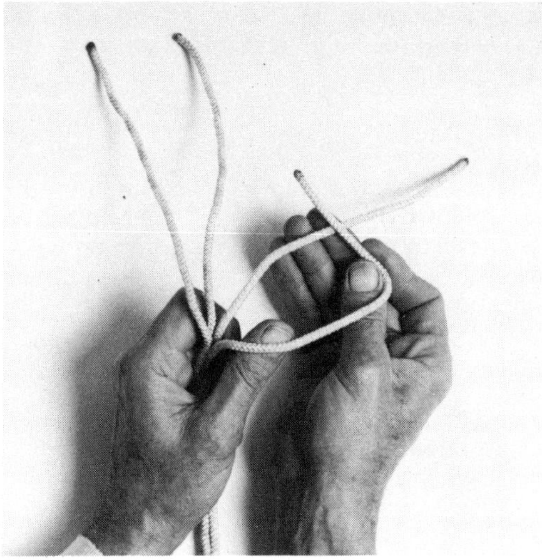
1

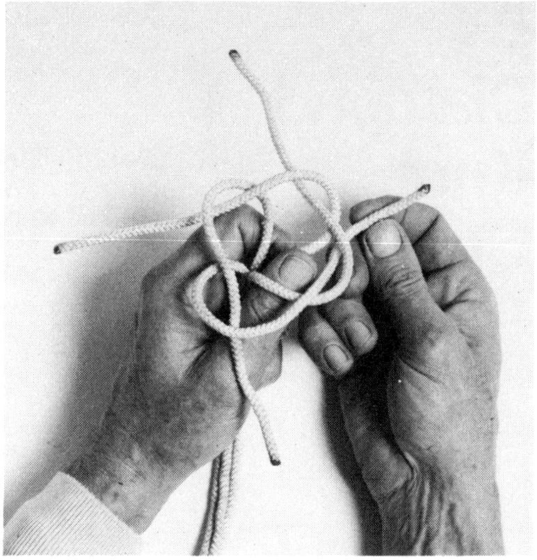
2

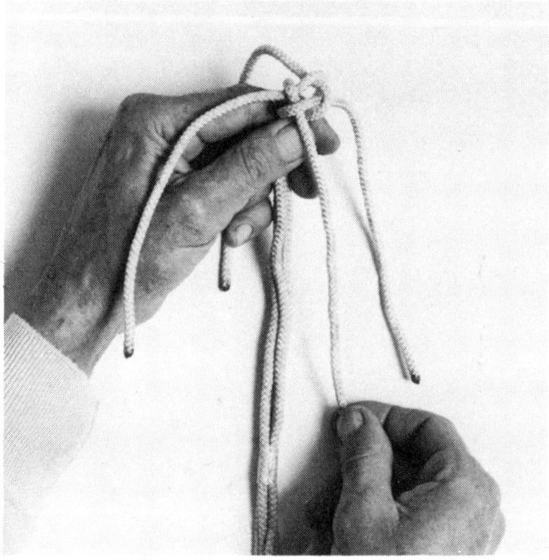
3

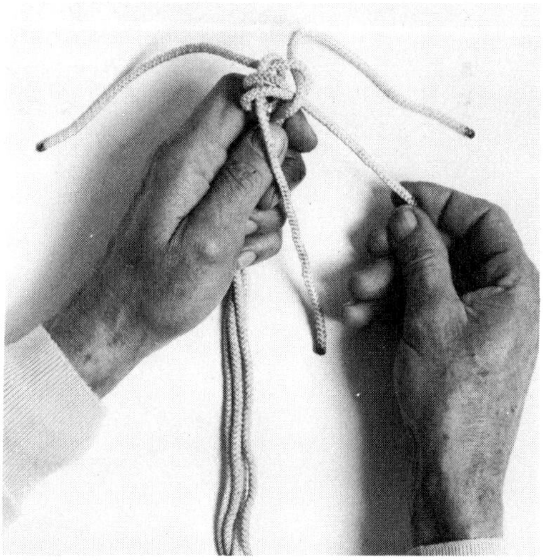
4

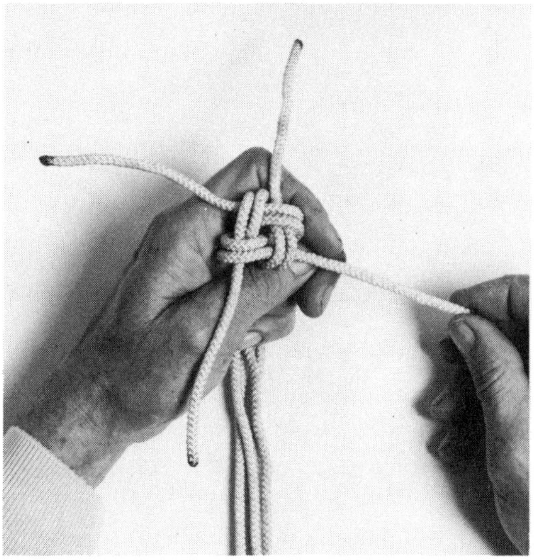
5

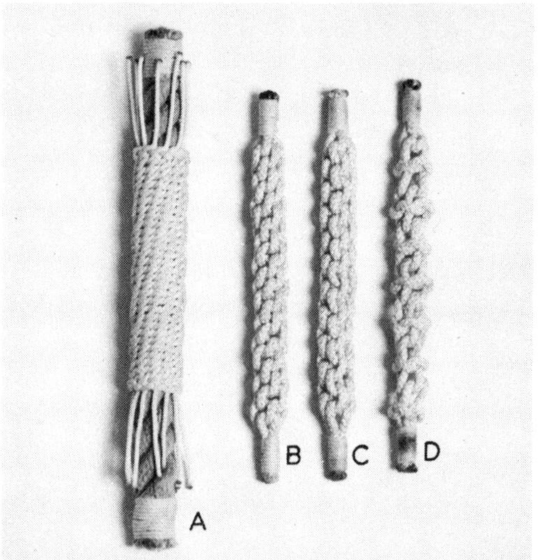

6

54 Diamond Knot, On Four Strands*

A bight is formed in all strands, Fig 1. Each strand is then taken anti-clockwise past the adjacent bight and up through the next, Figs 2 to 6.

Double Diamond Knot*
From the single diamond, each strand is 'followed around' until all again emerge from the top. Because the original knot was made by passing one bight before going up through the next, each 'follow around' strand passes under two parts, the last under two double parts, Fig 9B.

Diamond Hitching
Continuous diamond knotting can be used to cover any cylindrical object, and consists of one diamond knot on top of another, Fig 9A.

Diamond Plait
This can be made with one diamond knot on top of another but a tighter plait is obtained if crowns are made between the diamonds. Fig 9C shows single and double diamond knots with crowns between.

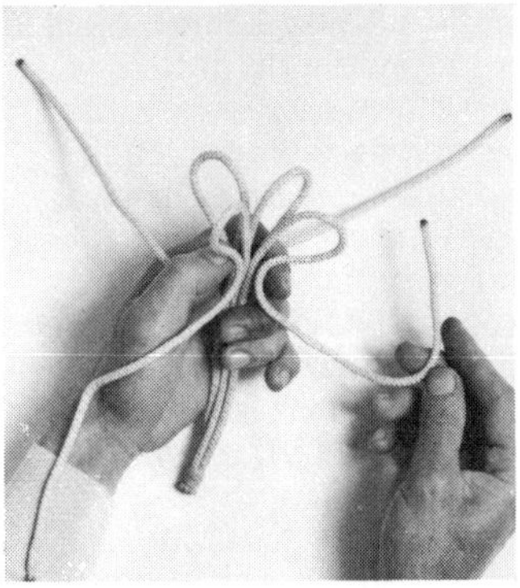

1

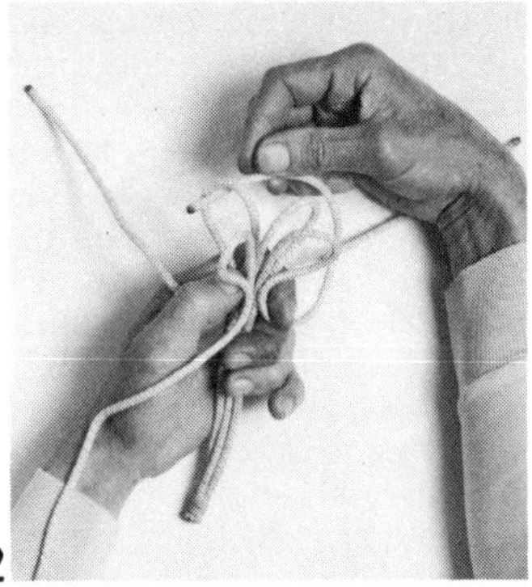

2

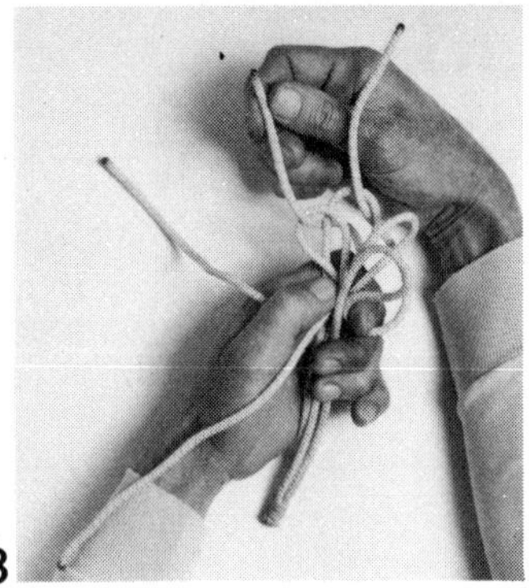

3

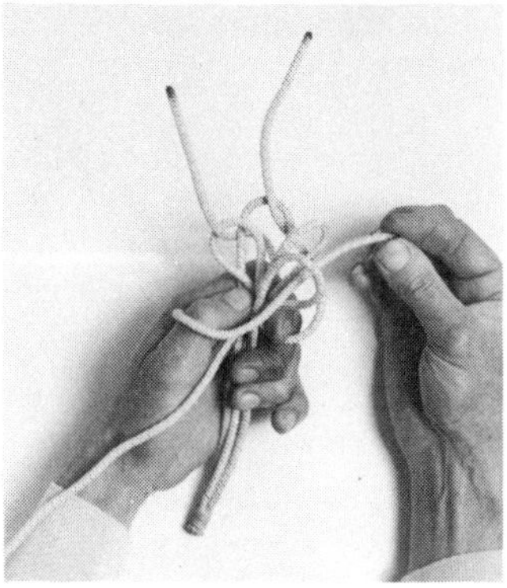

4

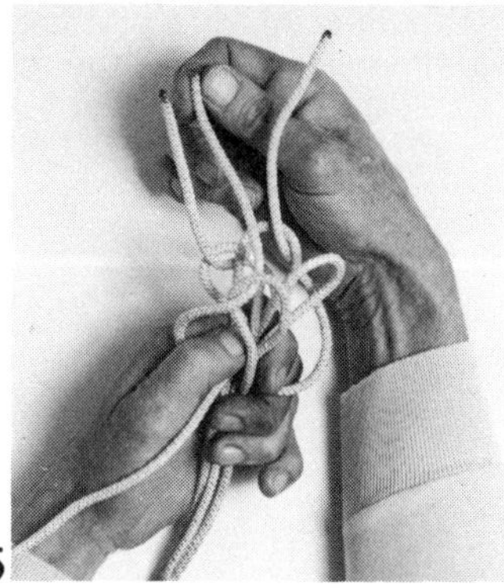

5

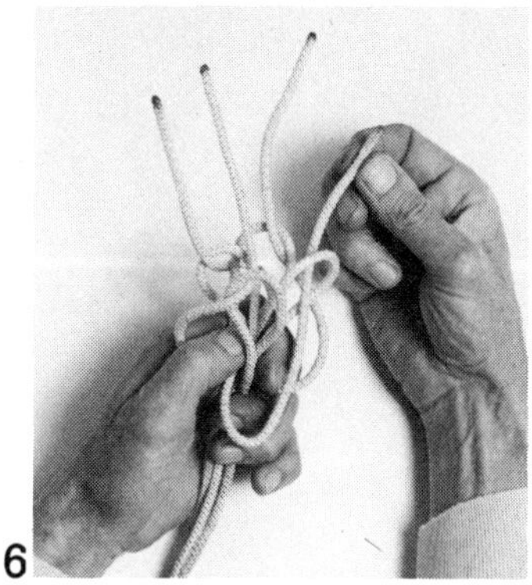

6

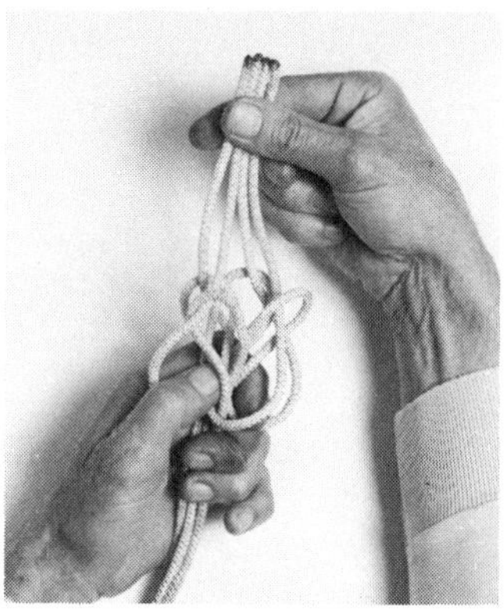

7

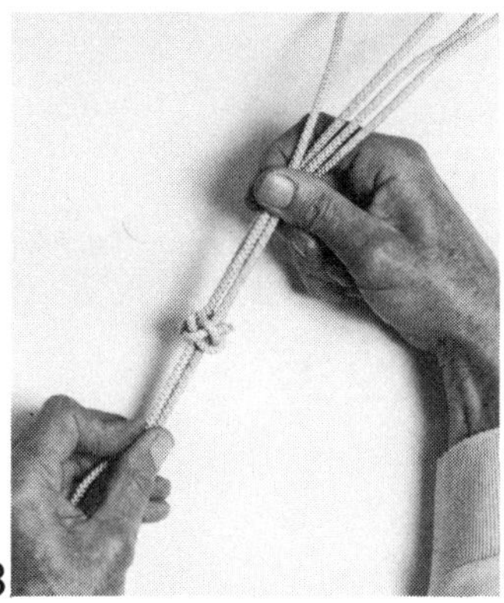

8

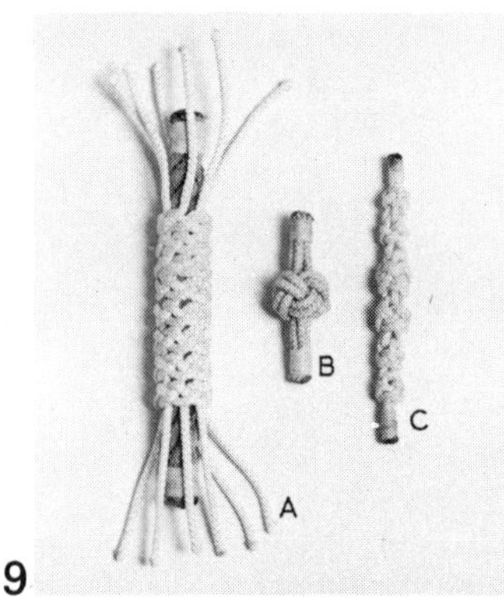

9

55 Star Knot, Six Stranded

All strands are looped *backwards*, Figs 1 and 2, and the tails brought up through the next loop working anti-clockwise, Figs 3 and 4. All are next crowned *backwards*, Figs 5 and 6. Reverting to anti-clockwise working, each strand is brought back around and up under its own part, Fig 7, forming six more loops above the originals, Fig 8. Each strand will be found to lay alongside a previous tuck, pointing directly to an appropriate pair of loops down through which all are tucked, Figs 9 and 10. The knot is turned upside-down, Fig 11, all strands again following a previous tuck, over two and down through the centre when they all emerge together, Fig 12.

The more strands used the better the result, six being shown to do the knot justice whilst ensuring photographic clarity. Any fewer will be unsatisfactory, especially four, which will result in a glorified, un-starlike square knot, ideal however if that is the requirement.

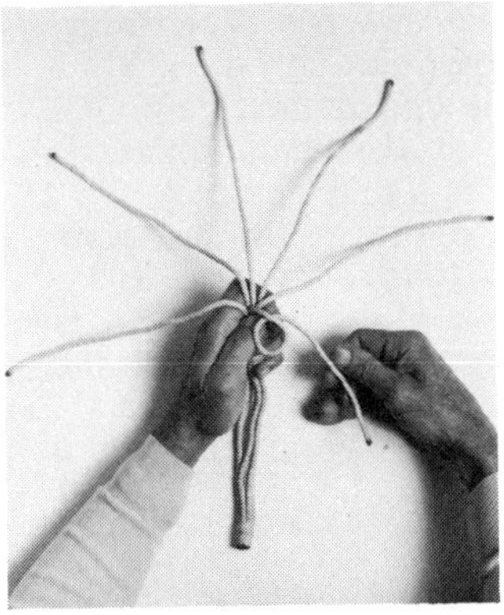
1
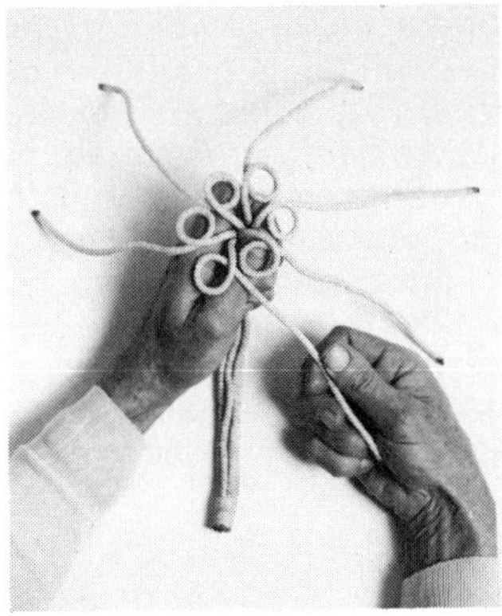
2
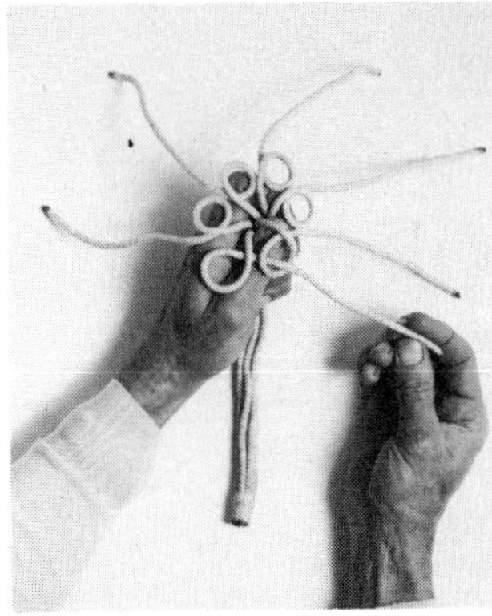
3
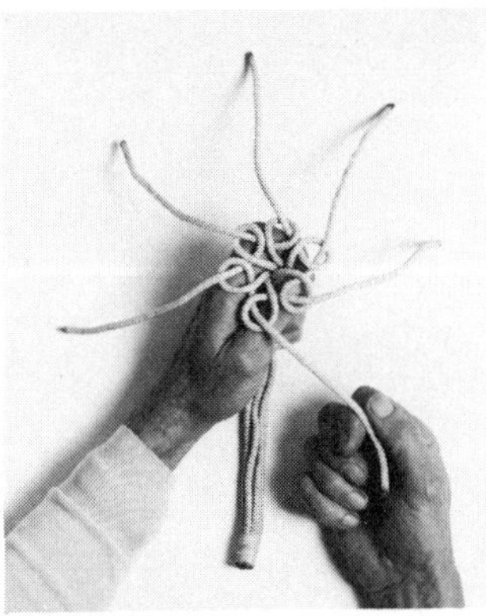
4
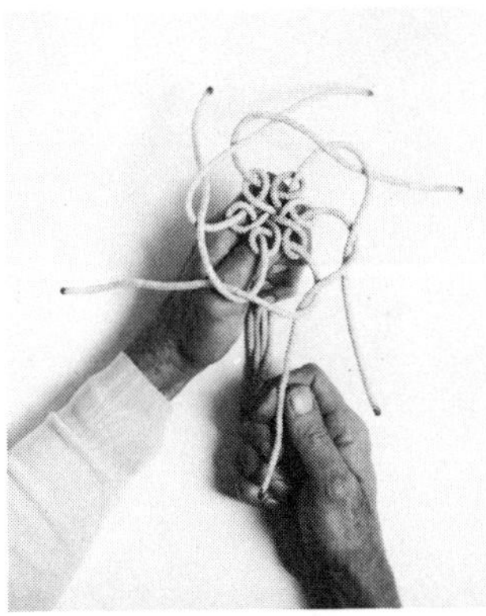
5
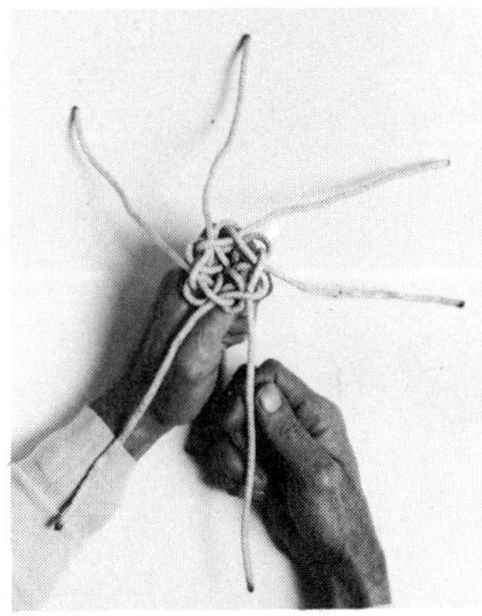
6
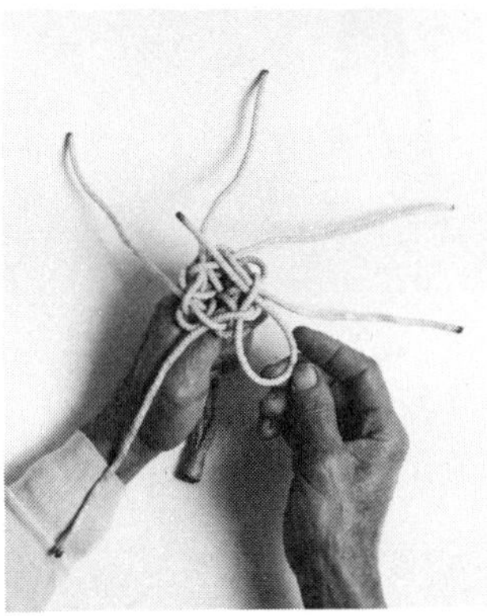
7
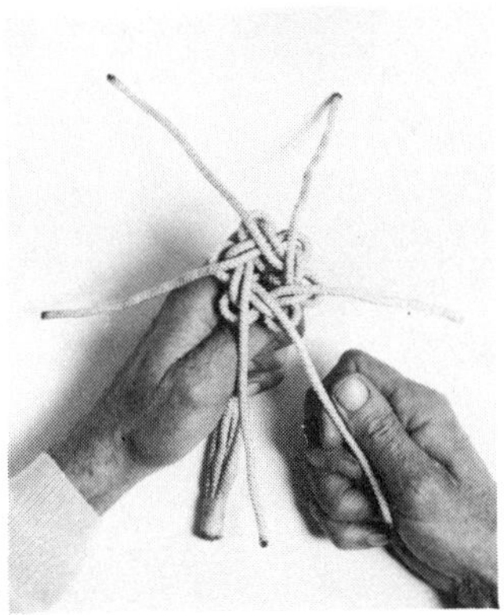
8
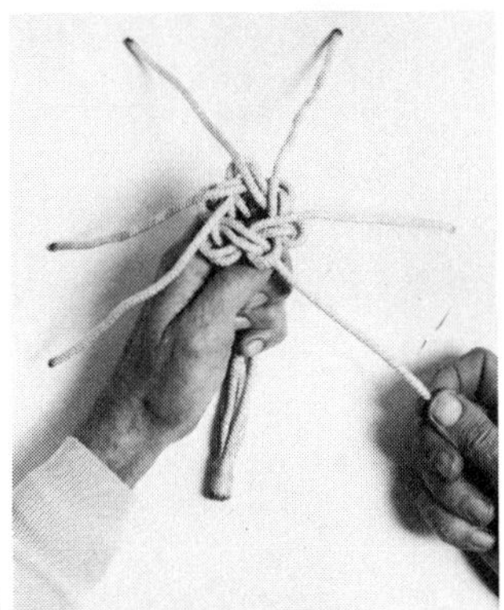
9
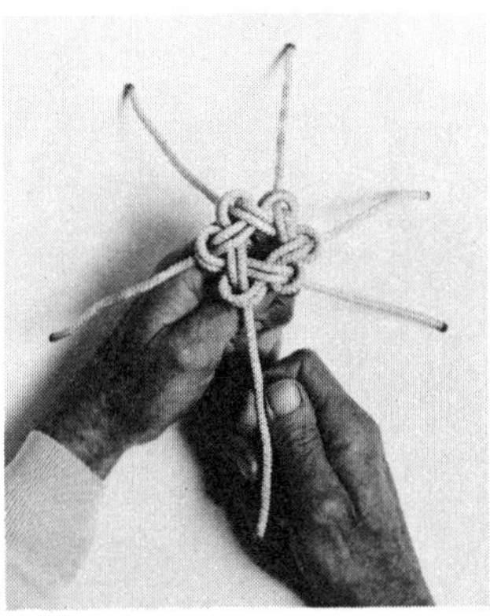
10
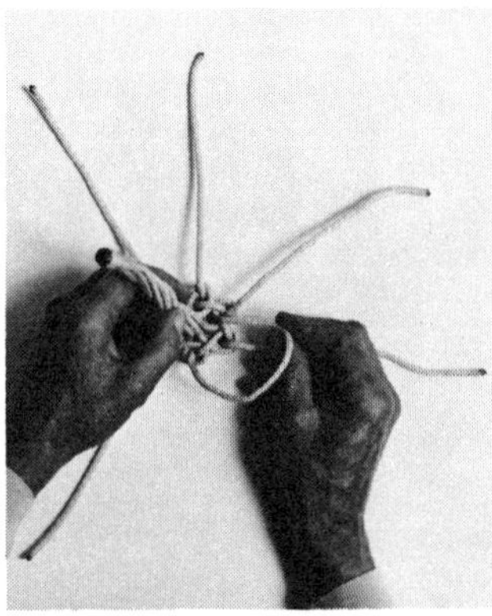
11
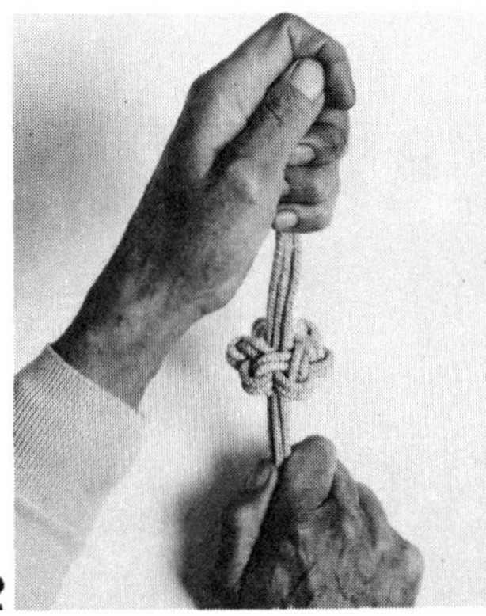
12

56 Pineapple Knot, Four Stranded

Form a crown (Knot 53), pass each strand over the adjacent bight, under its neighbour and down through the next bight, Figs 1 and 2. Turn the work upside-down and make a *backwards* crown, Fig 3, which, when tightened, leaves each strand laying alongside a previous tuck, Fig 4. 'Follow around', as in Figs 5 and 6, then return the work the right way up and continue to 'follow around', Fig 7, until all the ends emerge separately at the bottom, pointing downwards. Tuck all the strands up through the centre when they emerge together, Fig 8. If used as a terminal knot the ends can be cut short or combed into a tassel.

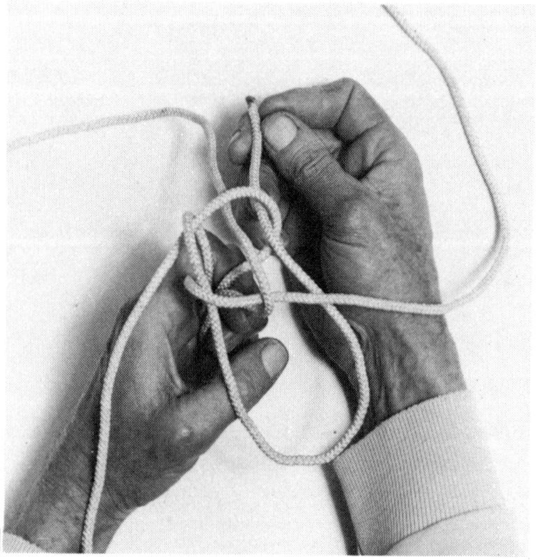
1

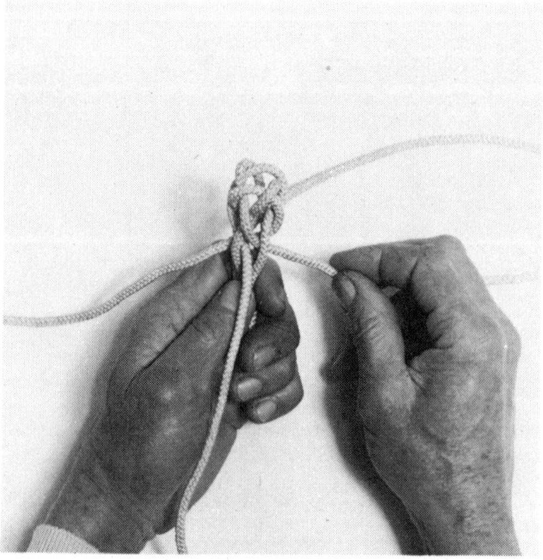
2

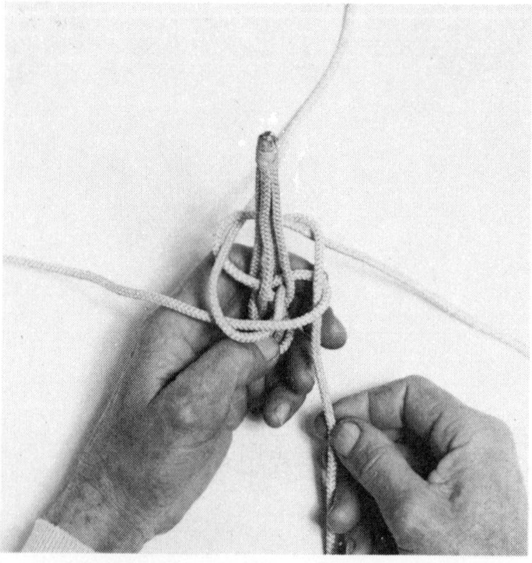
3

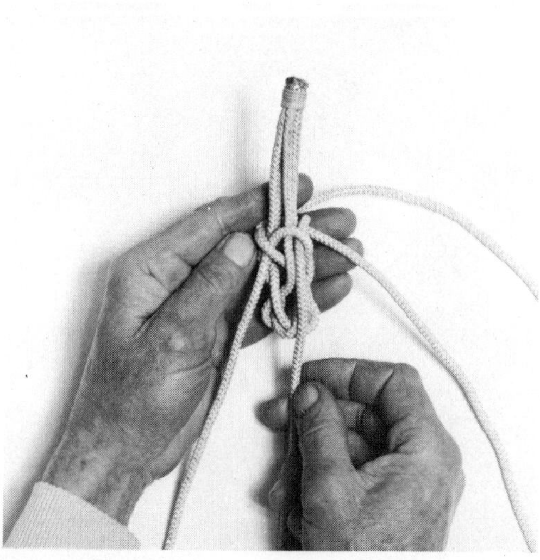
4

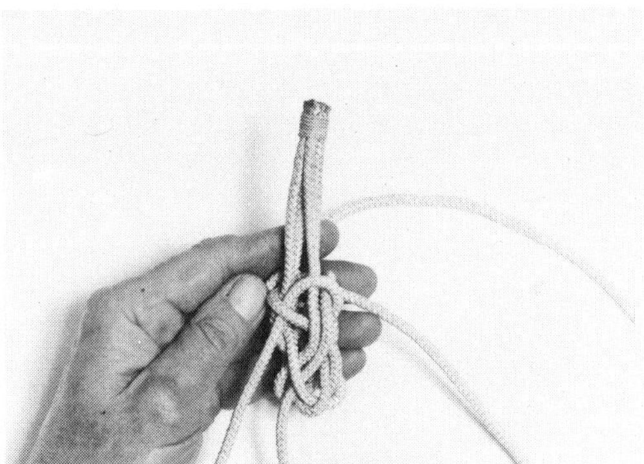
5

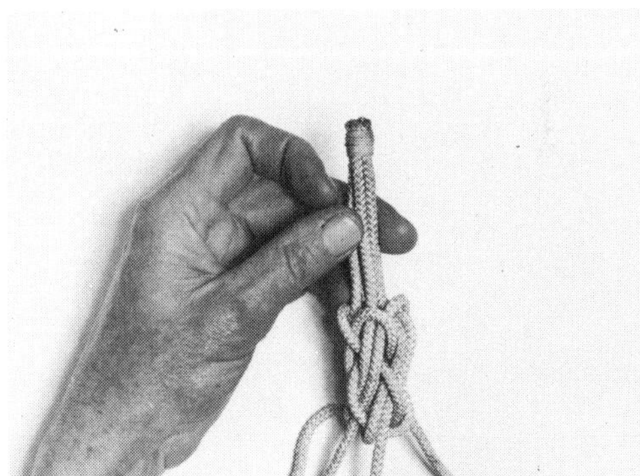
6

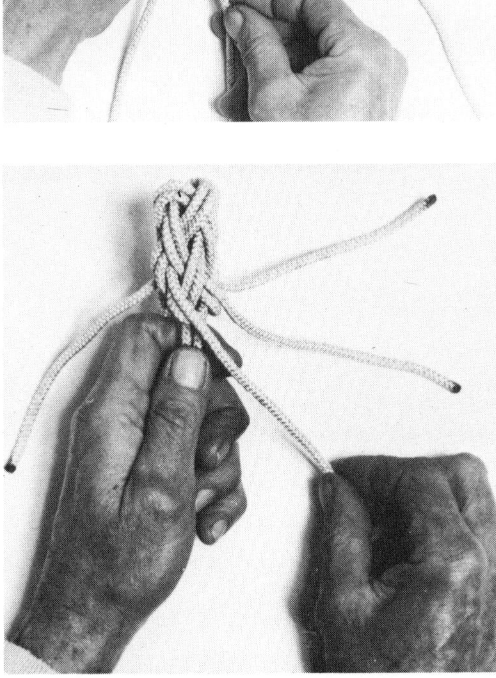
7

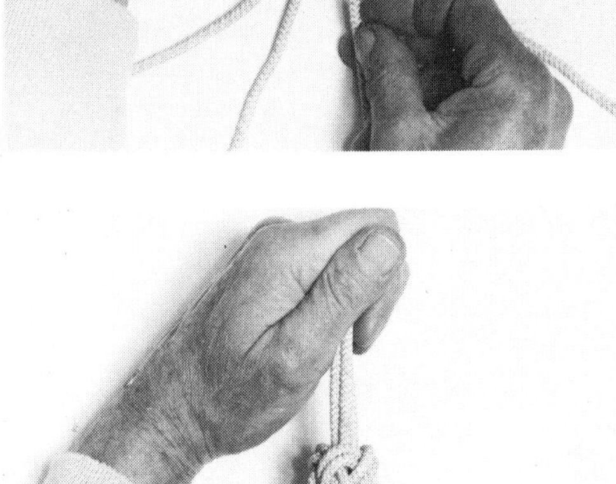
8

57 Rose Knot, Four Stranded*

Form a wall (Knot 52) and crown (Knot 53) as shown in Figs 1 and 2. Completely 'follow around' the wall, Fig 3, but only partially 'follow around' the crown, Fig 4. Pass all the strands down through the centre, Fig 5, to emerge separately as shown in Fig 6. Form a further wall, Fig 7, then a diamond knot (Knot 54), Fig 8, which is 'followed around', Fig 9, and all ends taken up through the centre and cut short, Fig 10.

Wall and Crown*
This is a knot in its own right, Fig 2, at which stage the ends would be cut short.

Manrope Knot*
If, after completing Fig 3, the crown was completely 'followed around' and the ends cut short, the result would be a manrope knot.

Stopper Knot*
This is made by forming the crown first, followed by a wall and both then being 'followed around' (not illustrated).

1
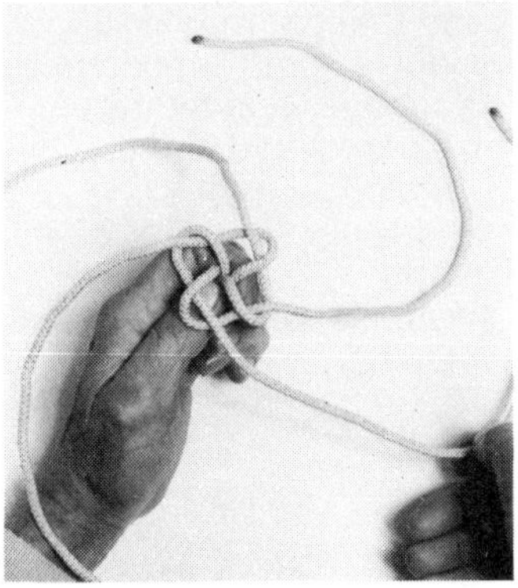
2
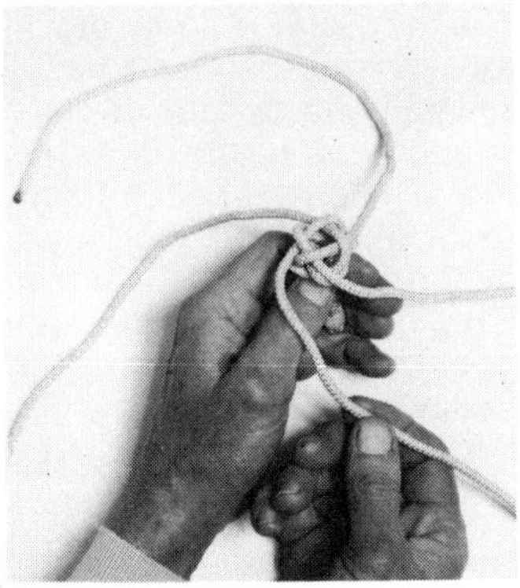
3
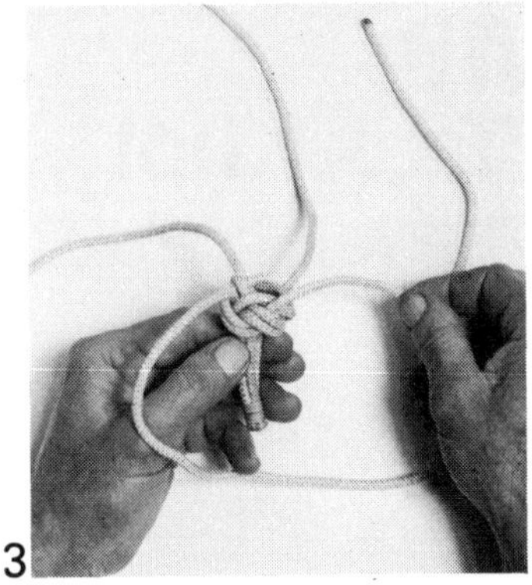
4
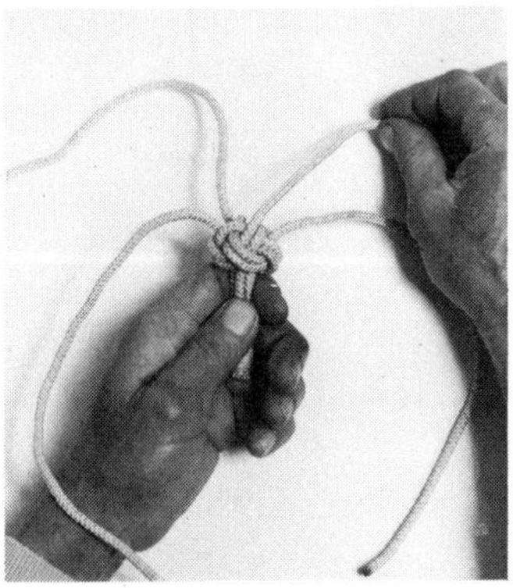
5
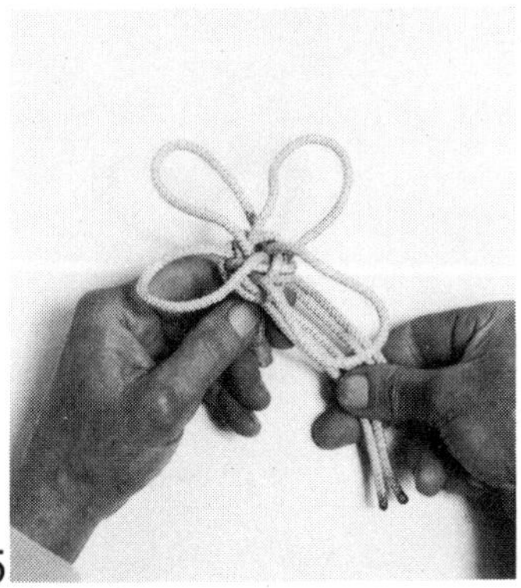
6
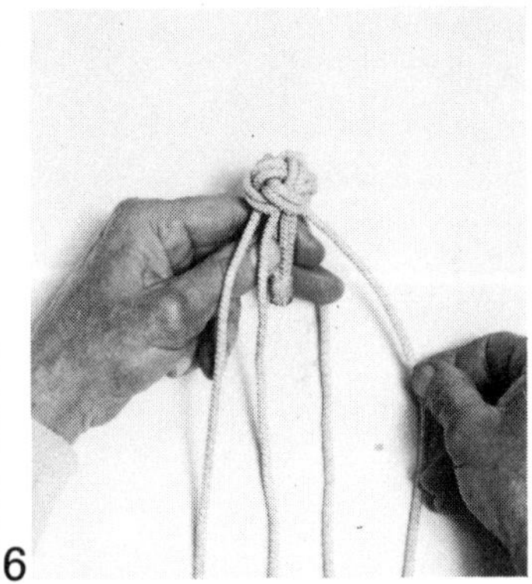
7
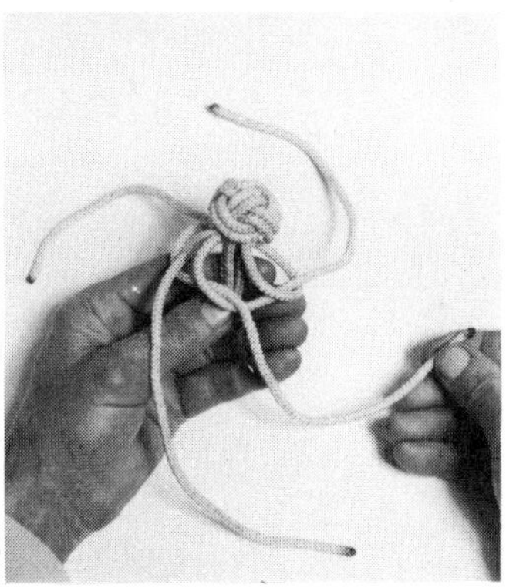
8

9
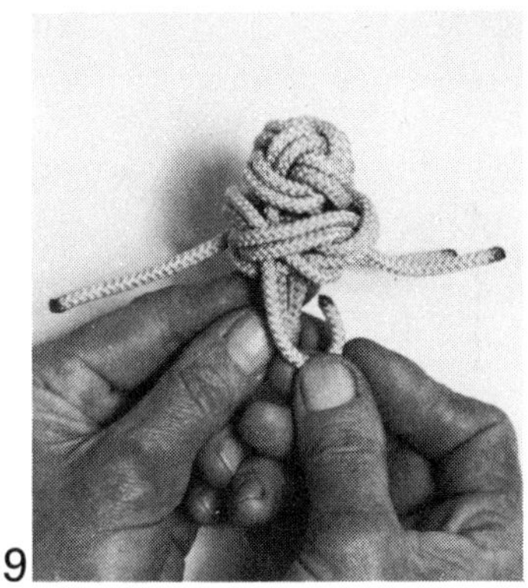
10

58
Tack Knot*

The tack knot is a real old-timer and though little used today is nonetheless a useful decorative knot. A modern sail still has its 'tack' even if it is no longer secured by a tack knot. It is invariably made on a rope's end and can easily be mistaken for a manrope or stopper knot.
As distinct trom either, it is a double wall (Knot 52), double crowned (Knot 53), Fig 1 showing the double wall and Fig 2 the double crown on top. The ends are then tucked down through the knot, Fig 3, tapered as Fig 4, and finally served, Fig 5.

1

2

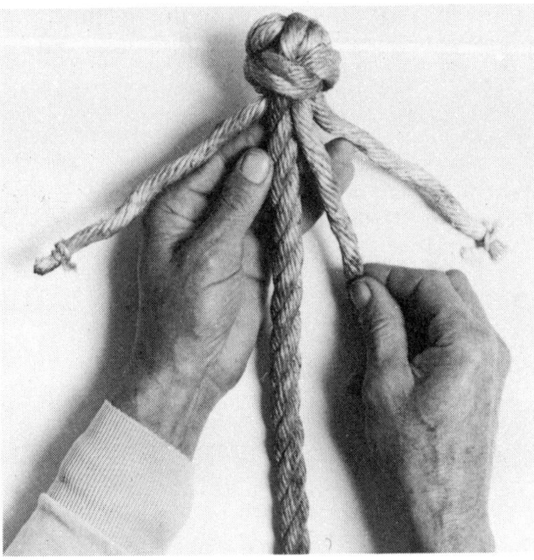
3

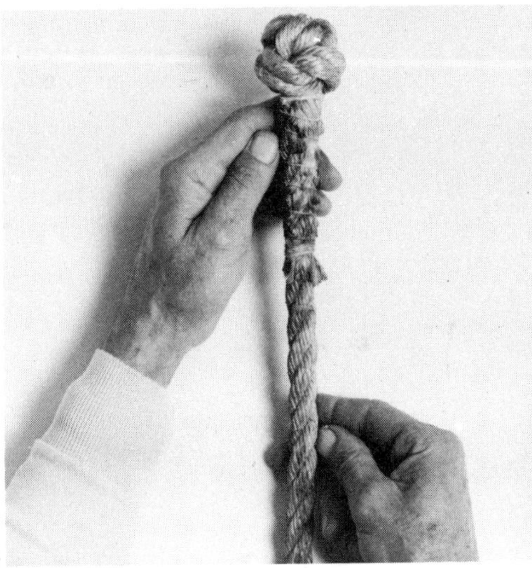
4

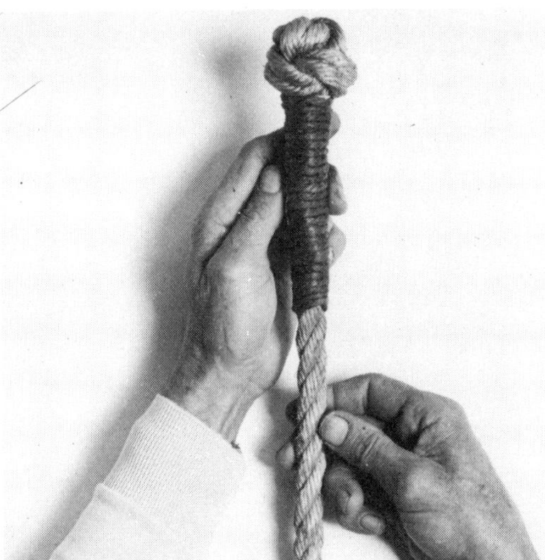
5

59 Single and Double Matthew Walker*

Single and double Matthew Walker knots are usually made on laid rope at some position throughout its length, the rope then being made up again as shown. However, they can be made on an end which is then whipped or even multi-stranded.
To make the single Matthew Walker any strand is taken around, under the other two and a bight retained, Fig 1. The second strand is taken around, passed up through this bight and a second bight retained, Fig 2.
The third strand is next taken around, up through the first bight, Fig 3, and on, up through the second bight, Fig 4, the finished knot when worked tight appearing as in Fig 9A.

Double Matthew Walker*
In this case any strand is taken around, under the other two and brought up through its own bight, Fig 5. The second is brought around, up through this bight, Fig 6 and on up through its own bight, Fig. 7. The last strand is brought around, up through both these bights in turn and on up through its own bight, Fig 8, the finished knot when worked tight appearing as shown in Fig 9B.

Note
These knots would normally be made 'in the hands' but have been shown 'flat' to ensure maximum clarity.

1

2

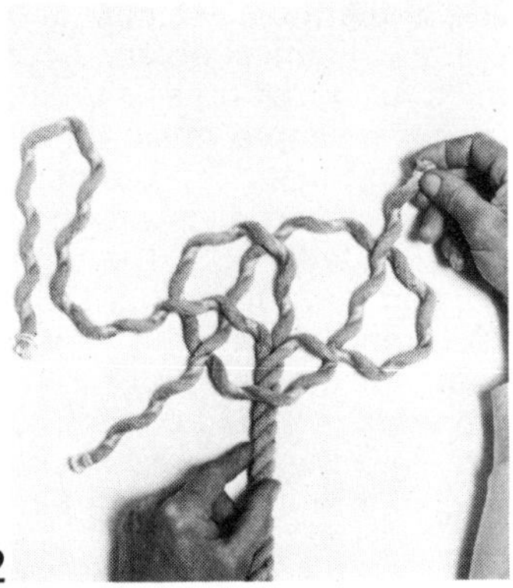

3

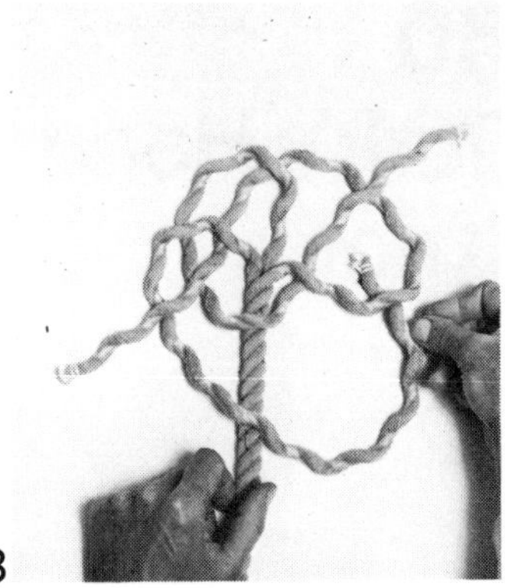

4

5

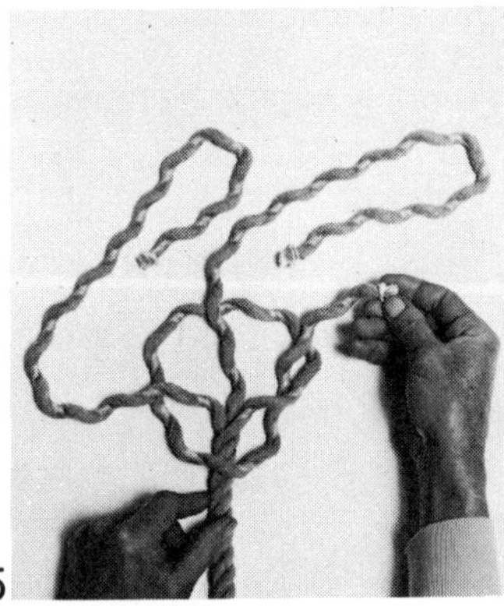

6

7

8

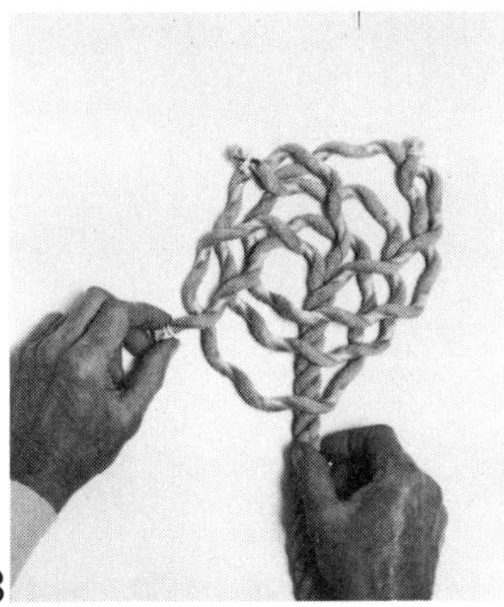

9

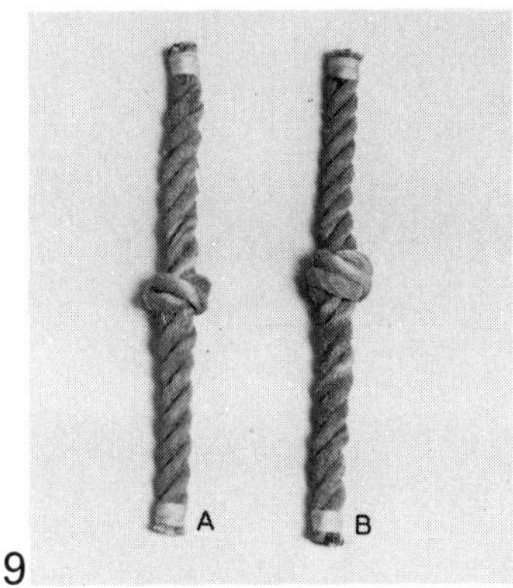

60 Turk's Head Knot

One of the most versatile decorative knots, usually applied to any cylindrical object, occasionally flattened into a turk's head mat or, as shown, tightened into a knot. The most simple version is illustrated (ie minimum *turns* and *parts*) made 'on the hand' to show the reverse side by rotation. The rope is set up as in Figs 1 and 2, then the hand rotated, Fig 3. The bights are then crossed, and the working end tucked right to left, Figs 4 and 5, then back, left to right as in Fig 6, at which point the working end meets the standing part in parallel for the first time, Fig 7. The work is 'followed around', Fig 8 showing the first and Fig 9 the second full circuit, the whole then being worked into a tight knot, Fig 10.

Turk's Head

This is complete in Fig 9, and may be transferred to any cylindrical object, being worked tight in the normal manner.

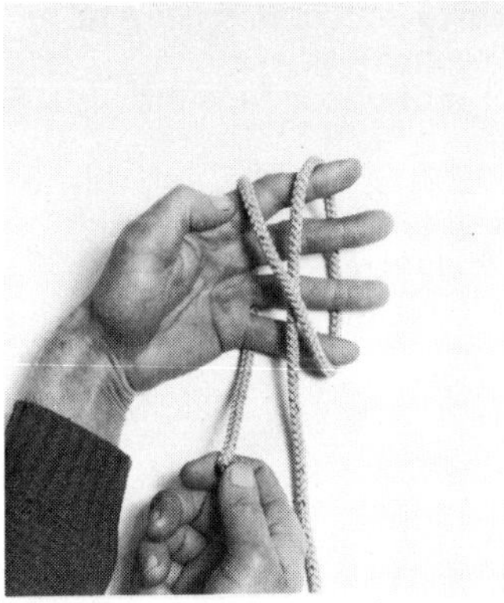
1

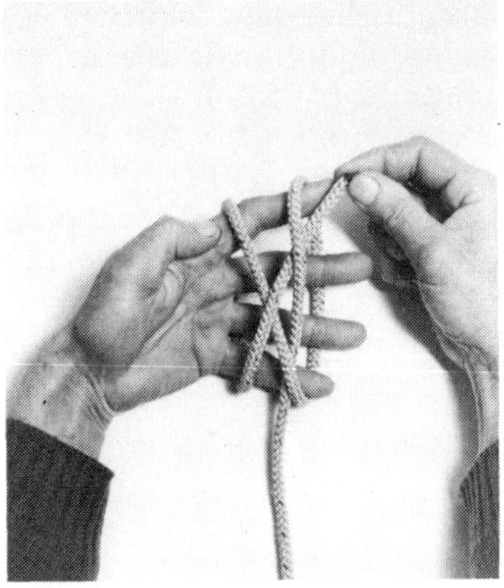
2

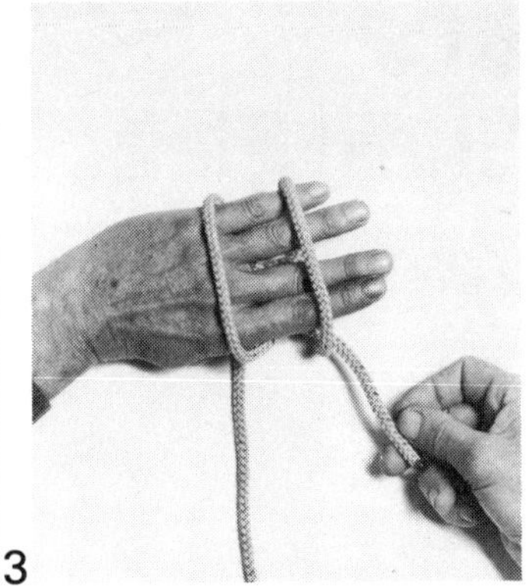
3

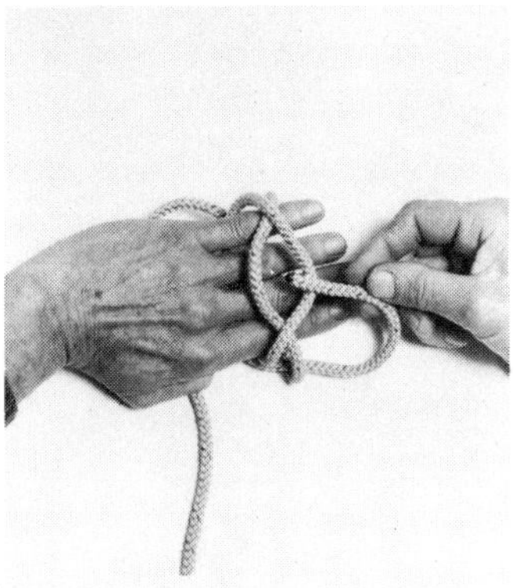
4

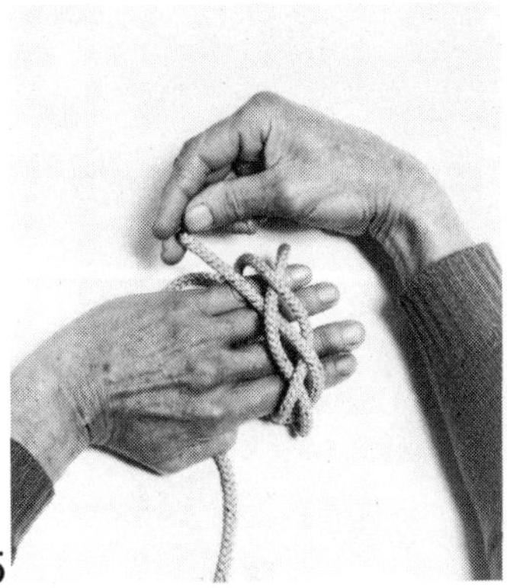
5

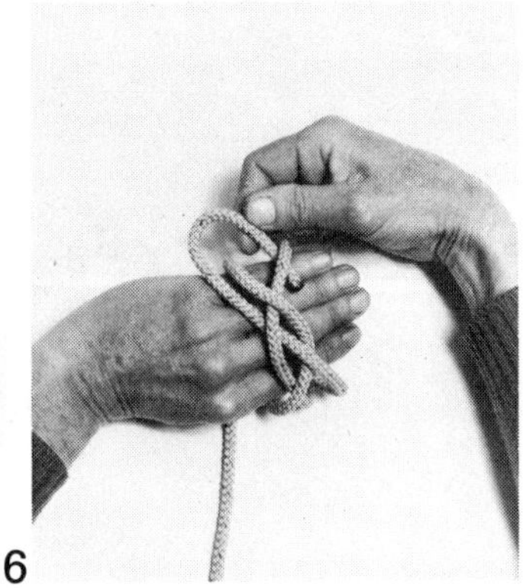
6

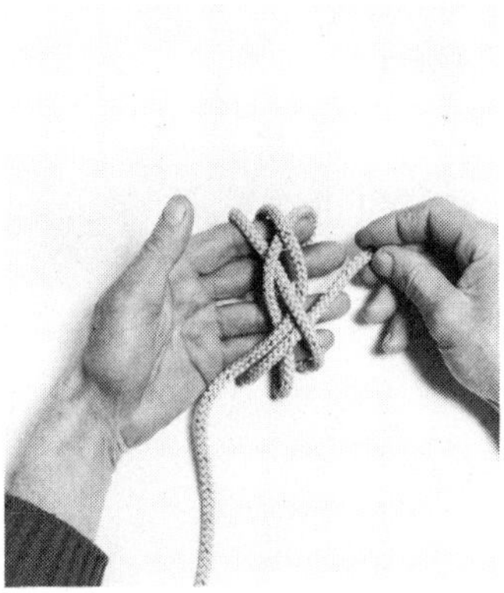
7

8

9

10

61
Chain Plait

Sometimes called a drummer's plait when it was used to decorate such instruments, it is commenced with an overhand (or thumb) knot except that one side is a bight, not an end, Figs 1 and 2.
Thereafter it is simply a question of raising bight through bight, Figs 3 and 4, for the required length of plait which is then finished off by reeving the end through the last bight as can be seen in the completed work, Fig 5.

1

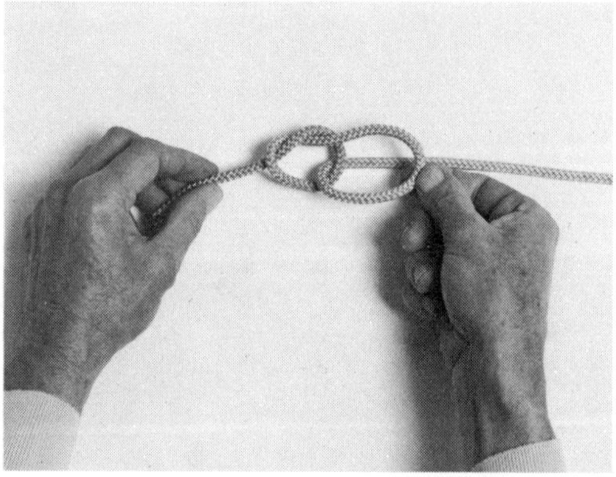
2

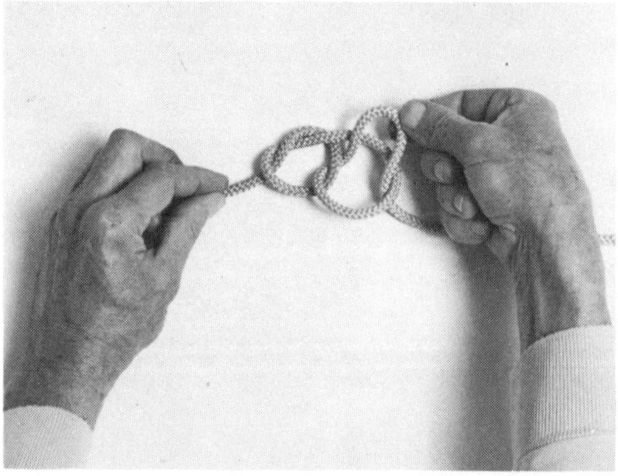
3

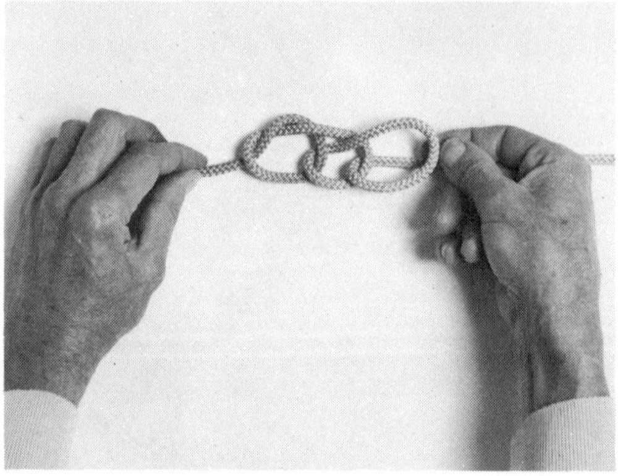
4

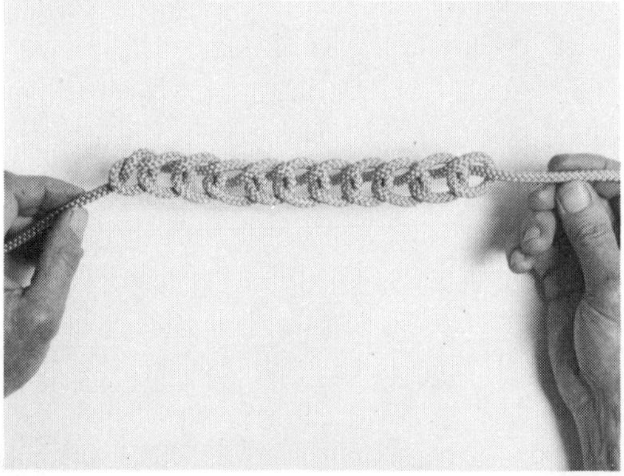
5

62 Double Chain Plait

The figure of eight is a knot in its own right and this plait is simply a series of such knots all interwoven. Figs 1 and 2 show the initial figure of eight, Figs 3, 4 and 5, the second, after which the process is repeated until the plait is of the required length.
The amount of tension is a matter of choice, the completed work, Fig 6, having been left loose for clarity. It could be 'followed around' indefinitely if so desired, by passing the working end back and forth, when it could become an elongated section of a mat.

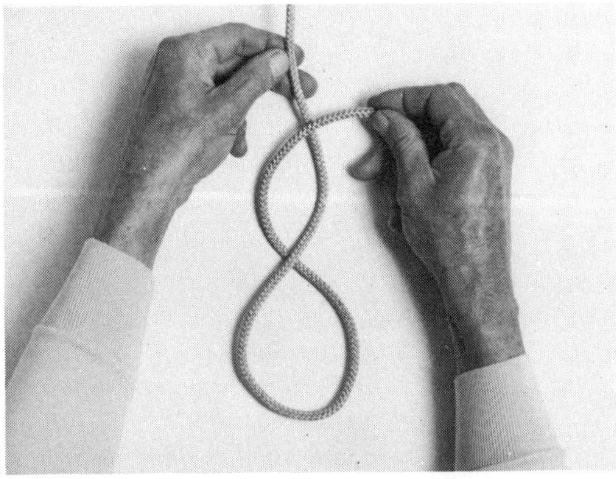

1

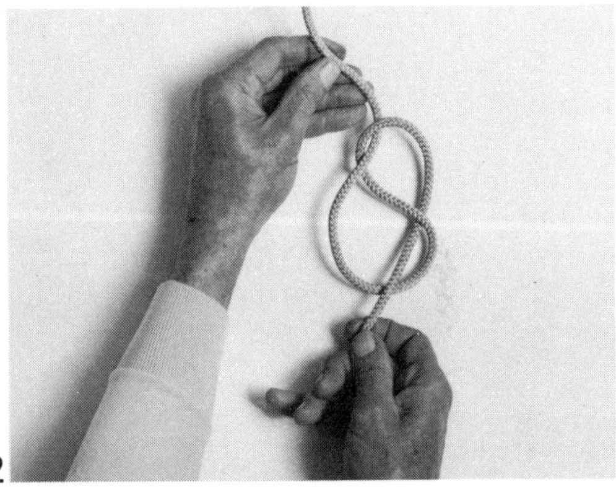

2

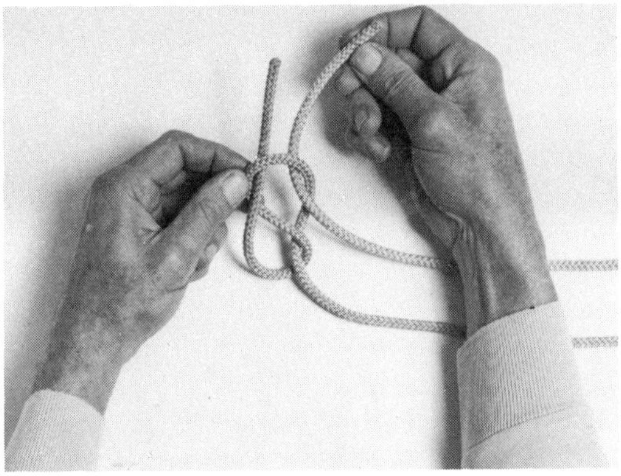

3

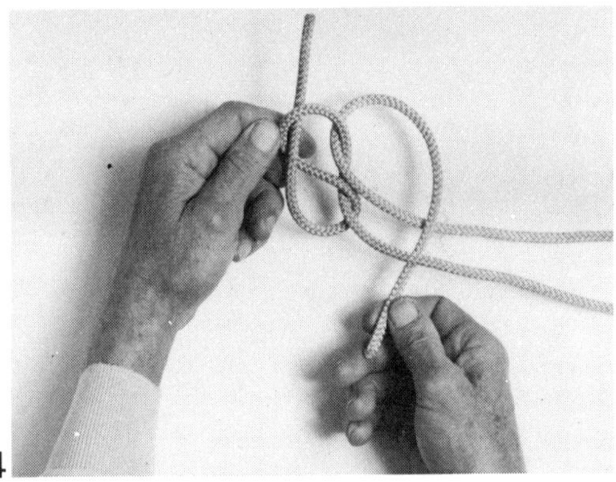

4

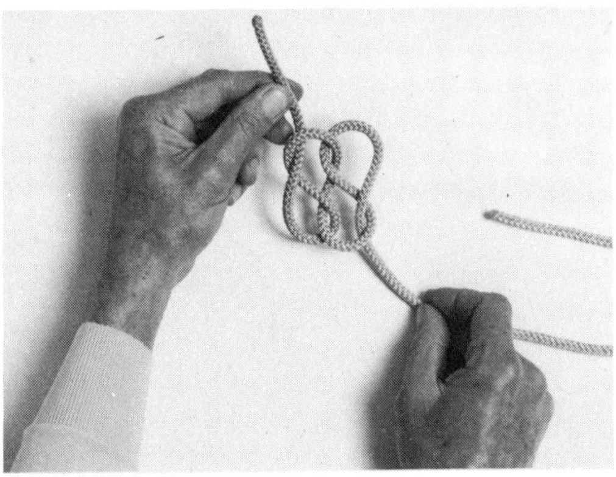

5

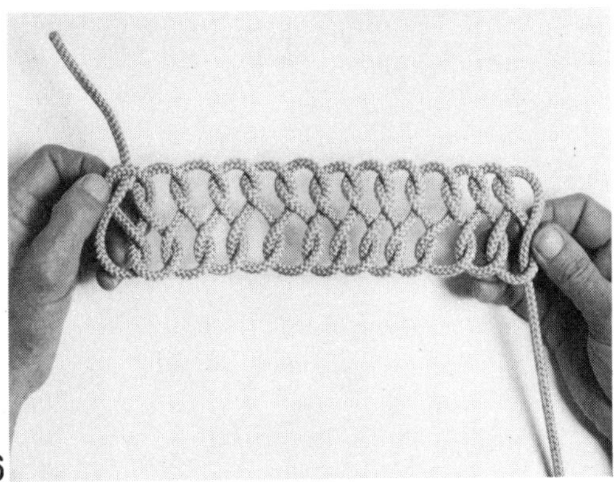

6

63 Square Plait

This plait has the appearance of square sennit with the advantage that it is made on a single strand much more quickly and easily.

A tom fool's knot (Knot 10) is made, Fig 1, after which a bight of the standing part is drawn through the right-hand loop, where it is gripped by pulling back on one strand of the left-hand loop, Fig 2.

The process is repeated with a bight through the left-hand loop, Fig 3, hauled tight by one strand of the right-hand loop and so on for the required length, working alternately from side to side, Fig 4.

To finish off the plait in such manner that it will not unravel, the end instead of the bight is passed through the last but one loop and back through the last, Fig 5, the finished plait appearing as in Fig 6.

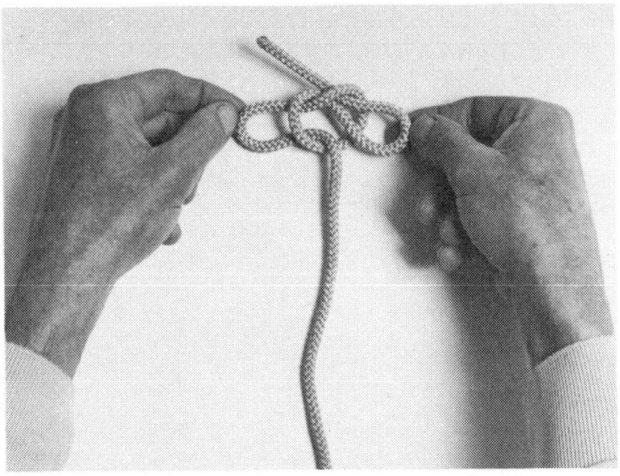
1

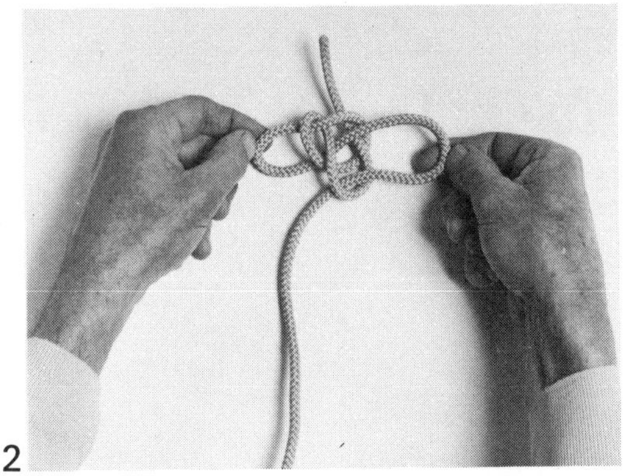
2

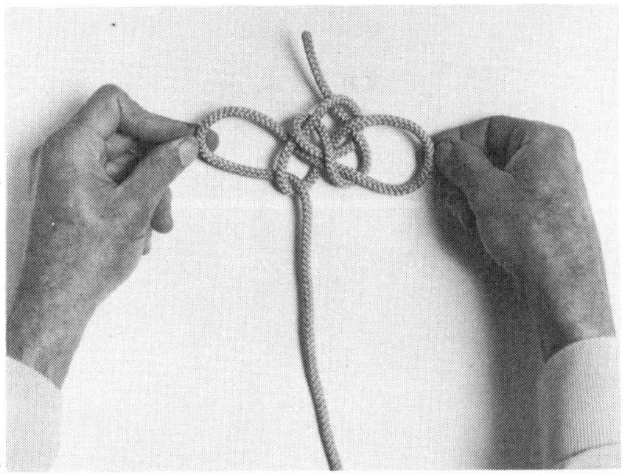
3

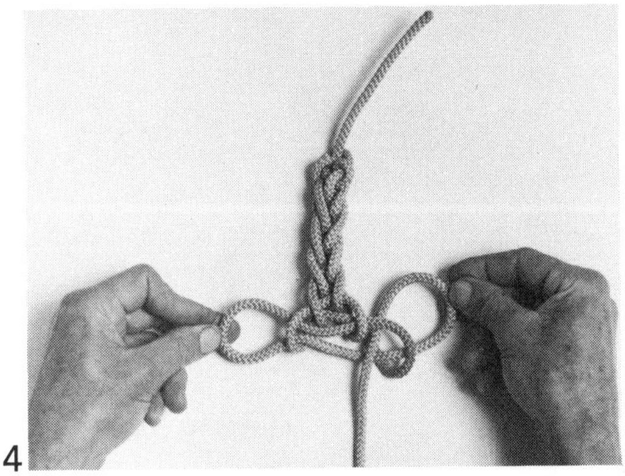
4

5

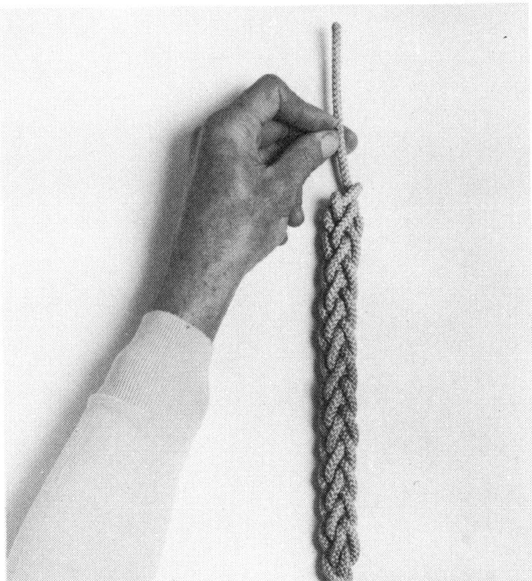
6

64 Twist Plait

The length of the plait is established by the size of the bight, Fig 1, which is then twisted in a clockwise direction, Fig 2, and the end passed through to the left, Fig 3. The bight is then twisted anti-clockwise, Fig 4 and the end passed through to the right, Fig 5, the whole process being repeated until the required length is completed, Fig 6.

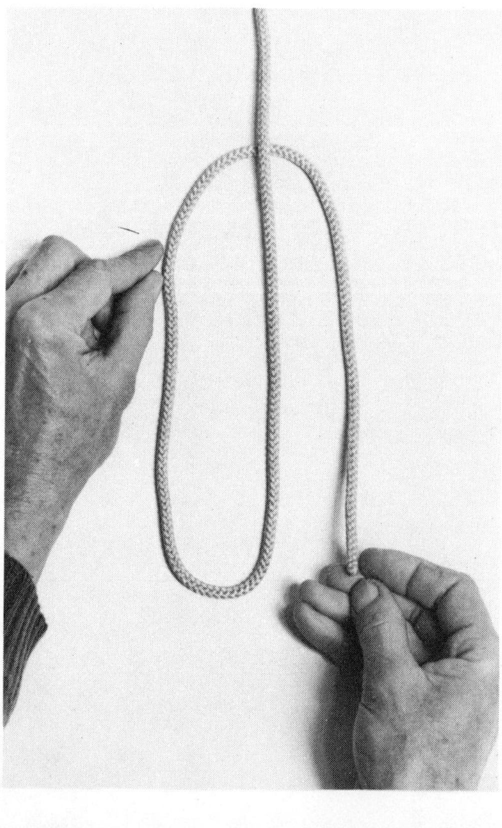

1

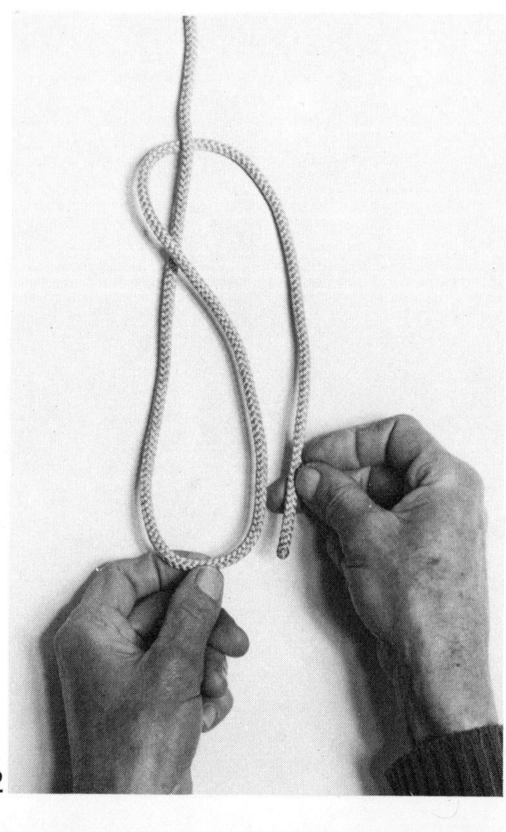

2

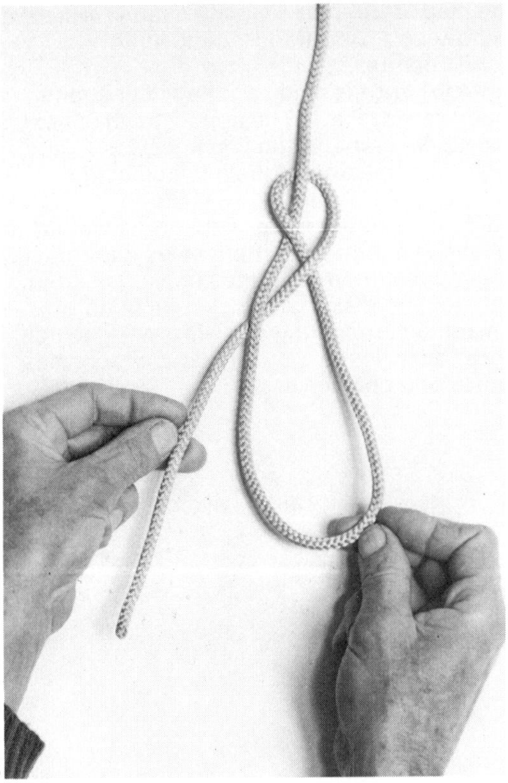
3

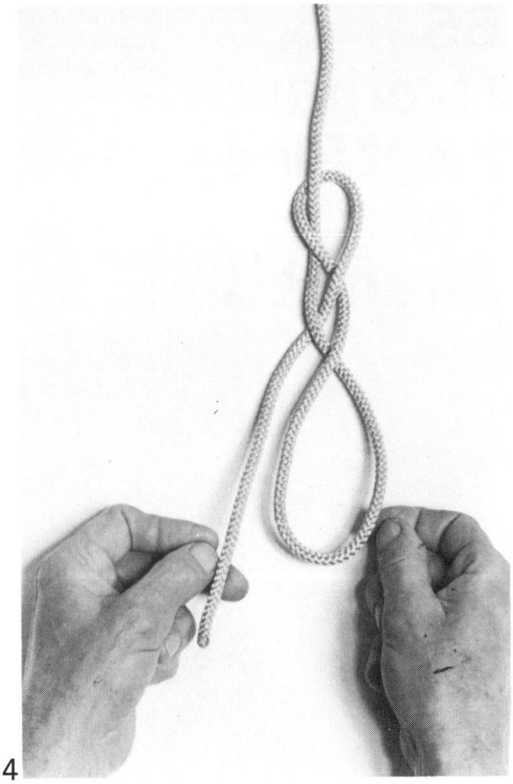
4

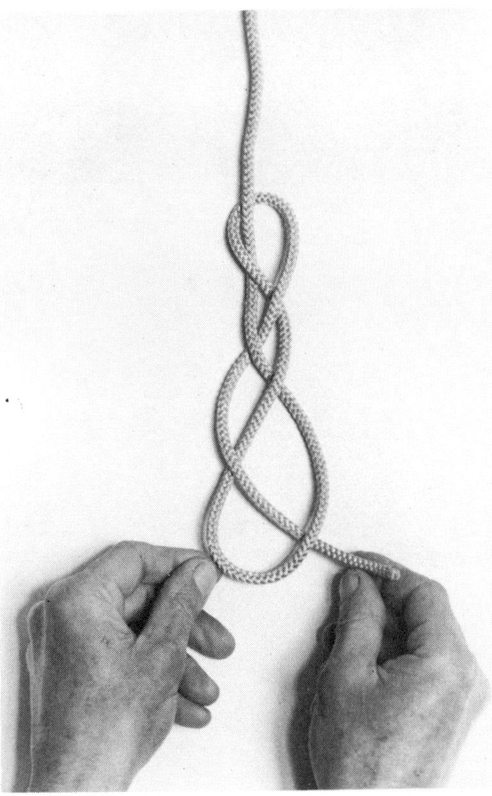
5

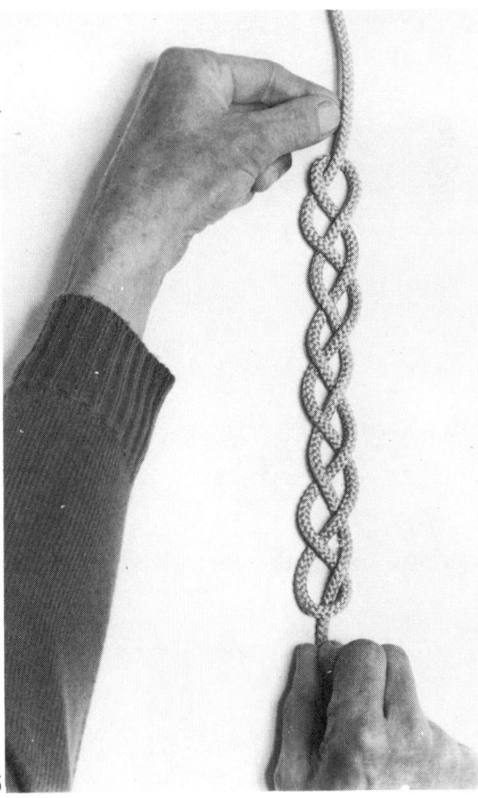
6

65 Overhand Knot Plait, Four Stranded

This plait can be made from four separate strands whipped together or, as shown on two strands, crossed at right-angles at their centres.
An overhand (thumb) knot is made on the lower strand trapping the upper strand, Fig 1. The upper strand is next knotted in the same way around the first knot, Fig 2, and so on, alternately to completion of the required length, Fig 3.
This is undoubtedly one of the most simple of plaits but to maintain a constant, symmetrical pattern every knot must be made in the same direction, ie, if the knots are started left over right all must be maintained so. A variation of pattern can be made by alternating the left over right/right over left sequence, but this must be regular and becomes a matter of practice and choice.

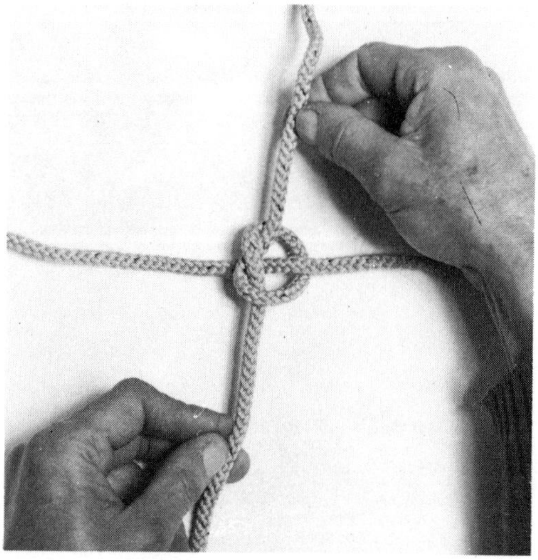

1

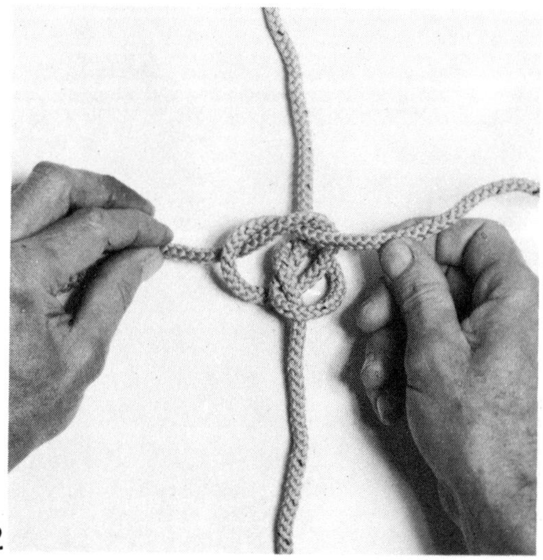

2

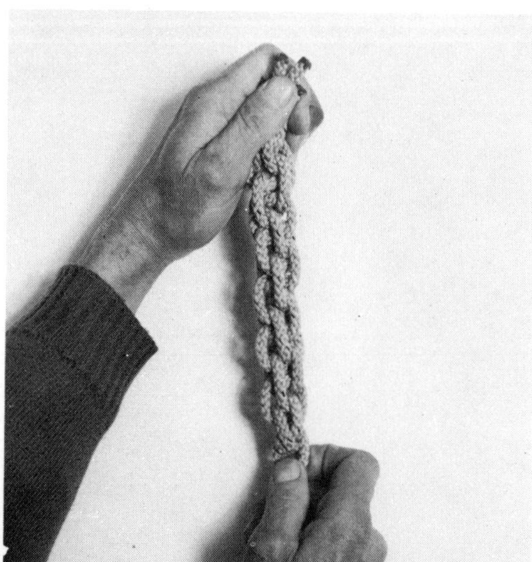

3

66 Overhand Knot Plait, Eight Stranded

As with the four strand version this plait may be made on the ends of eight strands or, as shown, on the bights of four. Thereafter it becomes a doubled version of the four strand, using pairs of overhand knots, care being taken to keep them symmetrical.

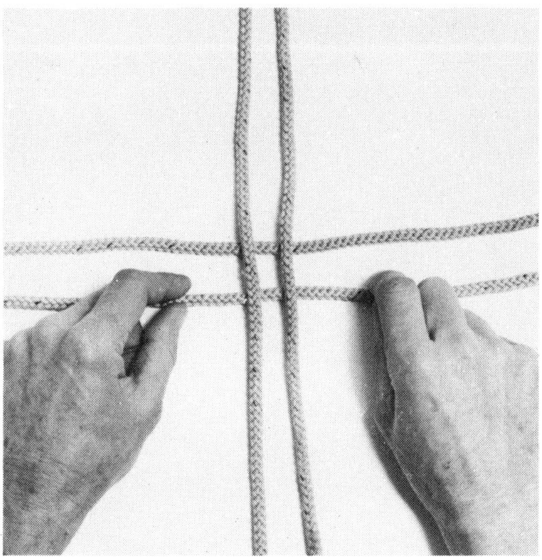

1

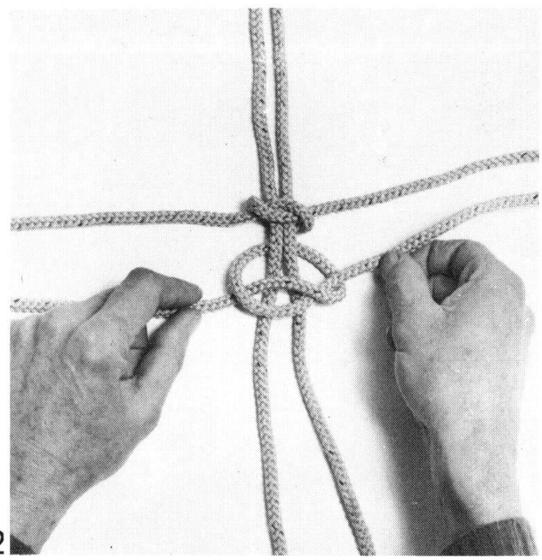

2

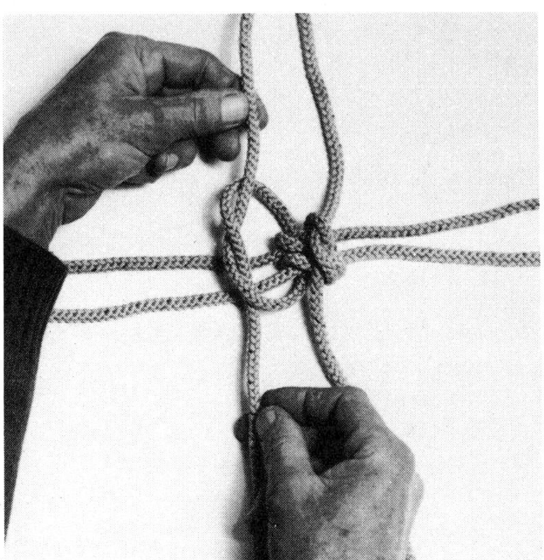

3

4

Sennits

Whether they be flat, round, square or spiral, common, English, French, Portuguese or Russian, sennits may be broadly divided into three groups: those that can be made with any number of strands; those that can only be made with any odd number; and those that require an even number. The square sennit is an exception, for although it requires an even number, it can be made only on eight, twelve or sixteen strands or a multiple, eight being the minimum.

A basic principle may be applied to the odd number group, in that the strands are divided with one more on one side than on the other, resulting in odd and even sides. Thereafter the outside strands each time, starting with the even side, are brought across to the centre and laid inside the previous odd number; thus the odd and even sides alternate as the work proceeds.

Note

As illustrated, a plastic binder such as is used to secure loose leaves of paper makes an ideal 'former' to secure any number of strands when making a sennit.

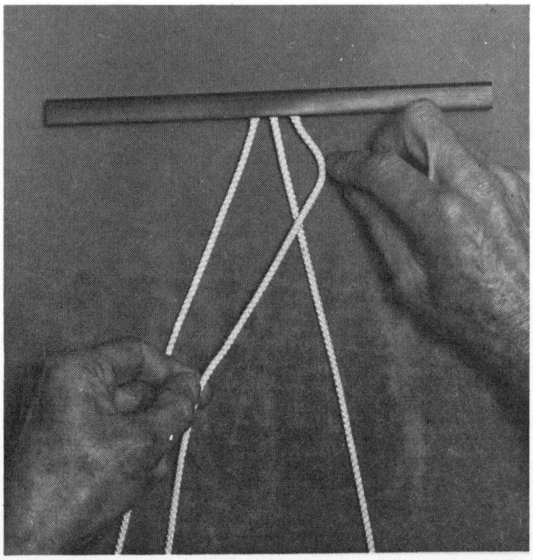

1

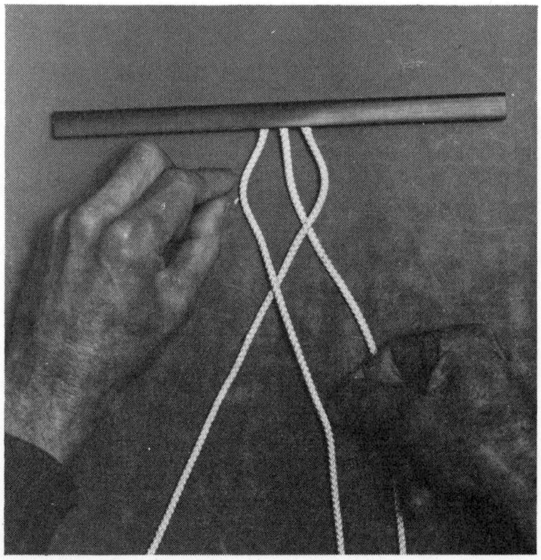

2

67 Common Sennit, Three Stranded

Figs 1 and 2 opposite

Obviously one of the odd number group, this is the most simple of all the sennit family, being most useful in mat-making when made up in long lengths. Strands are arranged, two to the right and one to the left, then the outside right is brought across to the inside of the left-hand strand, Fig 1. Outside left is next brought across to inside right, Fig 2, and the new outside right returned to become inside left, Fig 3.

All three strands have now been moved for the first time, Fig 4, showing them drawn tight, after which the process is continued to completion of any required length, Fig 5.

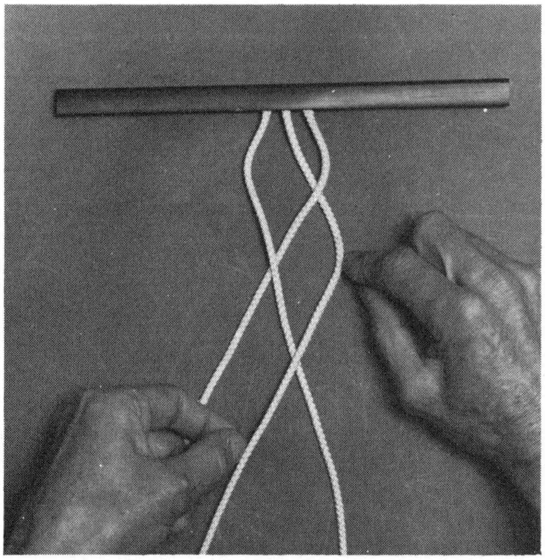

3

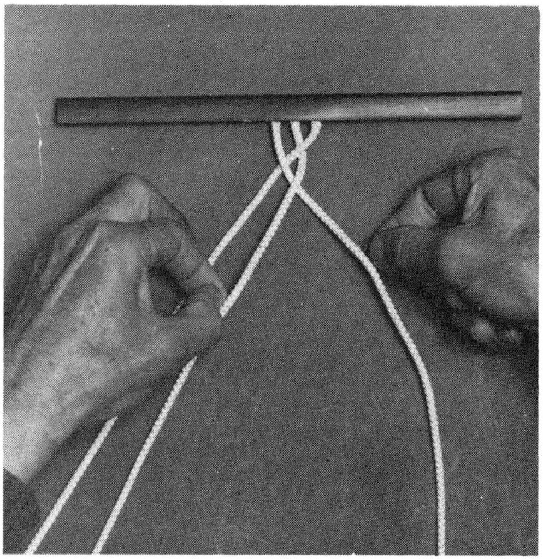

4

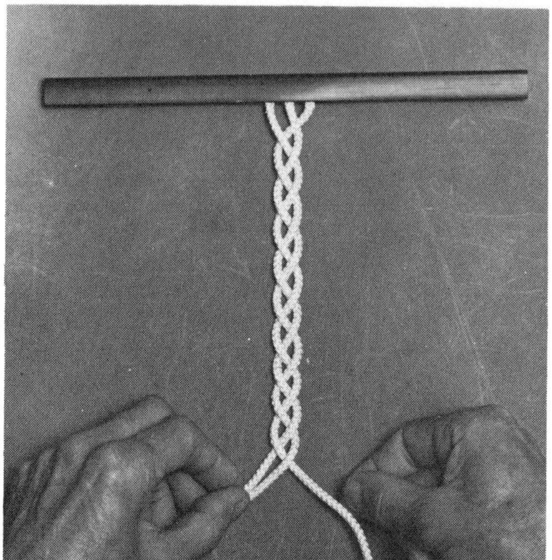

5

68 Common Sennit, Seven Stranded

Again one of the odd number group, it is a more elaborate version of the three strand, the same principles being applied. Figs 1 to 4 show the movements of the first four strands after which the 'lay' becomes automatic, all seven having been woven loosely in, Fig 5, and completed, Fig 6.

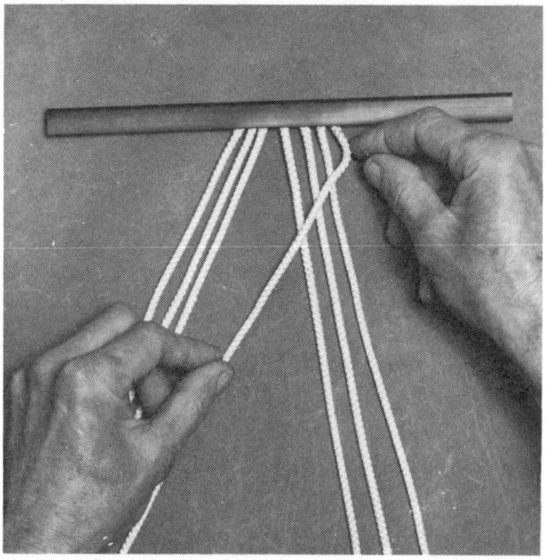

1

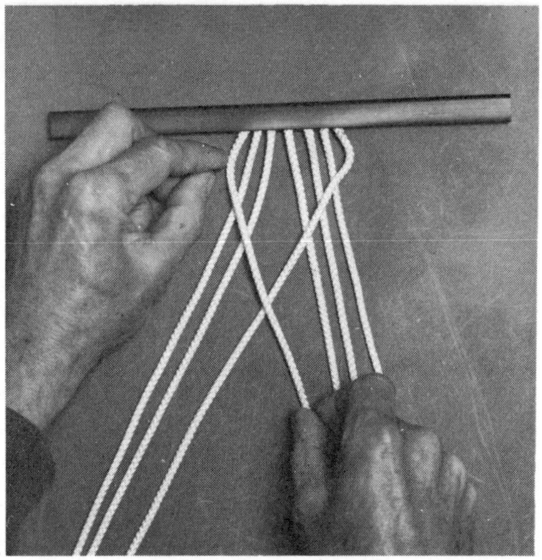

2

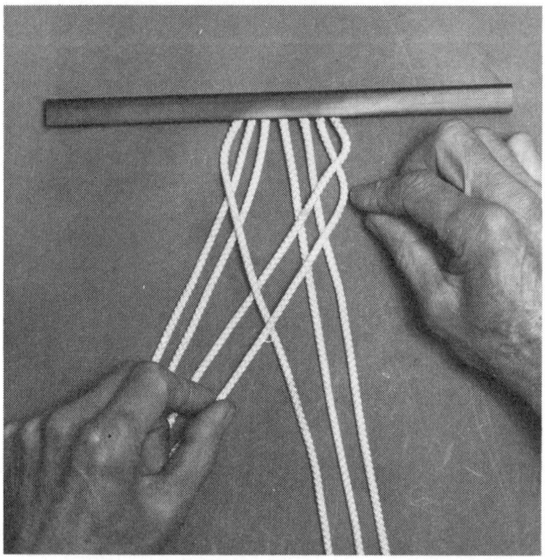

3

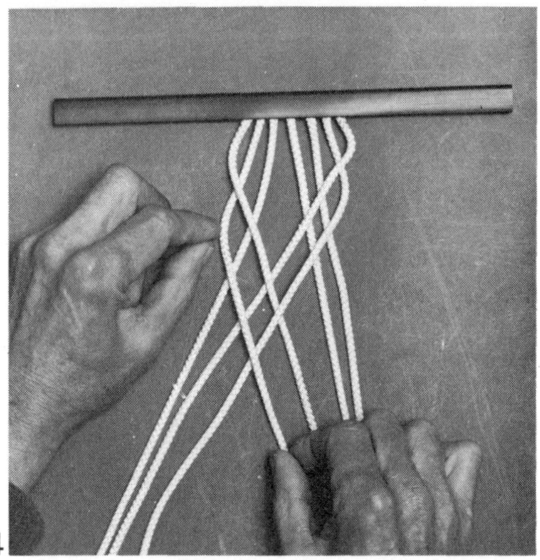

4

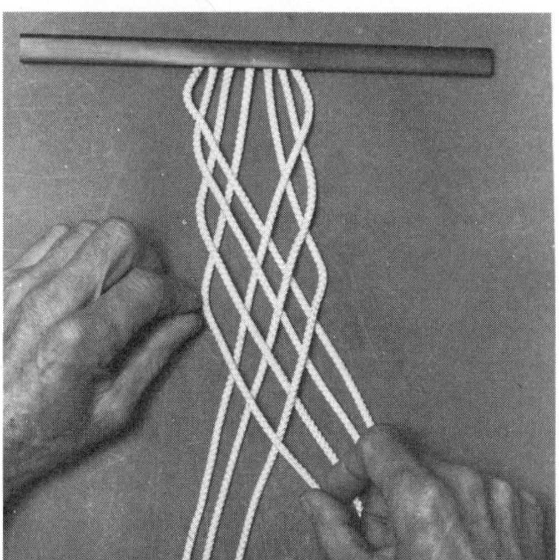

5

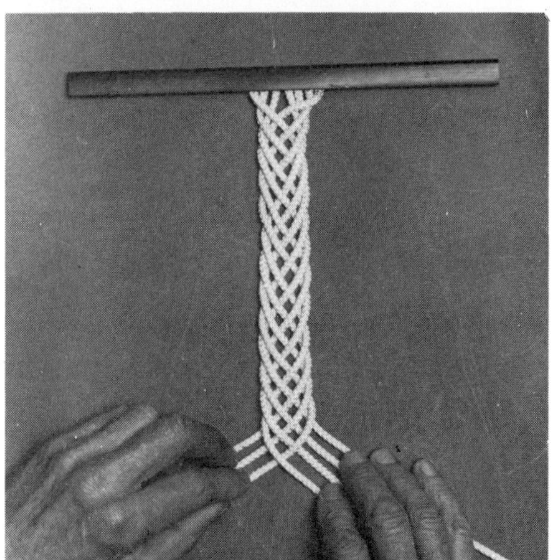

6

69 Round Sennit, Six Stranded

Four strands being the minimum, this sennit is made with any even number of strands and although it would normally be made vertically, it is shown 'flat' for maximum clarity.

It consists of taking alternate strands anti-clockwise around and over their immediate neighbours, the first strand, Fig 1, and all three strands, Fig 2, after which each is drawn down, Figs 3 and 4, leaving three strands 'up'. The 'up' strands are next taken clockwise over each of the 'held down' strands (which are released in passing), Fig 5, showing the first and all three in Fig 6, before the clockwise strands are in turn 'held down', Figs 7 and 8. The first three are again taken anti-clockwise and the whole process continued, when the sennit begins to take shape, Fig 9, a completed length appearing as in Fig 10.

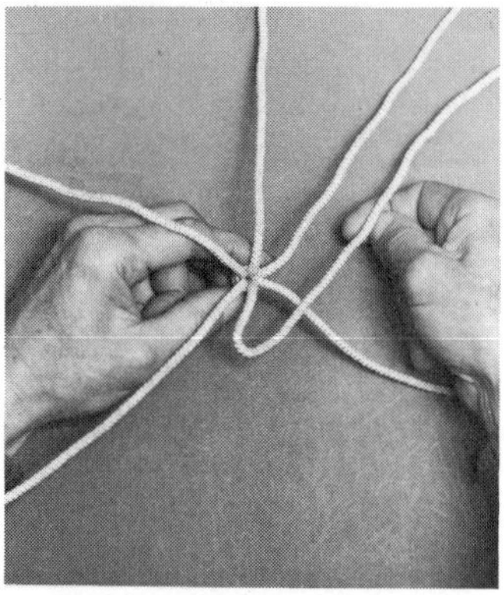
1

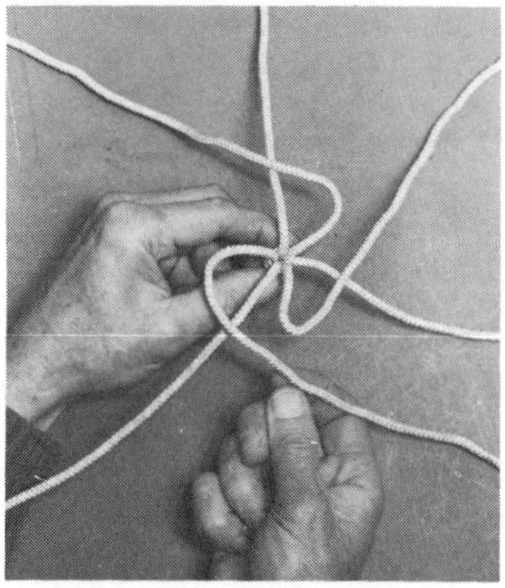
2

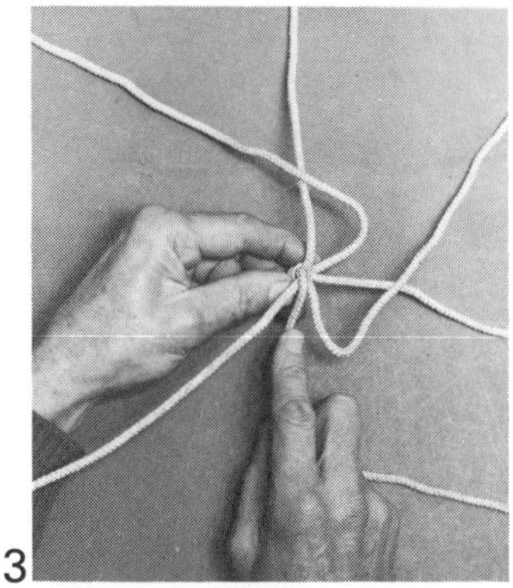
3

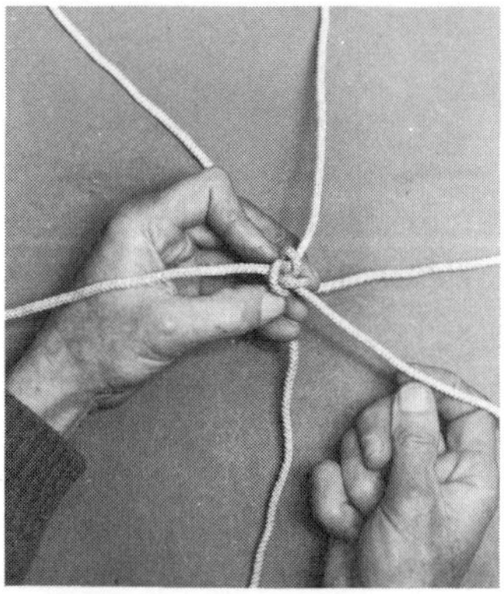
4

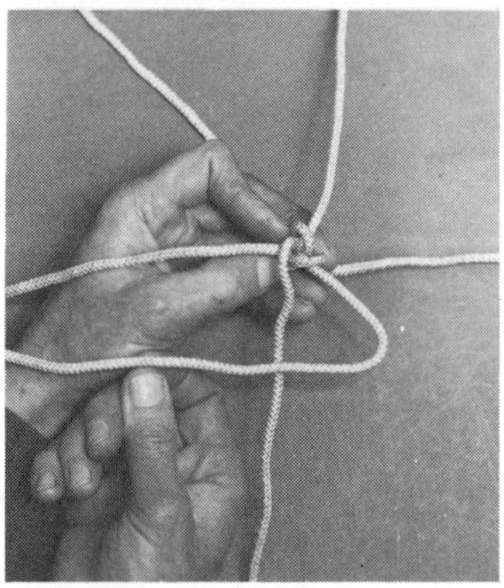
5

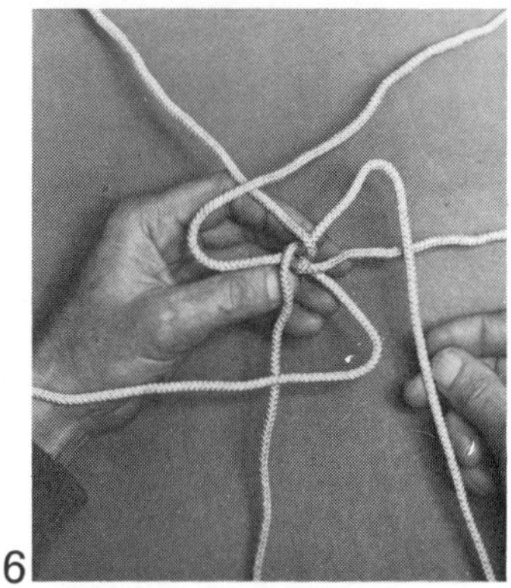
6

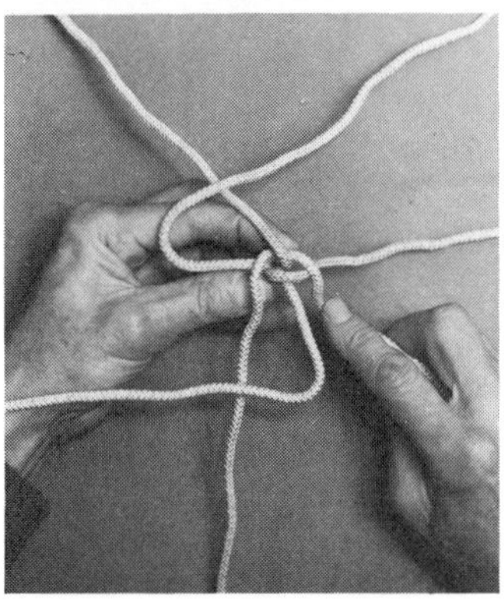
7

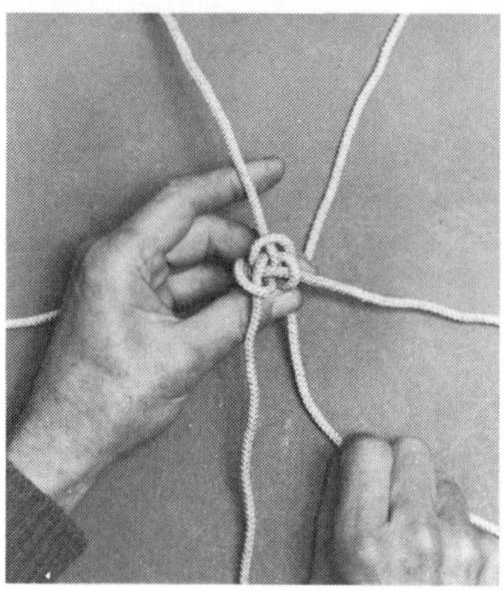
8

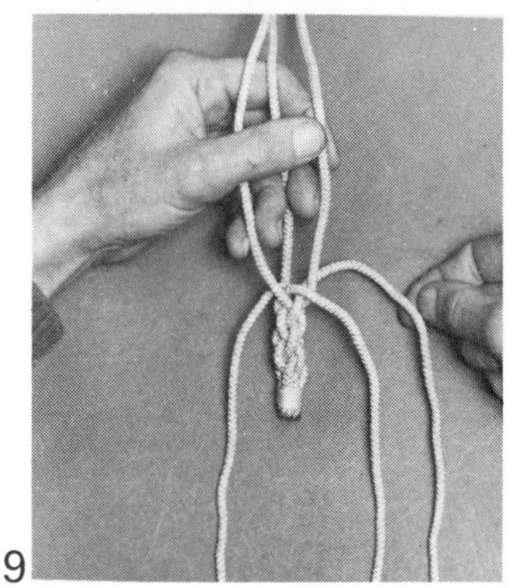
9

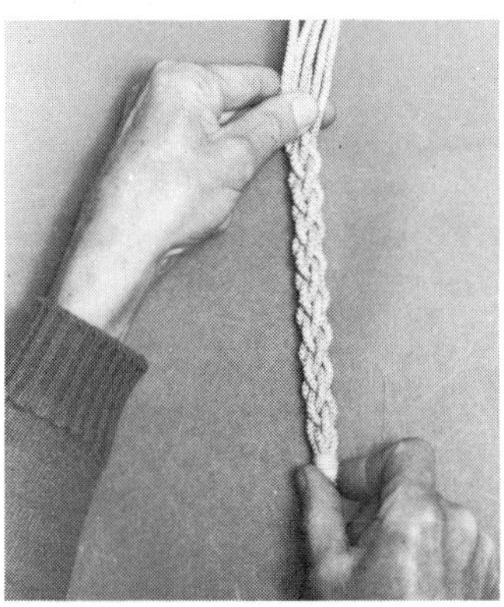
10

70 Square Sennit, Eight Stranded

This must be made, not only with an even number of strands but with multiples, either eight, twelve or sixteen, the minimum being shown to illustrate the basic principle. The strands are separated equally, as in Fig 1, the outside right-hand strand brought under its fellows and on, up through the centre of the left-hand four, Fig 2, drawn tight, Fig 3, before being returned to its own side, where it is laid on the inside of the existing three, Fig 4. The outside left-hand strand is treated in the same way, emerging in the centre of the four right-hand strands, Figs 5 and 6, before being returned to its own side, Fig 7. Working alternate outside strands the sennit is continued, Fig 8, drawn tight in Fig 9, and to completion of any required length, Fig 10.

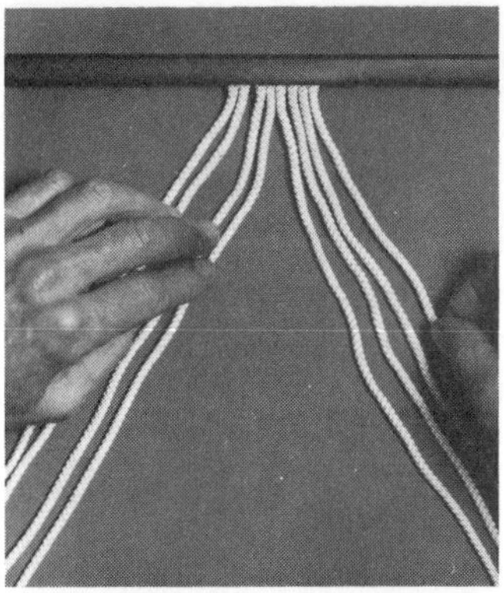
1

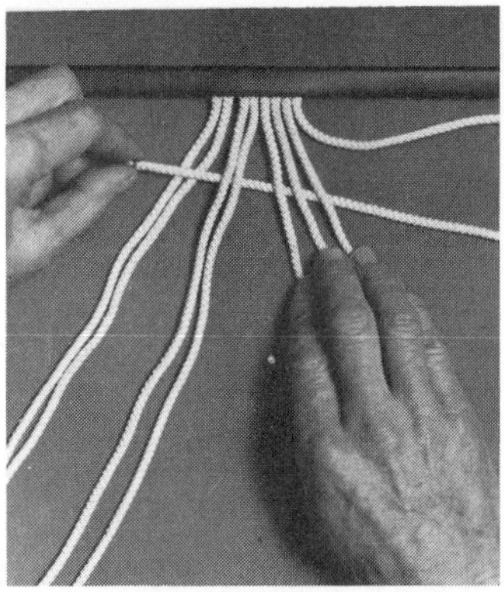
2

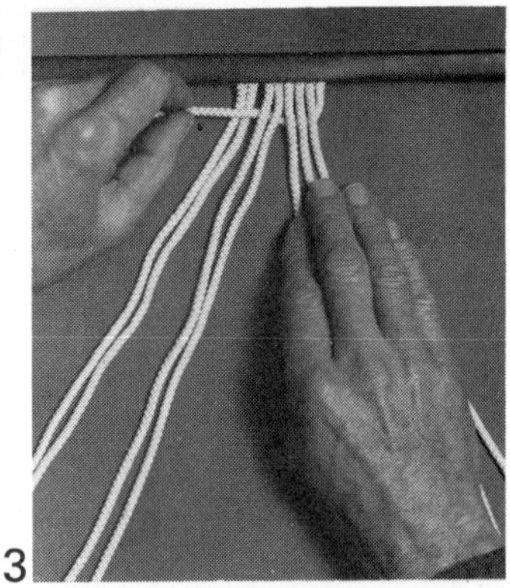
3

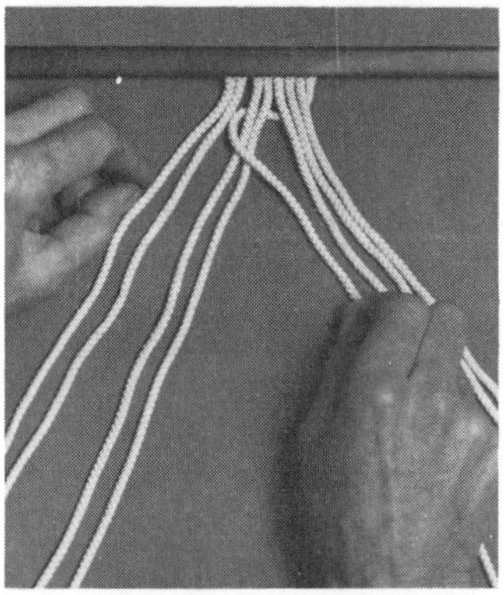
4

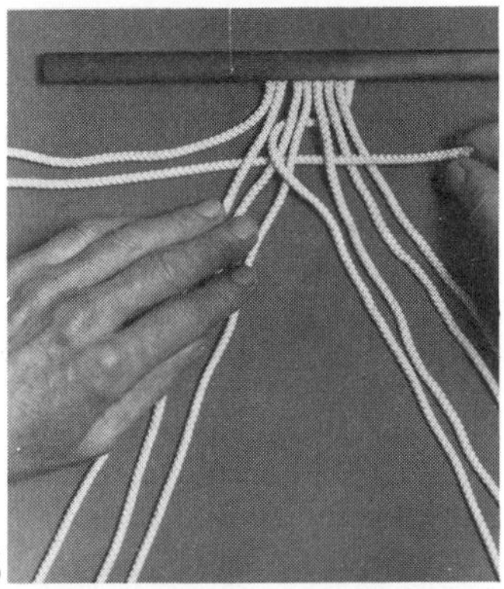
5

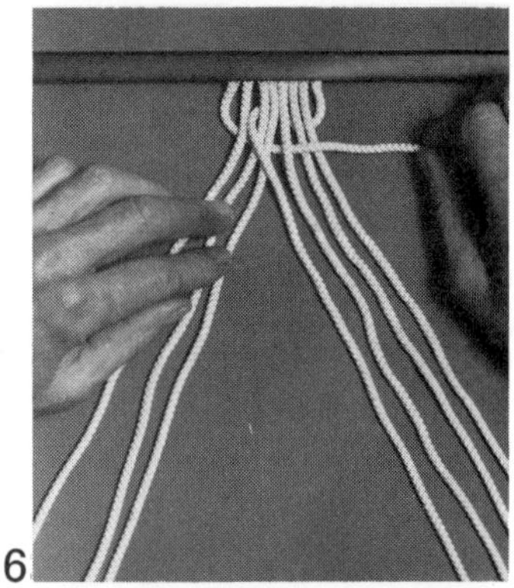
6

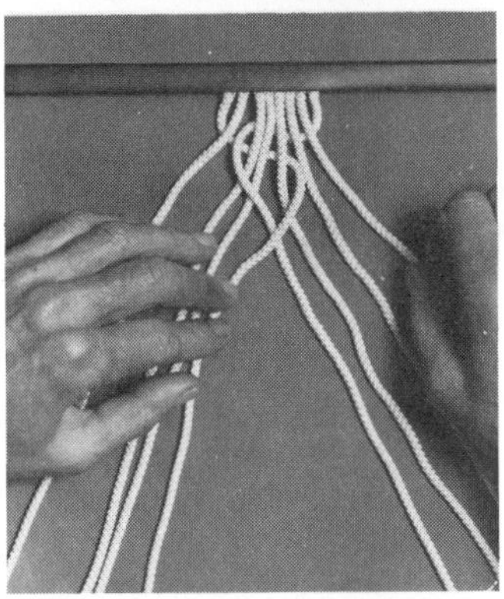
7

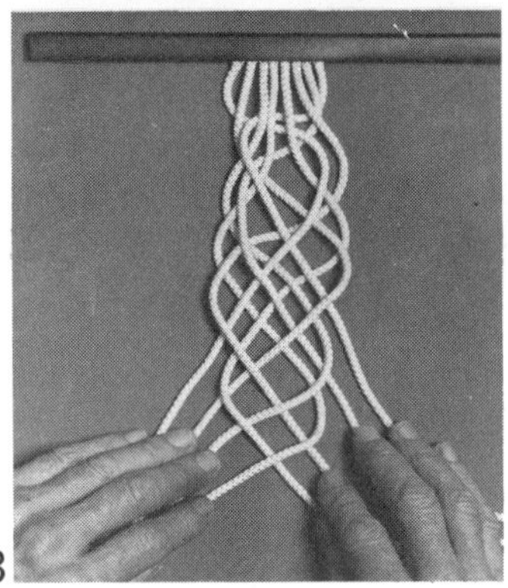
8

9

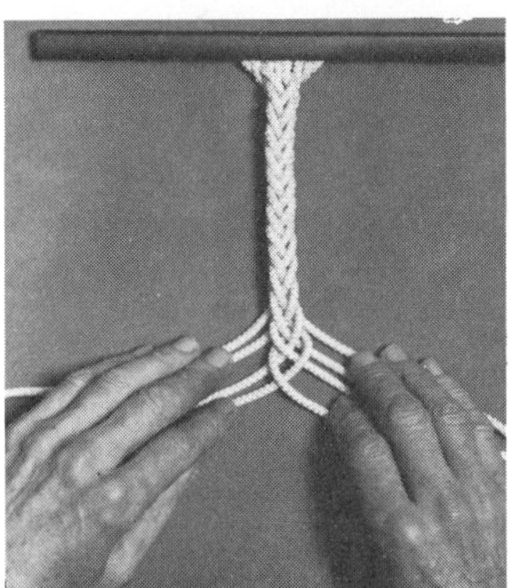
10

71 English Sennit, Seven Stranded

Seven strands have been used for no particular reason as this sennit can be made with any number, odd or even, with a minimum of four (three reverts to being a common sennit).

Each outside right strand is used in turn, being reeved under one/over one until it emerges on the opposite side where it is laid parallel and becomes the extreme left-hand strand. Figs 1 and 2 show the first and second strands so treated, all seven strands having been reeved for the first time in Fig 3, whilst Fig 4 shows a completed length, suitably tightened.

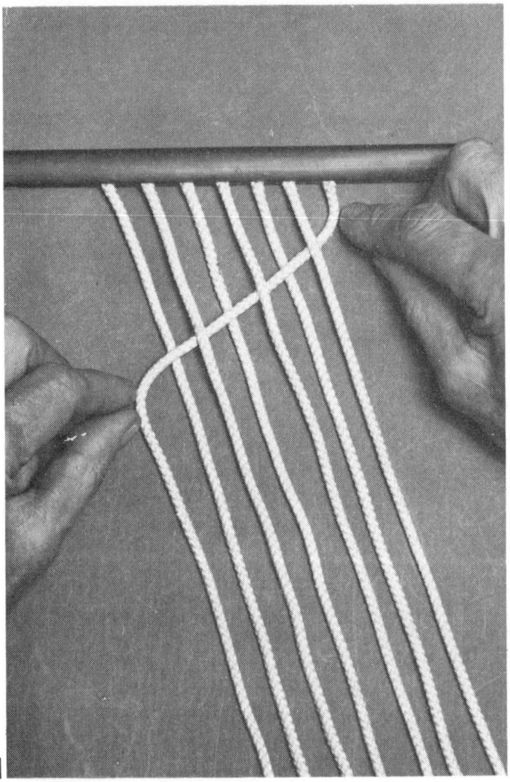

1

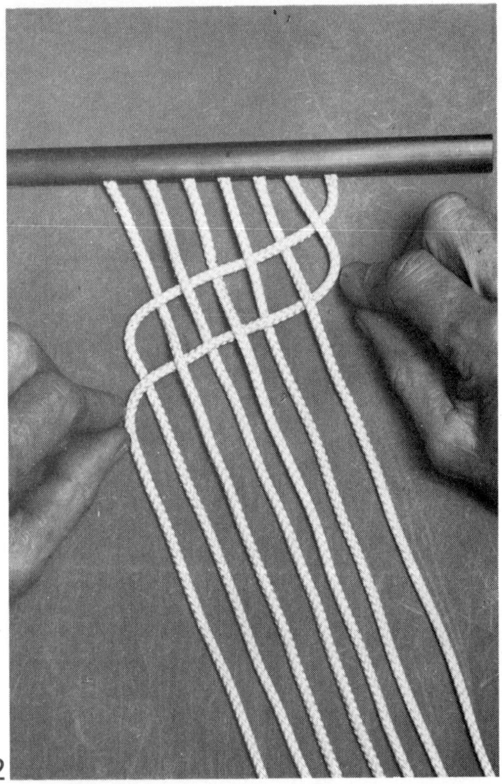

2

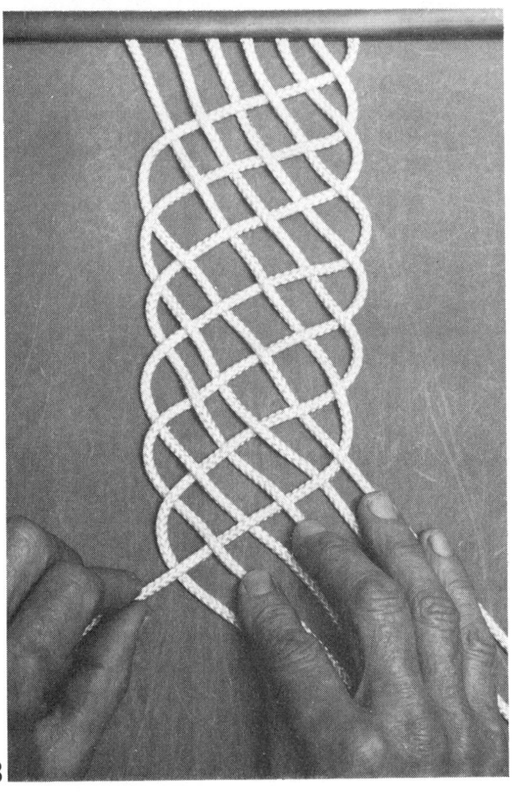

3

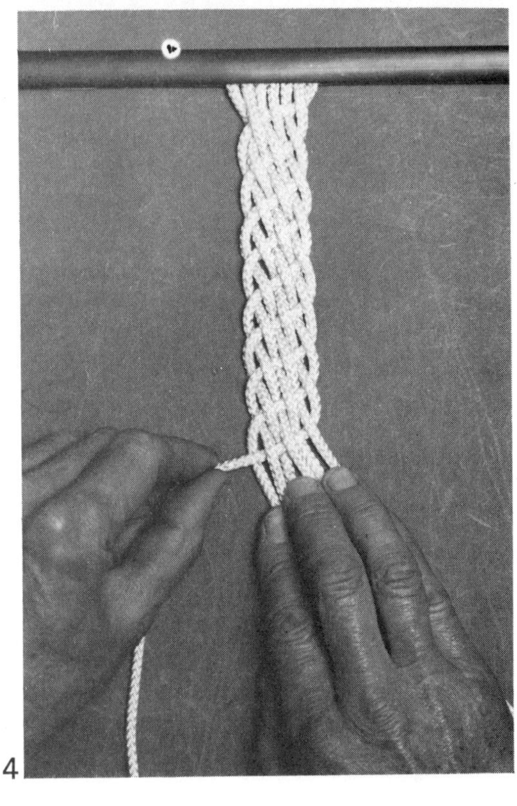

4

72 French Sennit, Seven Stranded

As with the English sennit (Knot 71) the strands of the French are reeved under one/over one, but an odd number is necessary (five being the minimum) and they do not pass across the full width of the sennit, but arrive from alternate sides at the centre, to become left- or right-handed respectively.
Strands are laid out, three to left, four to right, Figs 1 and 2 showing the first strand (the outside of the right-hand group) reeved through to the centre and laid with the left-hand group. Figs 3 and 4 show the second strand (the outside of the left-hand group) similarly treated and laid with the right-hand group.
Strands three, four and five follow, figs 5 to 7, and this process is continued for the required length, Fig 8 showing the loosely woven strands, worked tight in Fig 9.

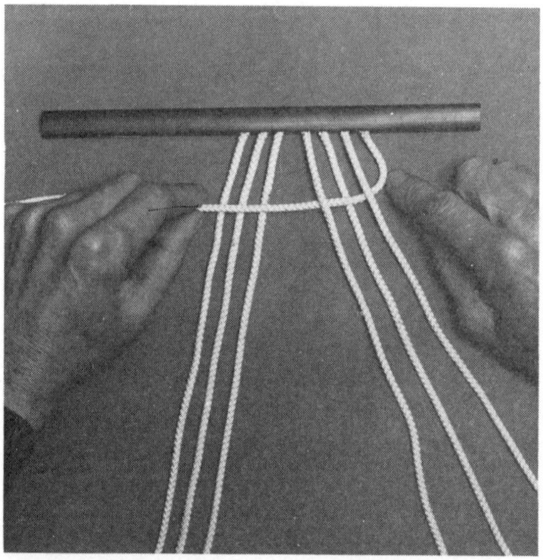
1

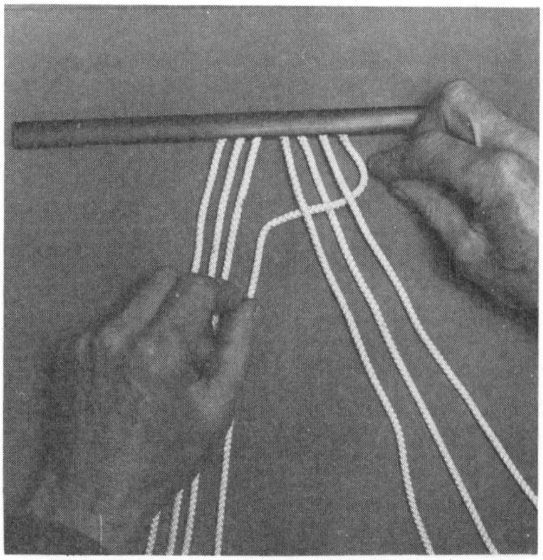
2

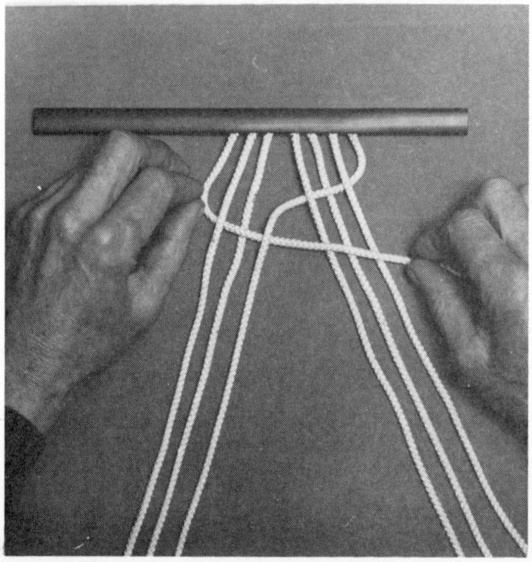
3

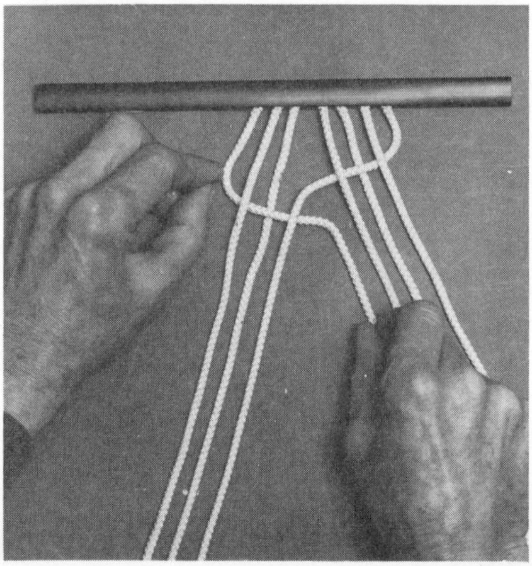
4

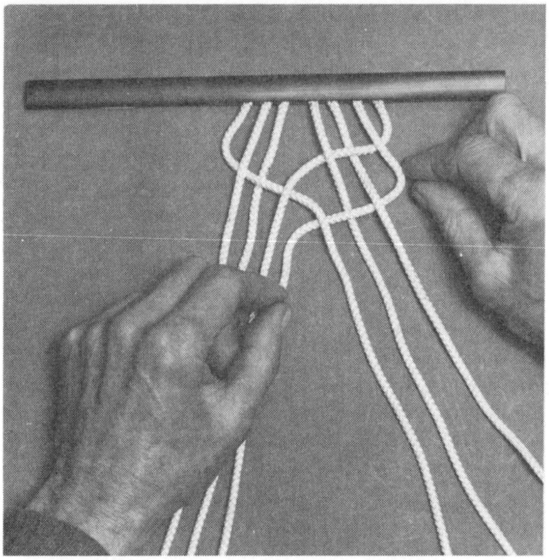
5

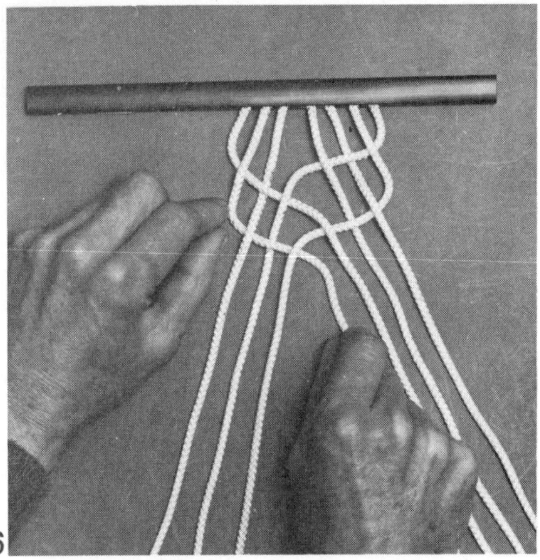
6

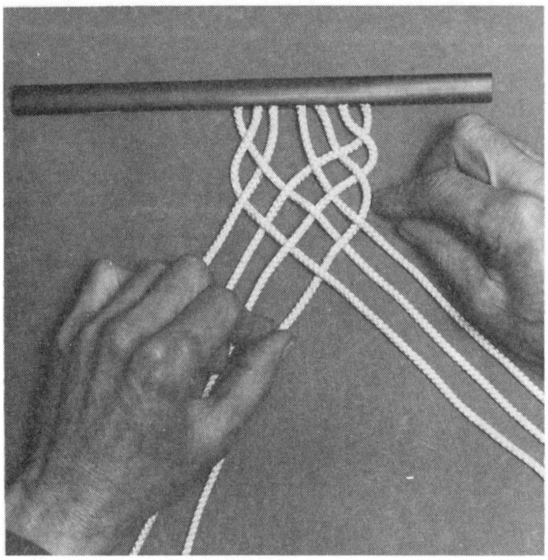
7

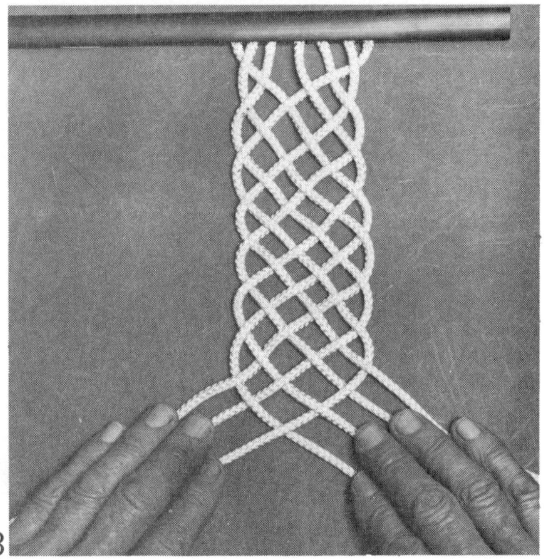
8

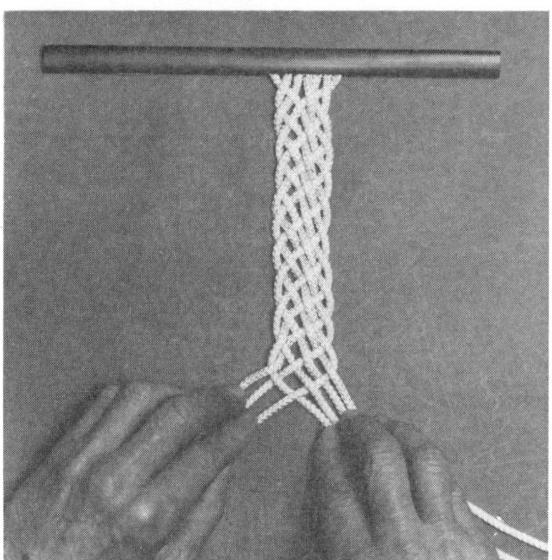
9

73 Portuguese Sennit, Spiral

There are only two working strands in a Portuguese sennit (these may be doubled if desired), one either side of a central heart, which can be any number of strands, usually two (more than three not being recommended).
The left-hand strand is passed under the hearts and over the right-hand strand, a bight being retained on the left, Fig 1. The right-hand strand is brought across, over the hearts, down through the bight, Fig 2, and both ends drawn tight, Fig 3. The left-hand strand is again passed under the hearts, Fig 4, the second knot being completed, Figs 5 to 7.
This process is continued, always using the left-hand strand first when the spiral will develop automatically, Fig 8, indeed it cannot be prevented or straightened out.

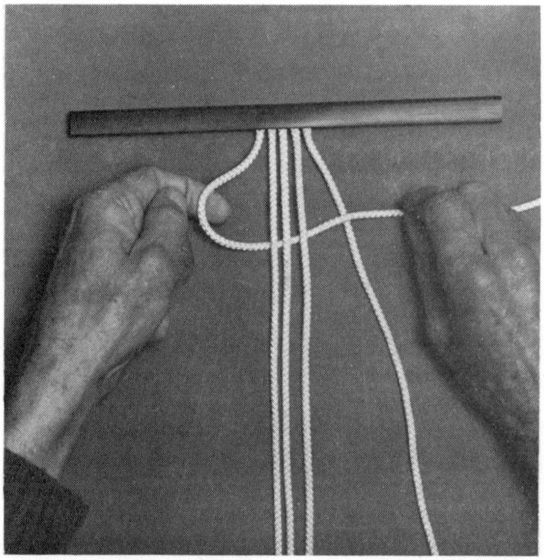
1

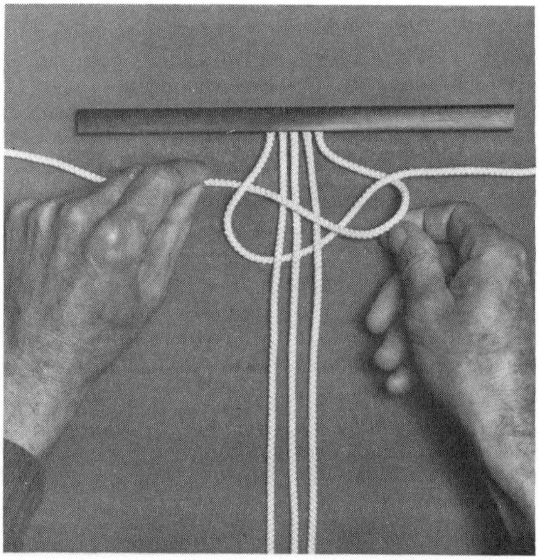
2

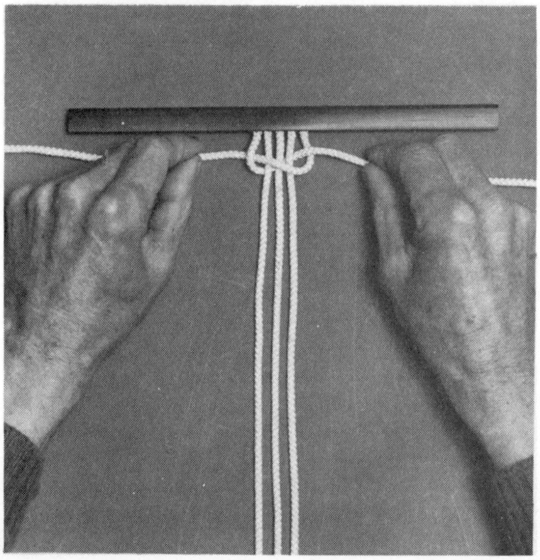
3

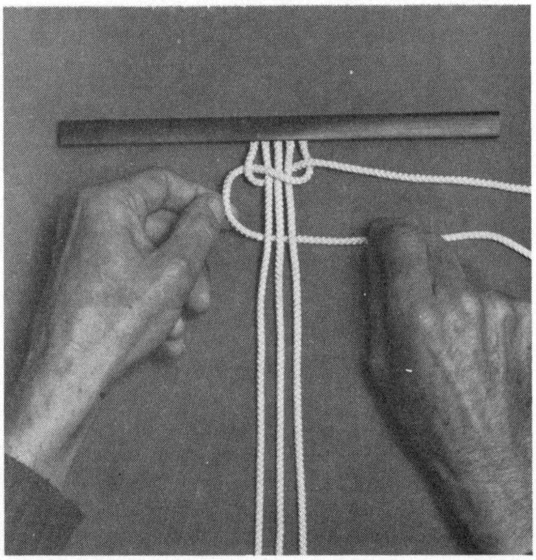
4

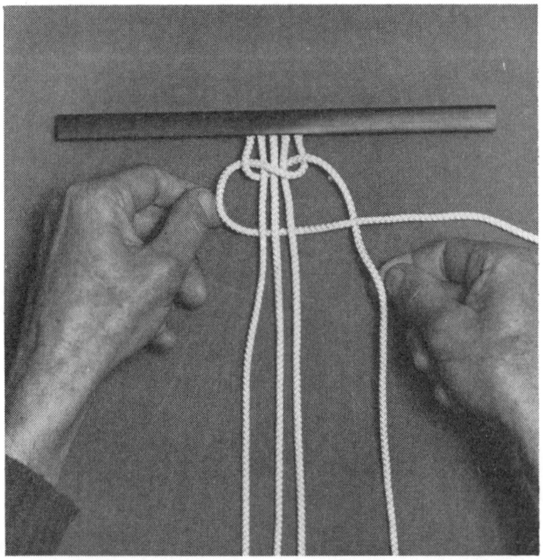
5
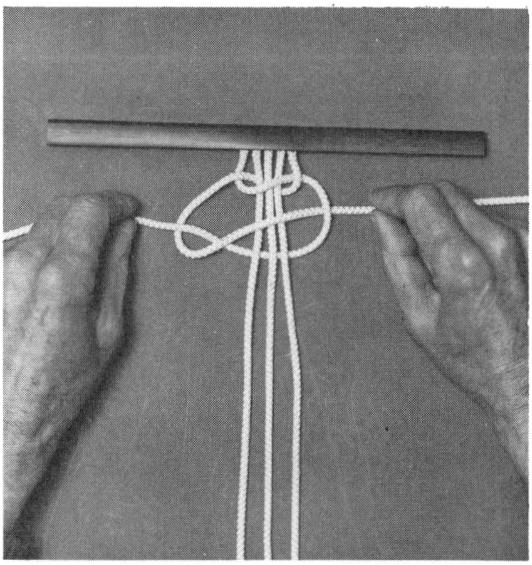
6
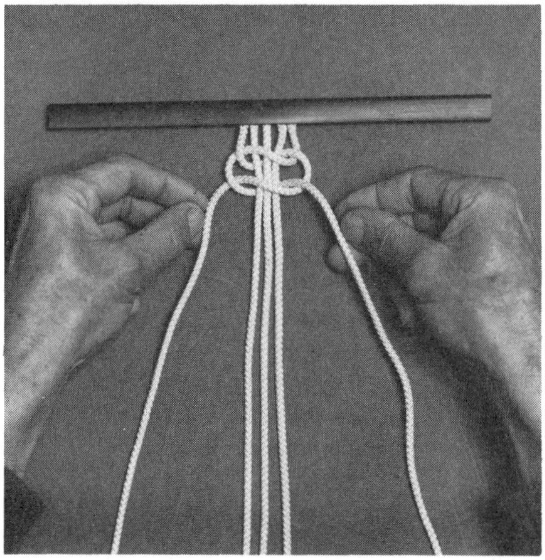
7
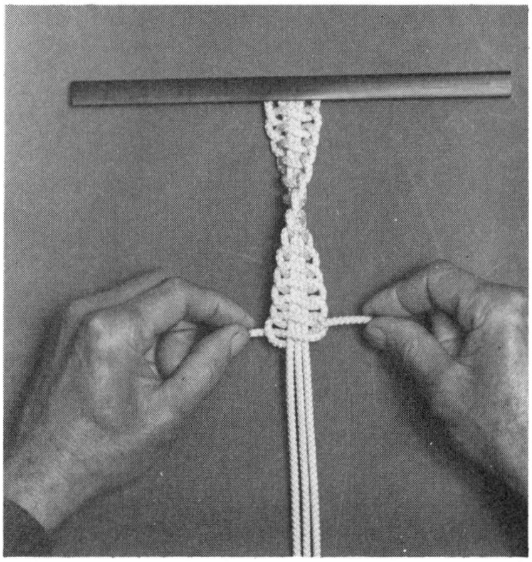
8

74
Portuguese Sennit, Flat

The arrangement of strands and formation of the first knot, Figs 1 to 3, are identical to the spiral version (Knot 73). The variation occurs at this point with the right-hand end being passed under the hearts, over the left-hand part, Fig 4, and the second knot completed as shown in Figs 5 and 6. The third knot is made in the same way as the first and so on with alternate left- and right-hand knots to completion, Fig 7.

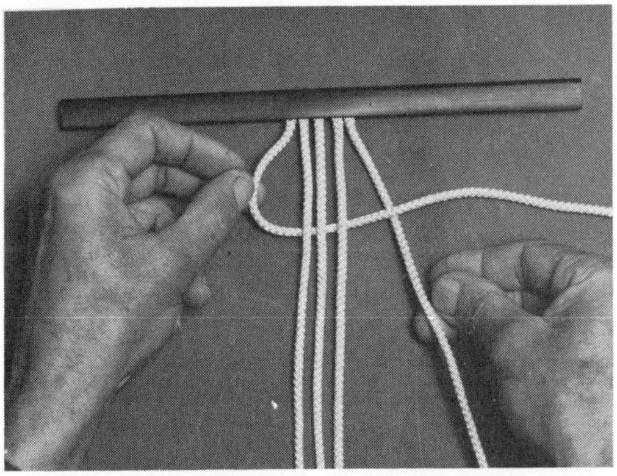
1

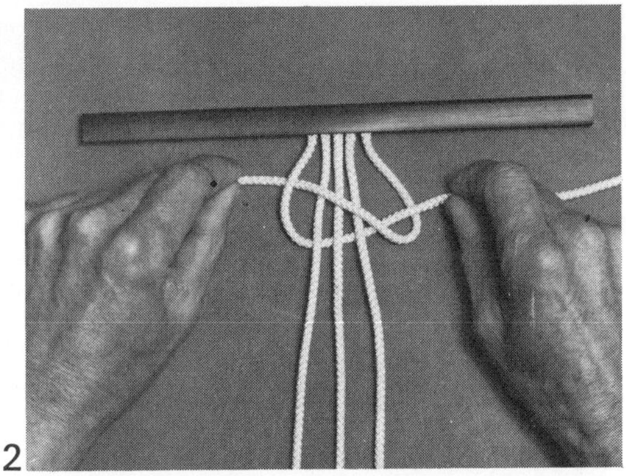
2

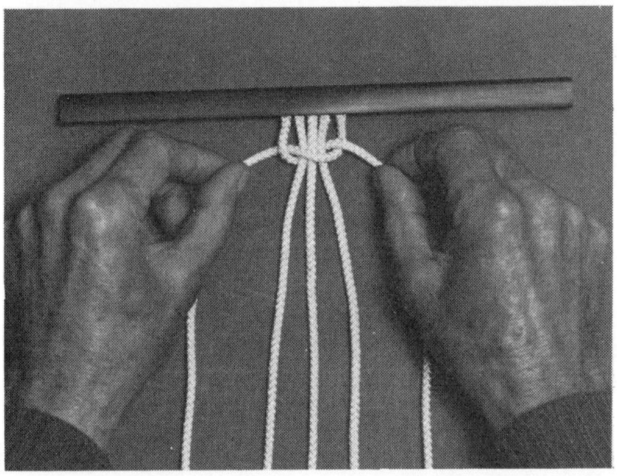
3

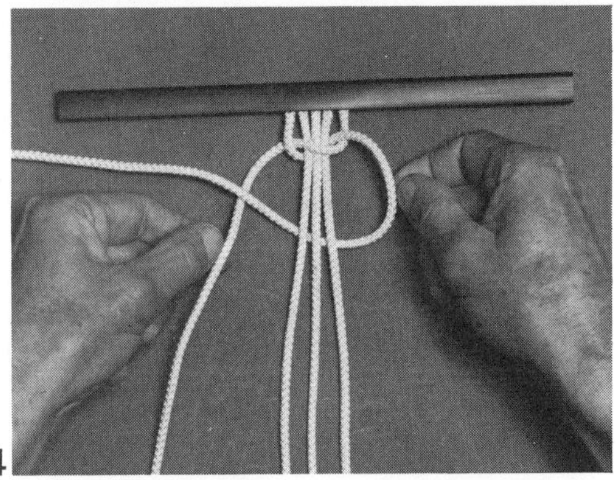
4

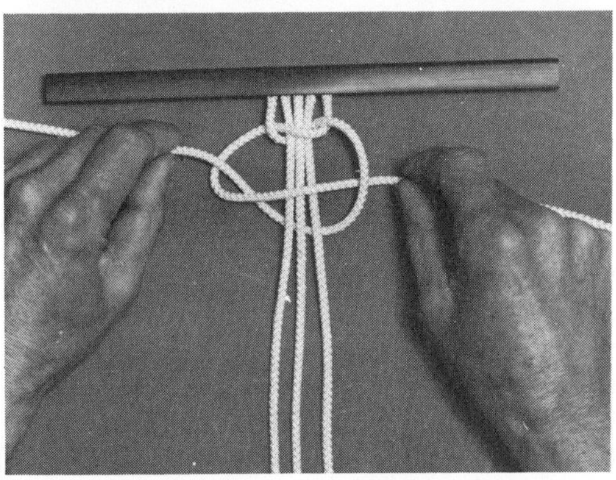
5

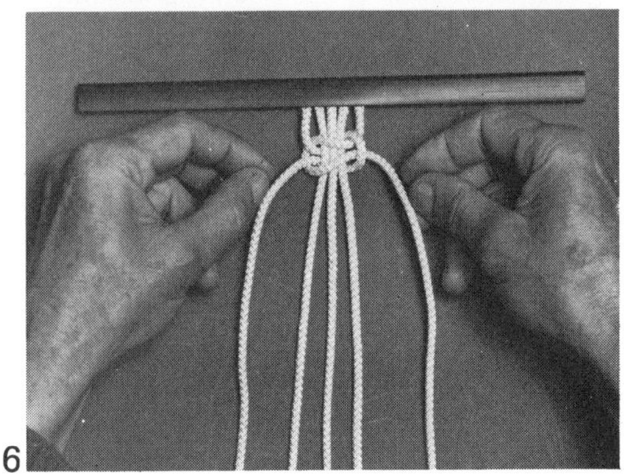
6

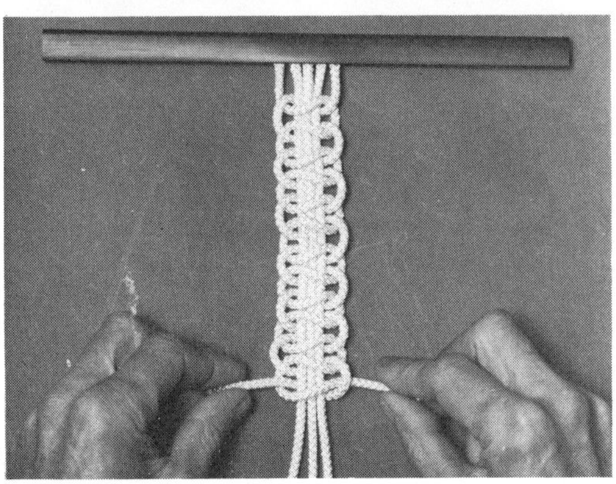
7

75 Spanish Hitching, Overhand and Reversed

There are two types of Spanish hitching, both being a means of covering any cylindrical object but, as distinct from continuous crowning (Knot 53), they involve the use of a 'warping strand' which is wound around and around the cylinder, interweaving the working strands, with every turn.
The latter are secured around the object in such numbers that they either completely fill the circumference or, as illustrated, with gaps between them. The thinnest possible warp would be used with the former, becoming almost indiscernible, whilst the heavier warp of the latter becomes an integral part of the pattern.
Fig 1 shows the working strands secured with a whipping and the 'warping strand' attached. The working strands must be kept *outside* the warp throughout. Pass the first working strand over the warp and back down, Fig 2, pulling both strand and warp tight. Rotate the work and repeat with the second strand and so on. Fig 3 shows the first full turn, Fig 4 the second, to completion in Fig 5.

Spanish Hitching, Reversed

A completely different pattern is obtained by keeping the working strands *inside* the warp and taking a full backwards round turn each time.
Fig 6 shows the warp and first working strand, with the turn taken in Fig 7.
This is repeated with each strand in turn, the first full rotation of the work being shown in Fig 8, the second in Fig 9, and the completed job, Fig 10.

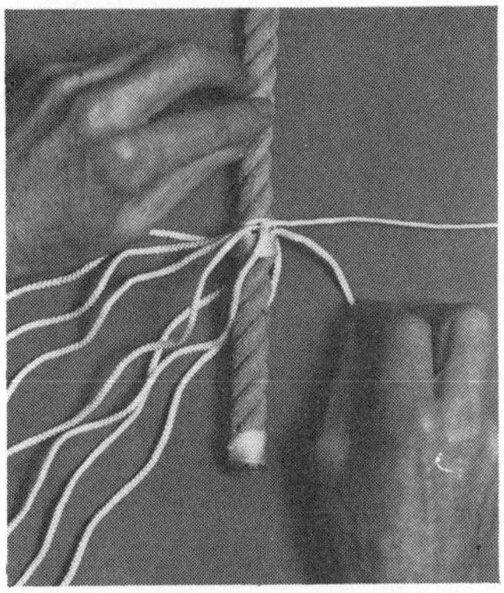
1

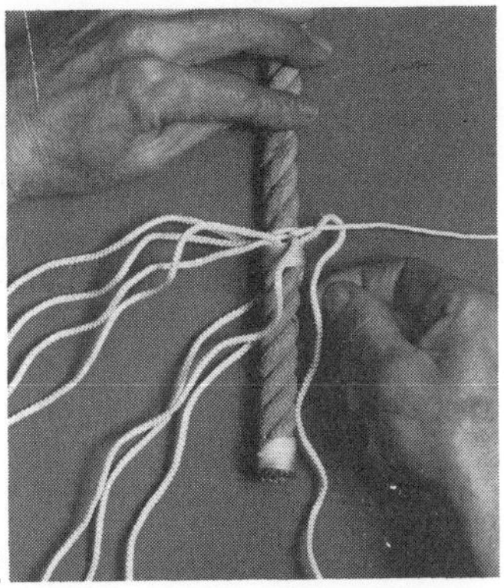
2

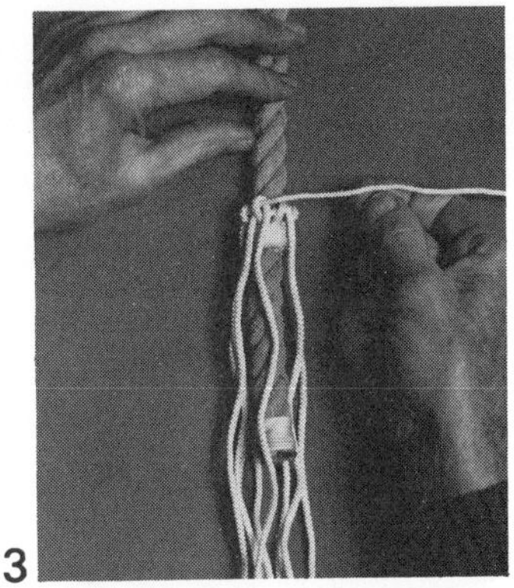
3

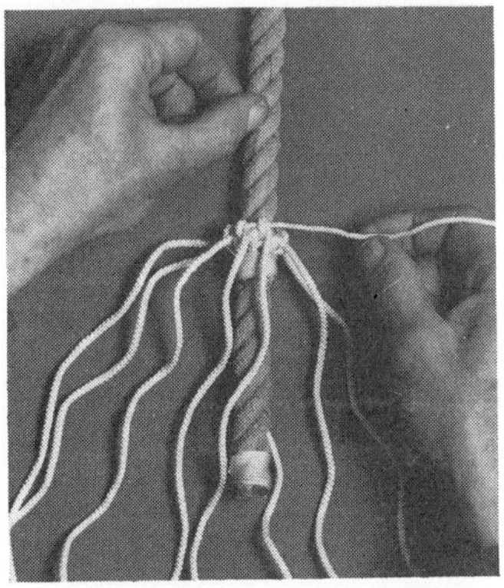
4

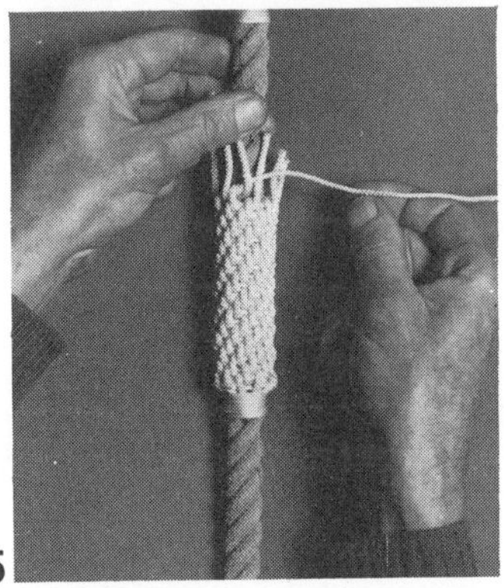
5

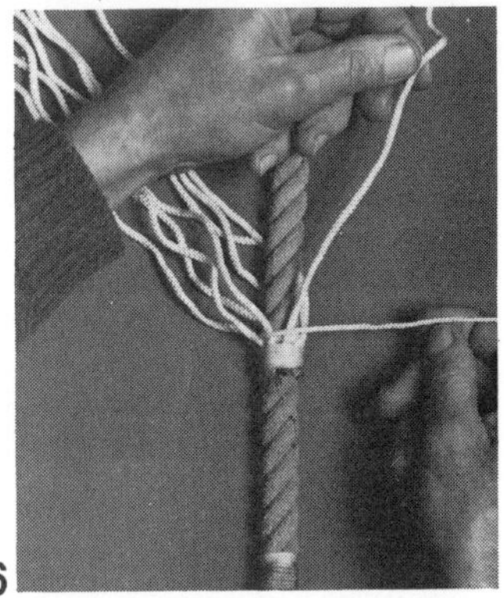
6

7

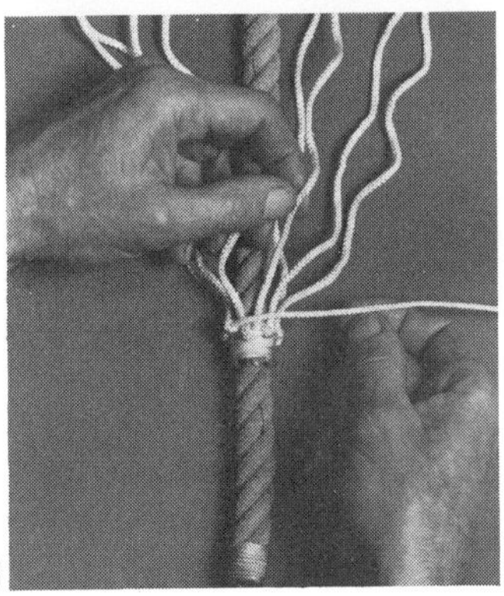
8

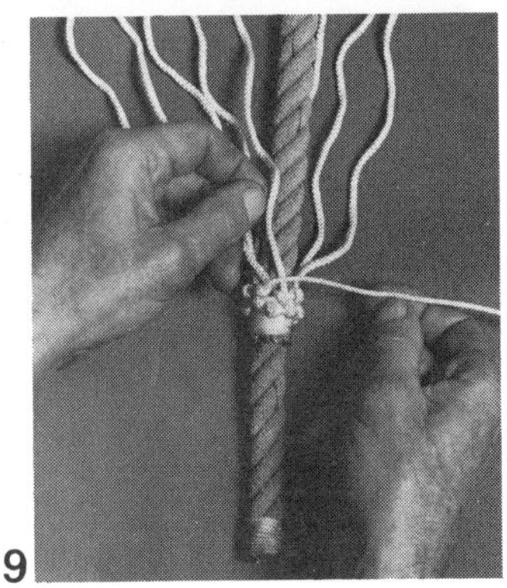
9

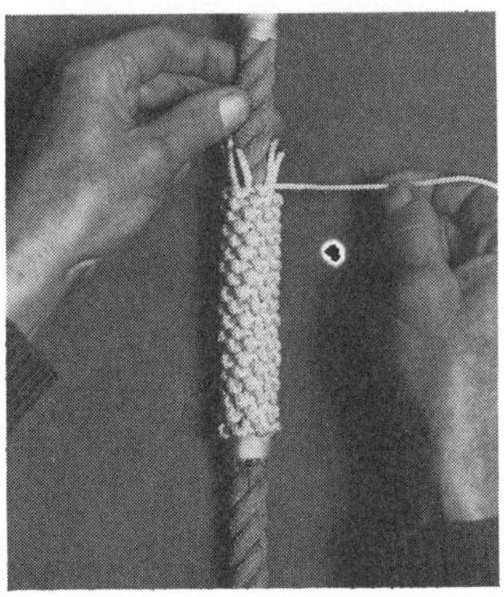
10

76 Russian Sennit, Six Stranded

The first and last strands form the border at each side around which the working strands are turned, four being shown, though any number may be used.
The first working strand is turned around the left-hand border and under the second working strand, Fig 1, before being laid away to the left, Fig 2. Each strand in turn, working left to right is tucked under its neighbour, also laid away to the left, Figs 3 to 5, and drawn tight with the last under the right-hand border, ready for the return, Fig 6.
All working strands are returned vertical and the border strand turned, Fig 7, after which the return reeving is made from right to left, Figs 8 to 10, thus completing the first 'over and back'. The completed length, Fig 11, is finished off by joining the border strands across the bottom and hitching the working strands to it (not illustrated).

Russian Mat
A square or rectangular mat can also be made on the same principle, using a large number of strands, obviously far too complicated to be photographed, even if necessary.

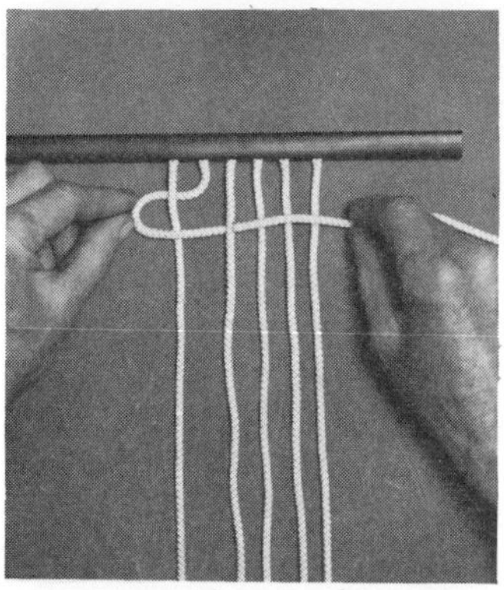
1

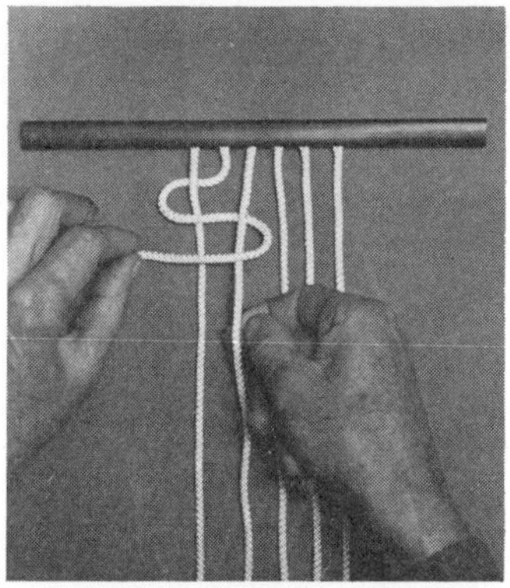
2

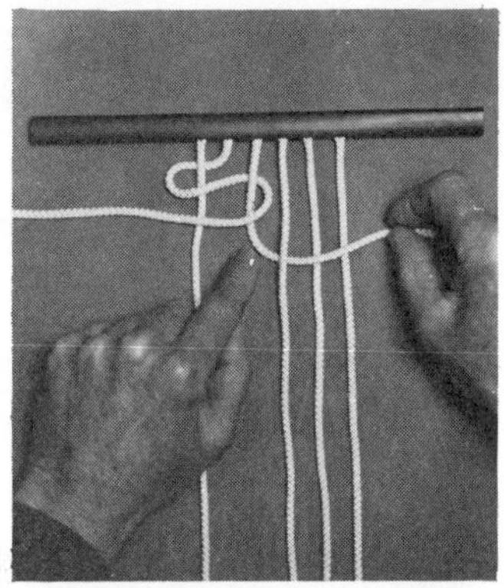
3

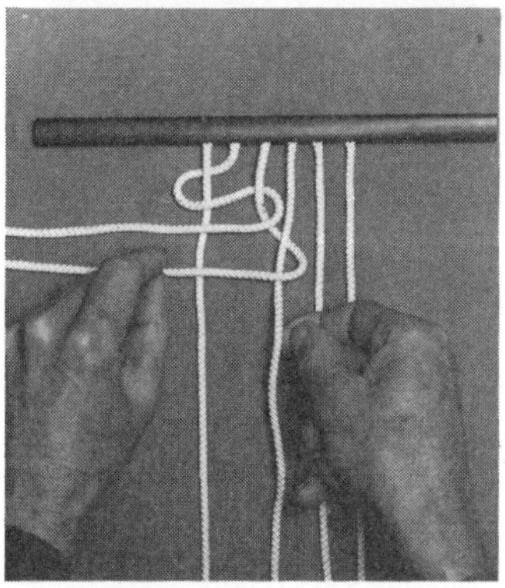
4

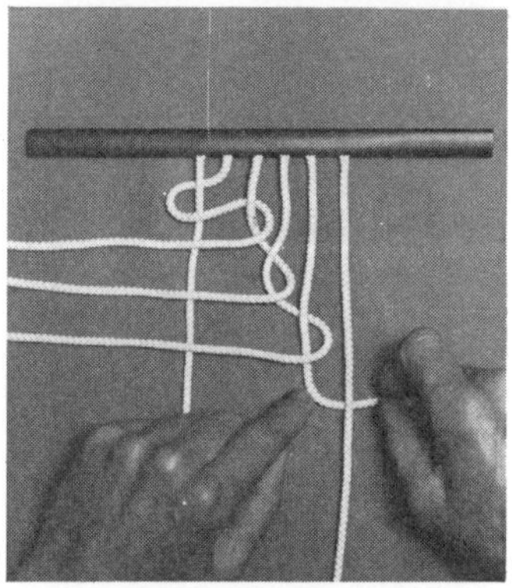
5

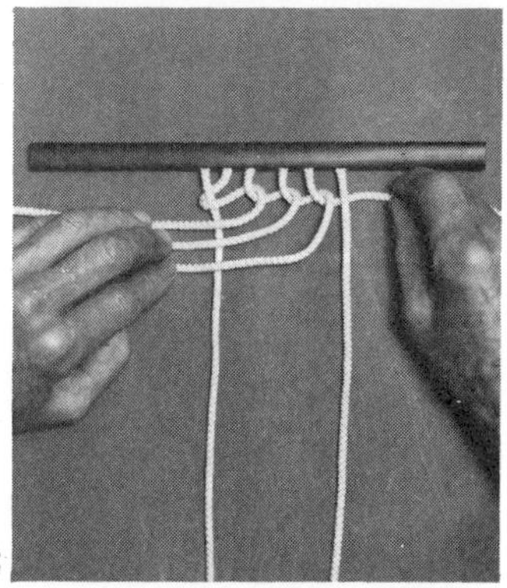
6

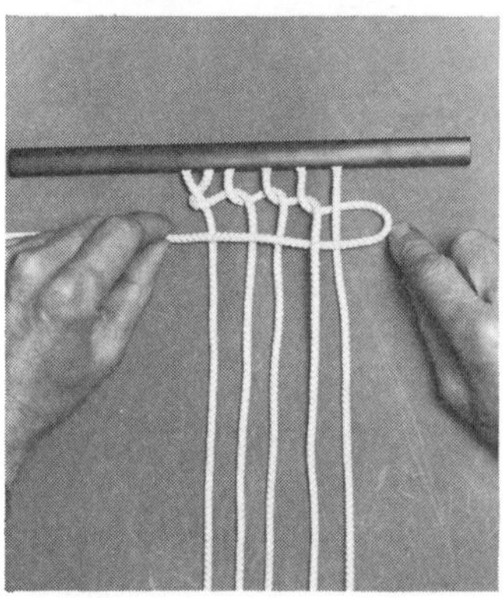
7

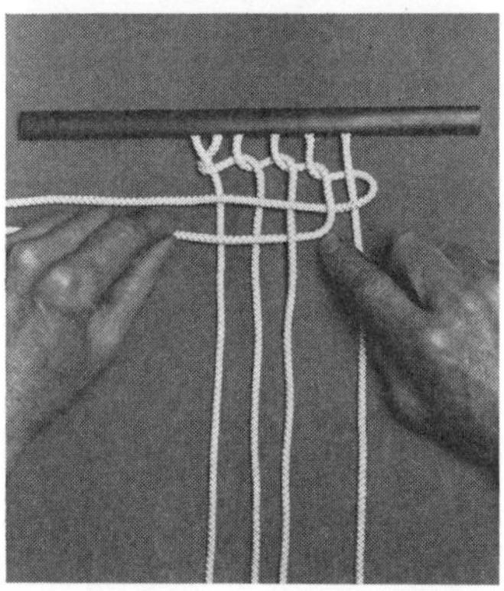
8

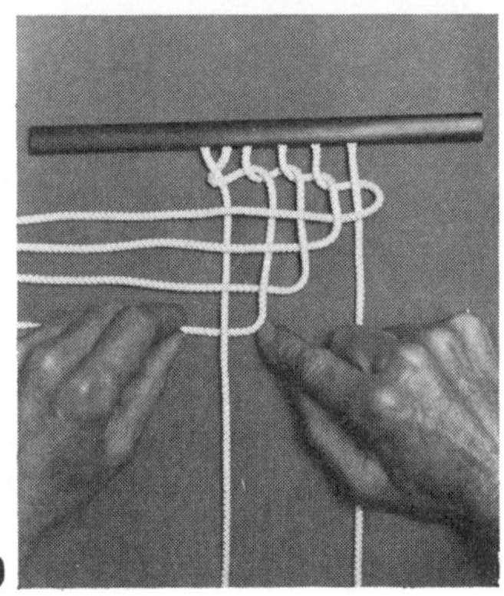
9

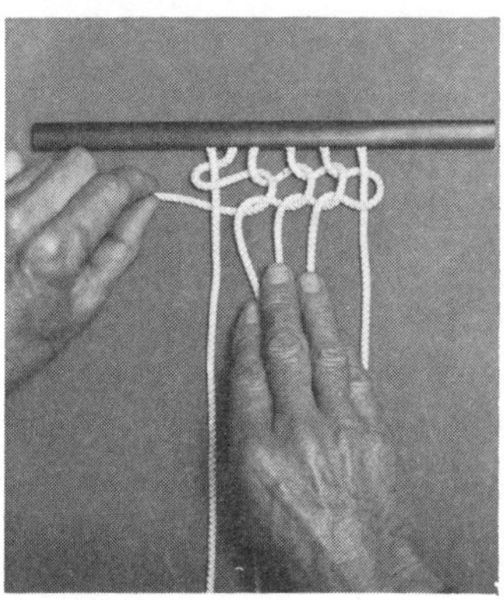
10

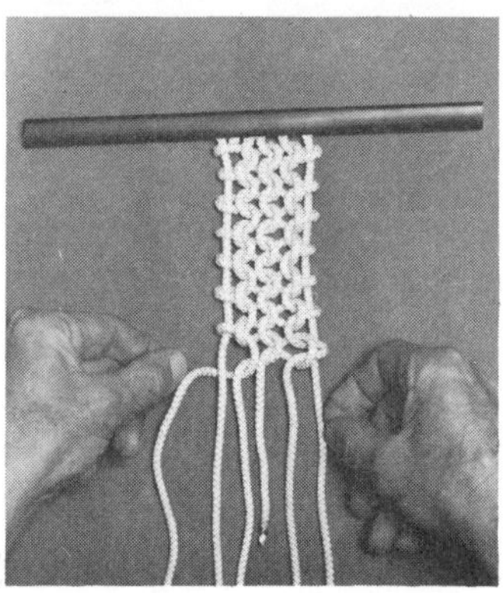
11

77 Cockscombing, Single Stranded

This is an ideal method of covering an object which is both cylindrical and circular as the gaps which form at the bottom of the bights are naturally taken up by the roundness of the ring.

It is essentially a question of making forwards and backwards hitches alternately, Figs 1 and 2, showing the formation of the first, drawn tight in Fig 3. The next hitch is made backwards, Figs 4 and 5, and so on alternately, Figs 6 and 7, until the ring is completely covered, Fig 8.

Cow Hitch

This is a useful knot provided that both standing parts share the load but usually it is the result of a wrongly made clove hitch, when it becomes useless. Fig 3 shows a typical cow hitch.

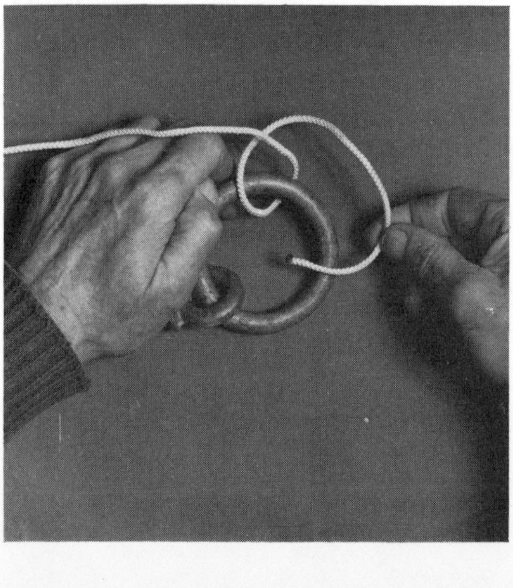

1

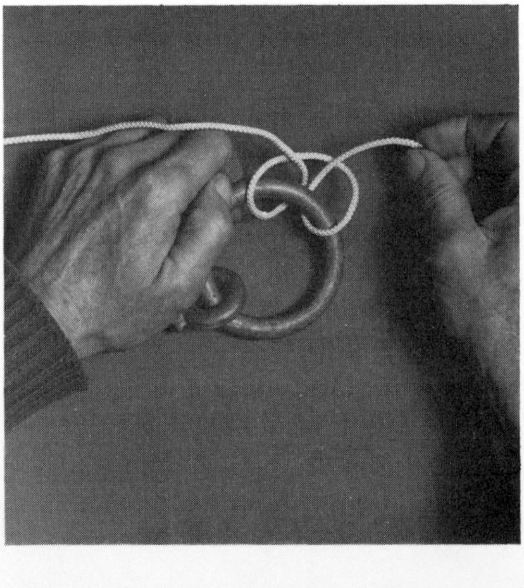

2

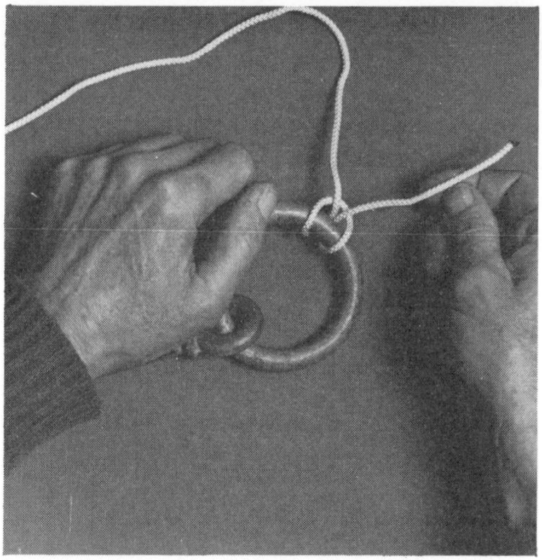

3

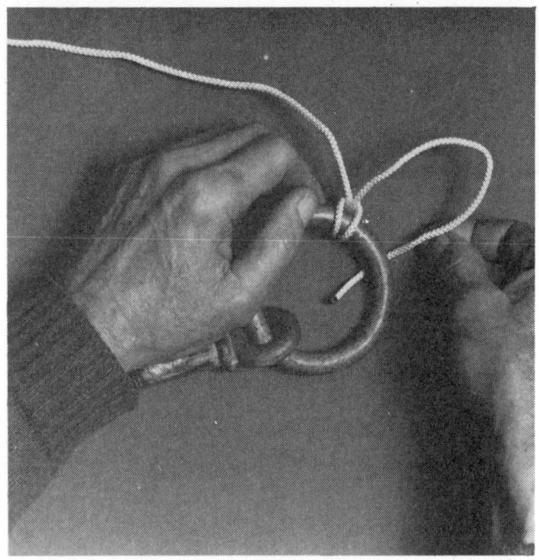

4

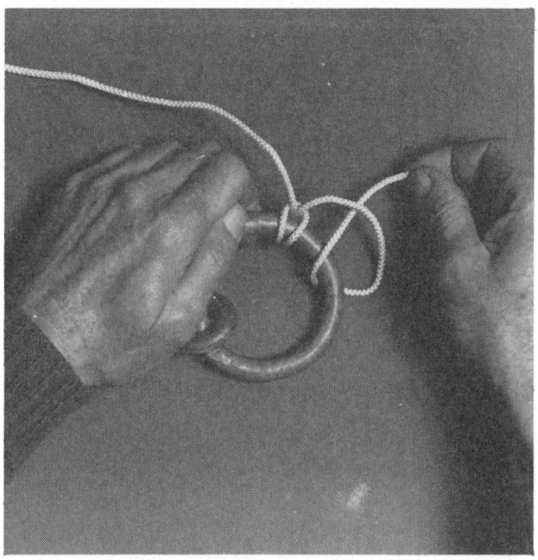

5

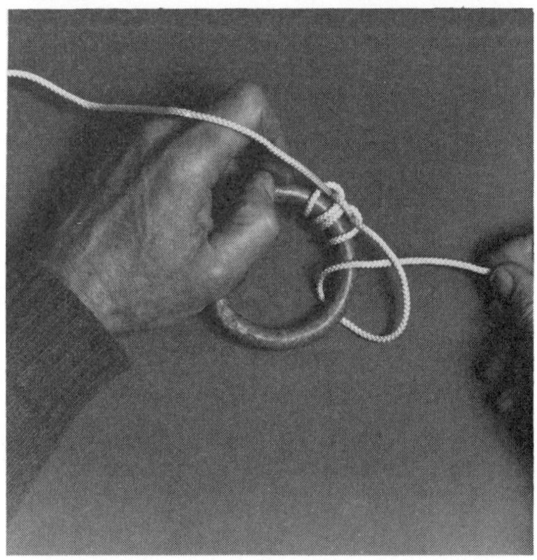

6

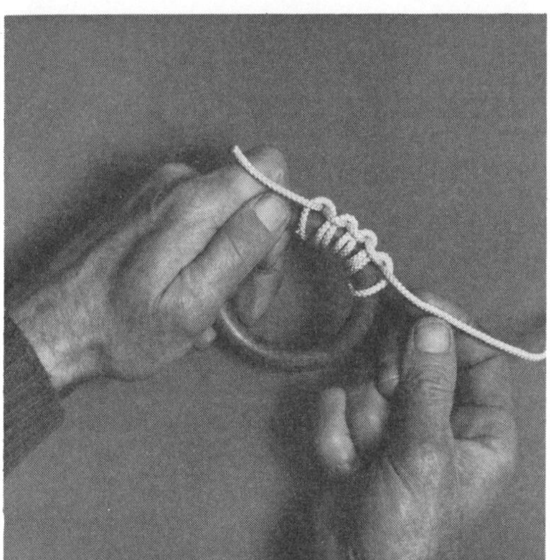

7

8

78 Cockscombing, Three Stranded

As illustrated three strands are normally used in this method of covering a cylindrical object, with the 'comb' being the feature. The three working strands are whipped to the object and a hitch made with the right-hand strand, Fig 1, drawn tight as in Fig 2.

The centre strand is then hitched in the same way but in the opposite direction and drawn tight, Figs 3 and 4, followed by the remaining left-hand strand, hitched in the same direction as the first, Fig 5. The process is then repeated, working each strand alternately right and left to completion, Fig 6.

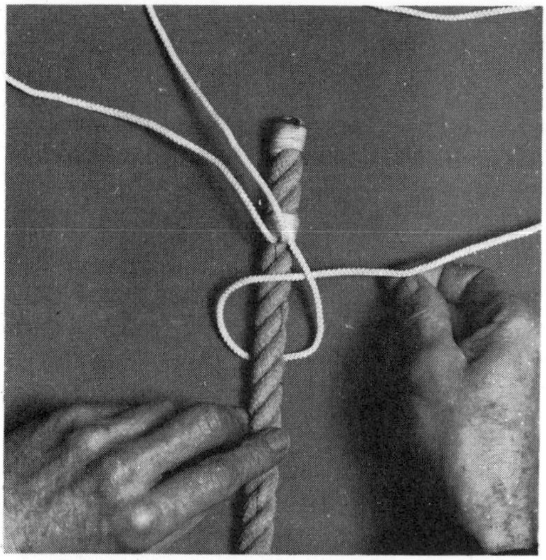

1

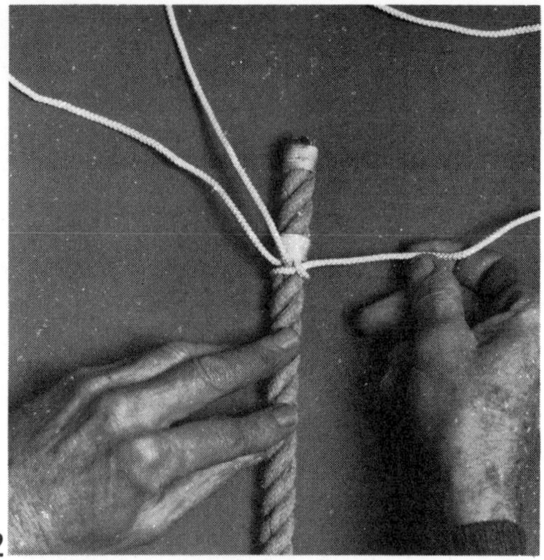

2

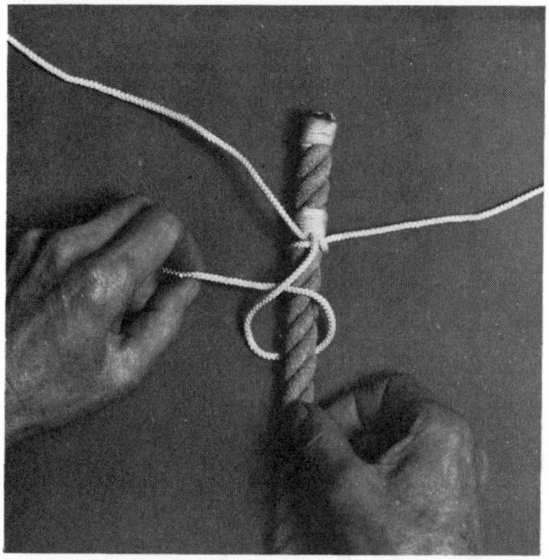

3

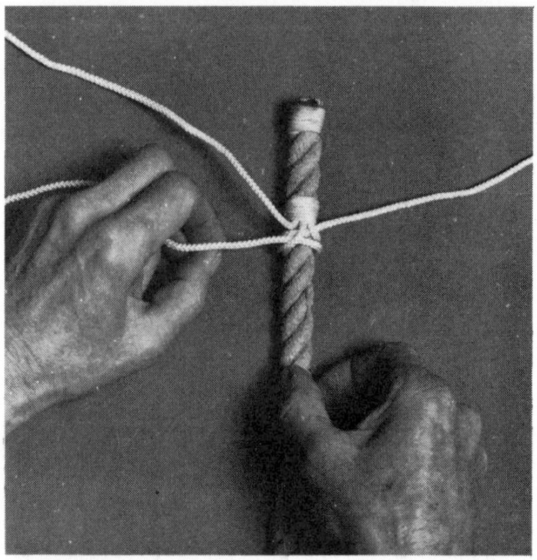

4

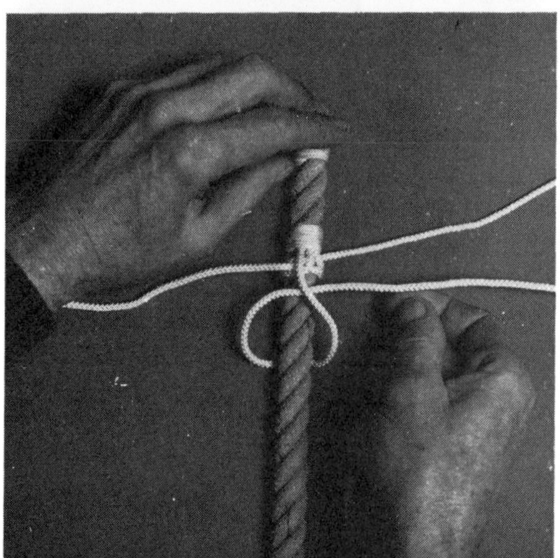

5

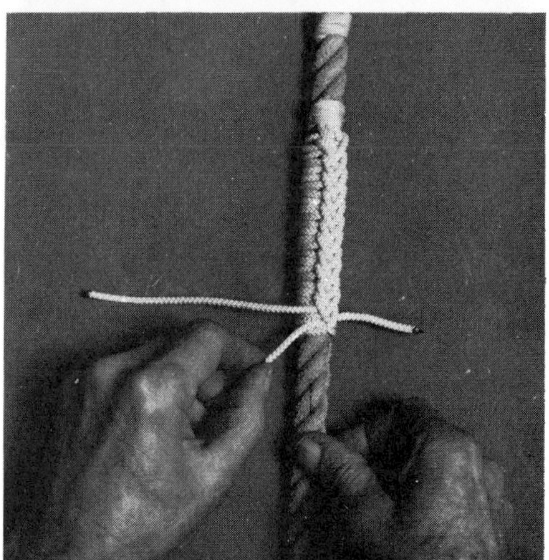

6

79 Thrum Sennit

A thrum is a short piece of cordage, usually rope yarn (four to six inches long), but no rules prevent the use of plaited cordage, as illustrated.

Two thrums are laid down, Fig 1, a third added, Fig 2, the left-hand end of which is brought around, trapping two bights, before being laid parallel with the three right-hand strands, Fig 3, the top one of which is brought down to the vertical, Fig 4, resulting in one pair and one odd strand pointing downwards.

A fourth thrum is added, reeved through the bights of the first two (to prevent the whole from unravelling), Figs 5 and 6, brought to the parallel, Fig 7, and the top strand brought to the vertical, Fig 8. This completes the start and end sealing of the sennit with two pairs and one odd vertical strand.

The fifth thrum is laid down with the left-hand end emerging between the last pair and the odd strand, Fig 9, drawn tight, Fig 10, passed to the parallel, Fig 11, and the next top strand brought down, Fig 12. All further thrums are added in the same way as in Figs 9 to 12. On completion of the required length, the ends are trimmed to a given length, Fig 13, and can be left as such or combed into a fringe, Fig 14.

A long length of this sennit wound into a circle or formed into a square and sewn together makes the conventional door-mat with the bristle appearance. In the past, with slight variations, it was used also as anti-chafing gear, when it was made around topping lifts for instance, to protect the sails and was known as a 'Bag o' Wrinkles'.

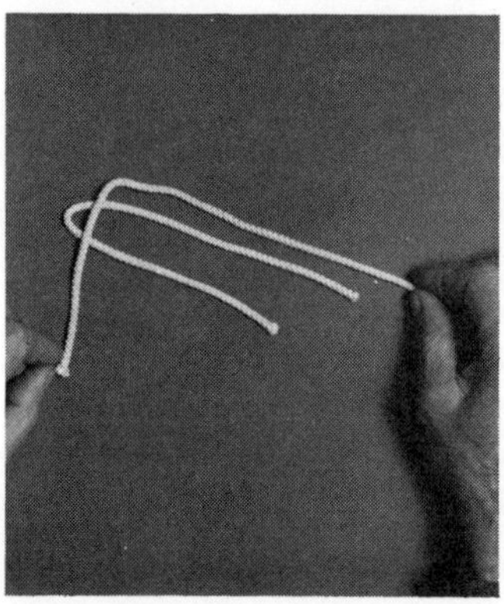

1

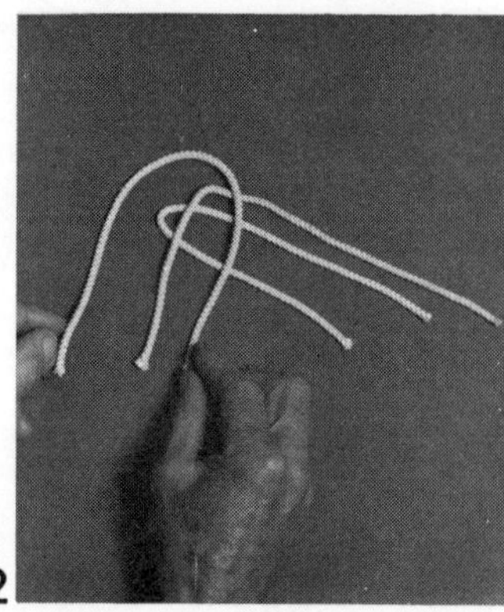

2

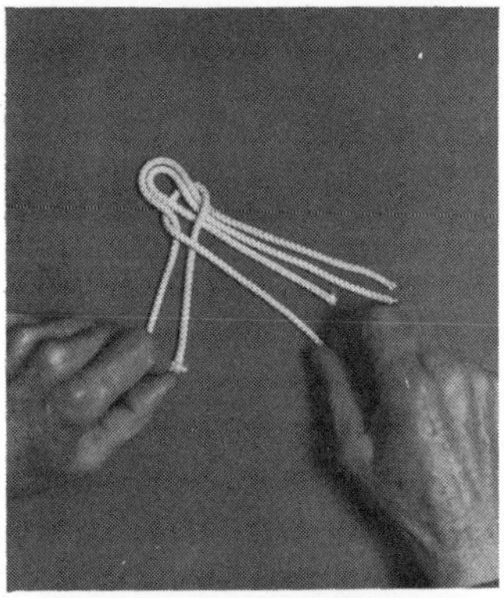
3
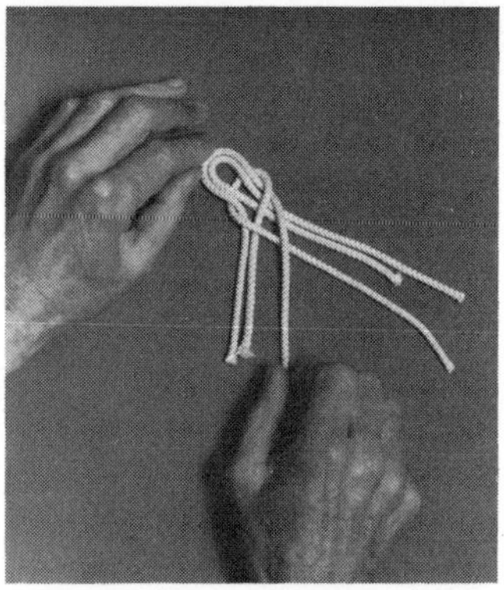
4
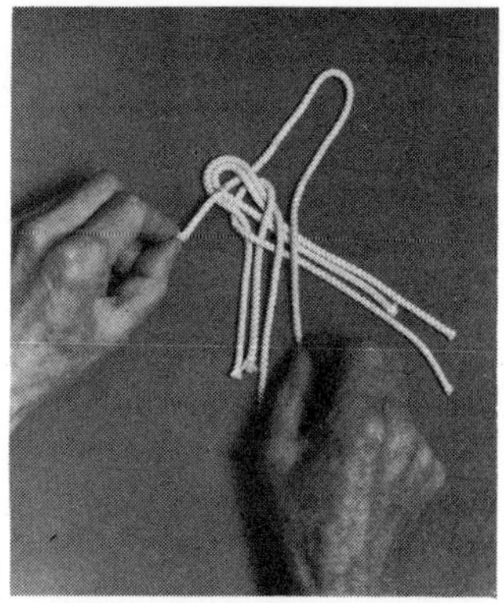
5
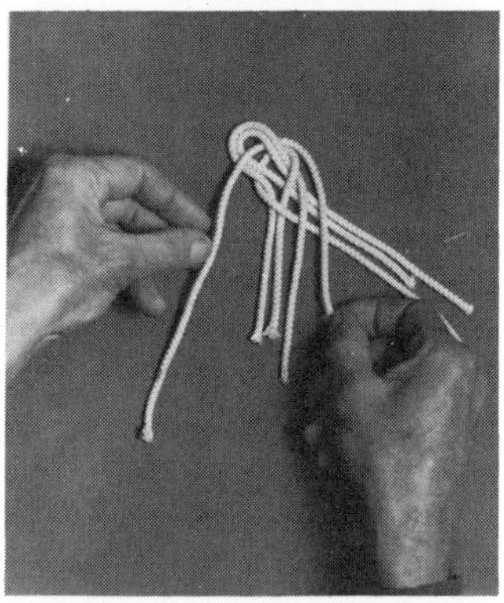
6
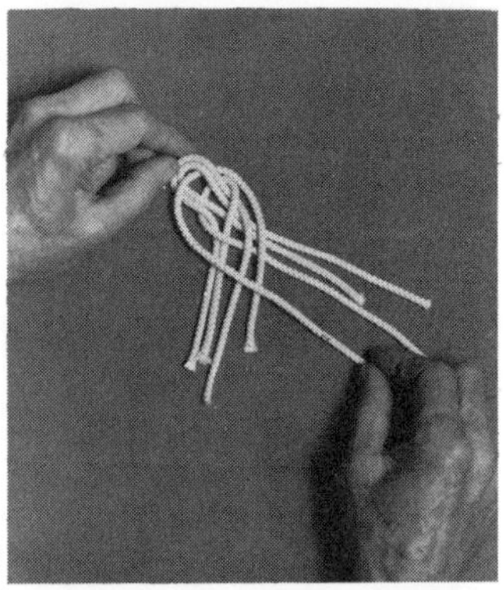
7
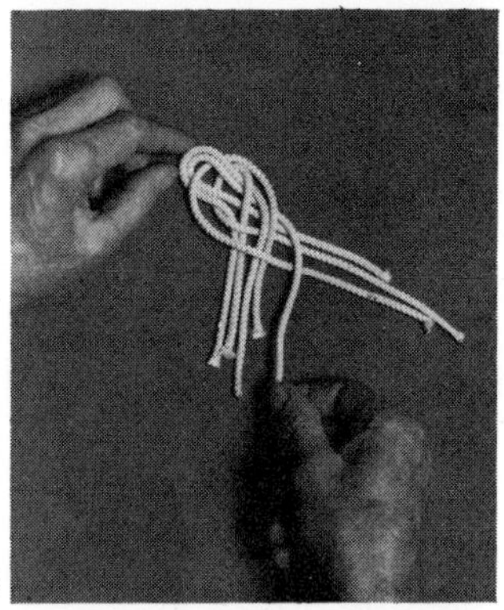
8
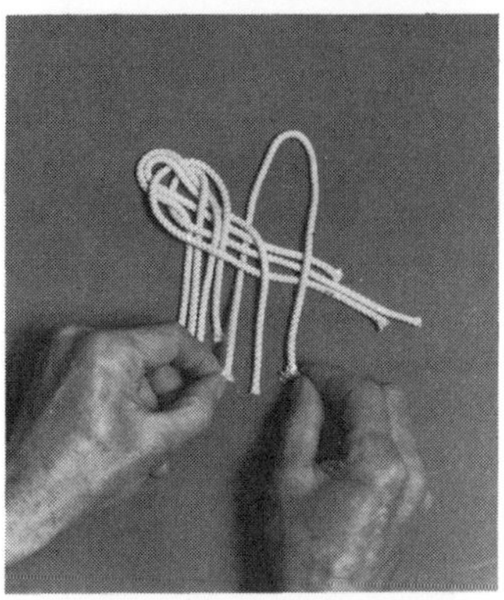
9
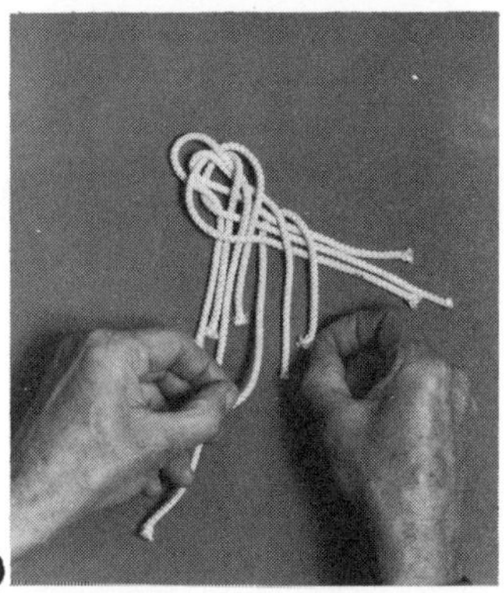
10
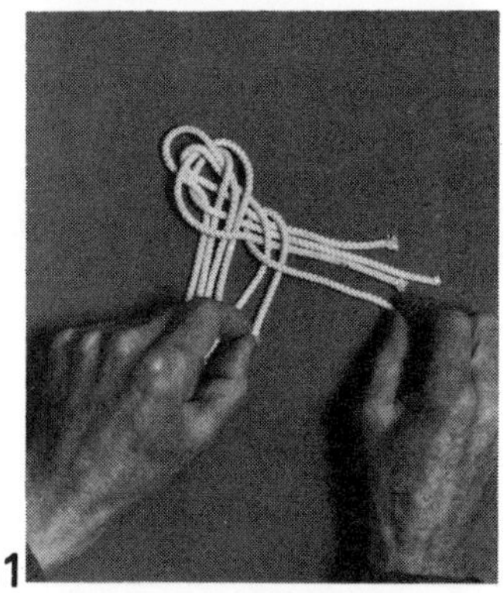
11
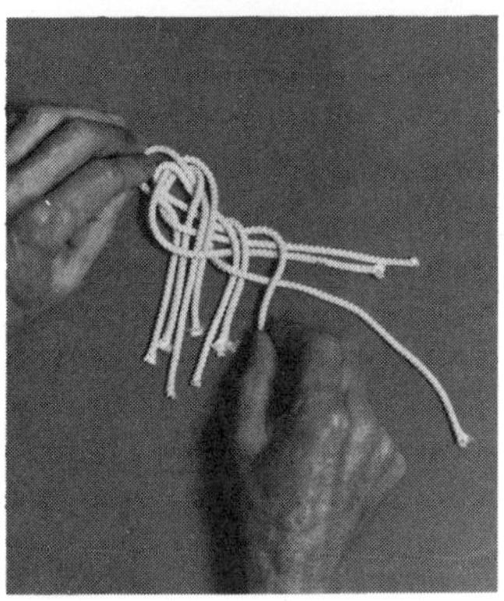
12
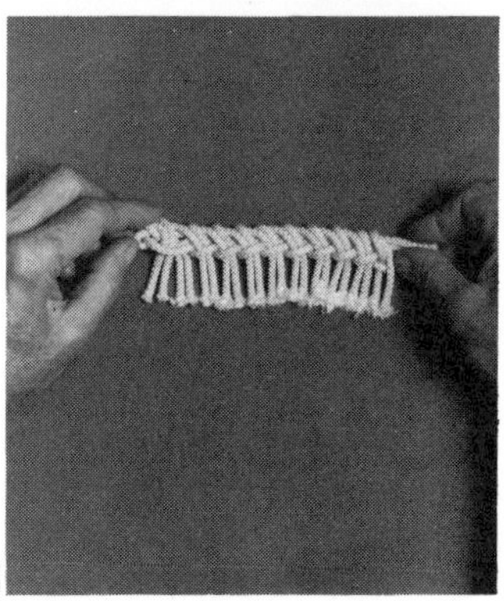
13
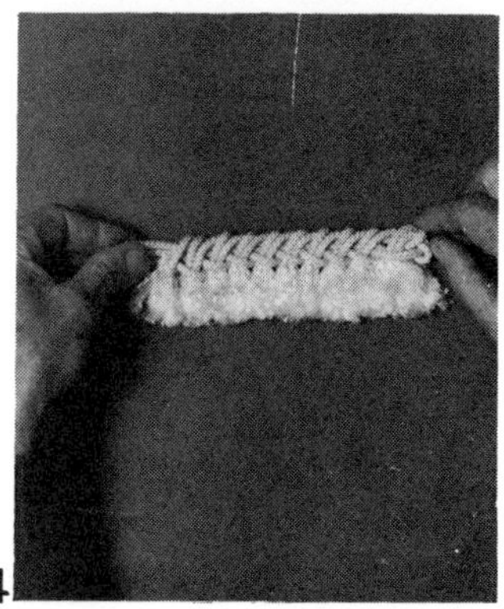
14

80
To Form a Spindle Eye

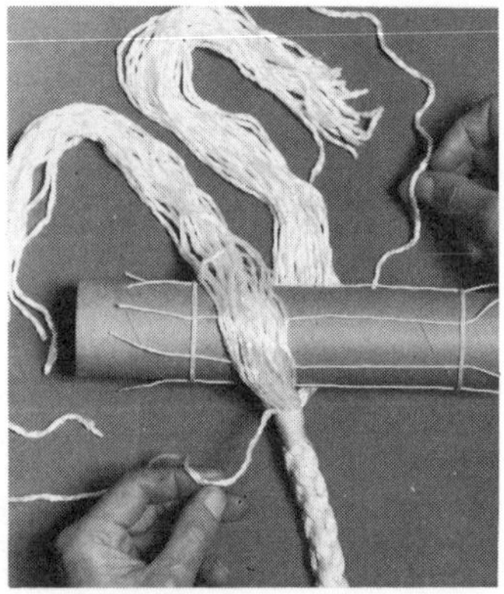
1

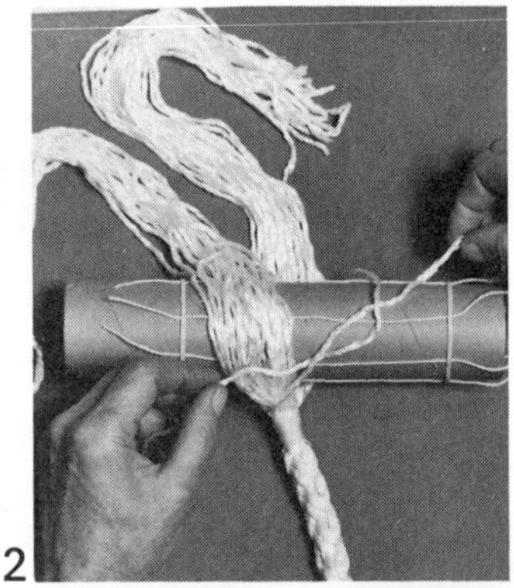
2

3

4

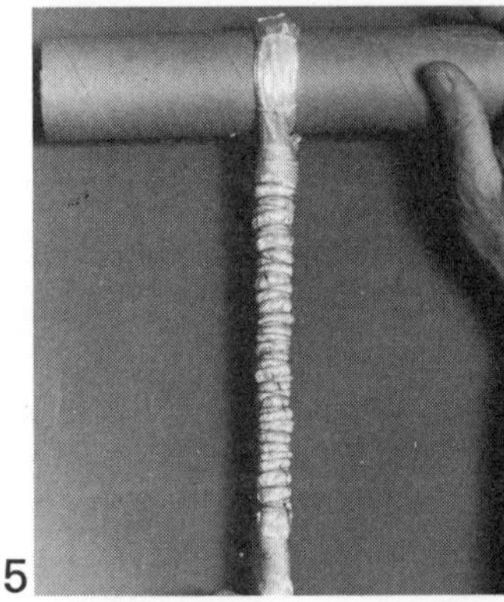
5

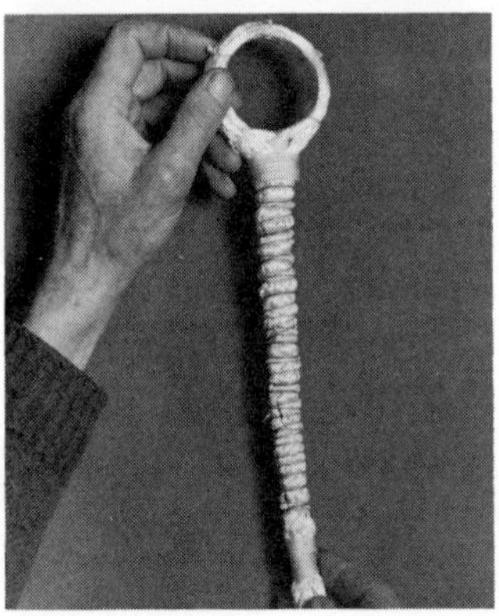
6

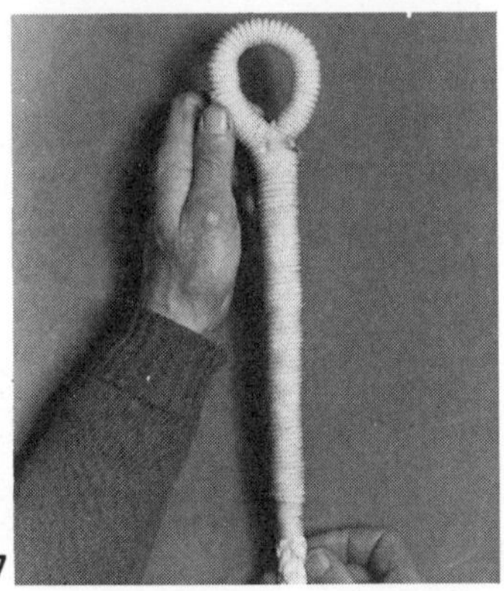
7

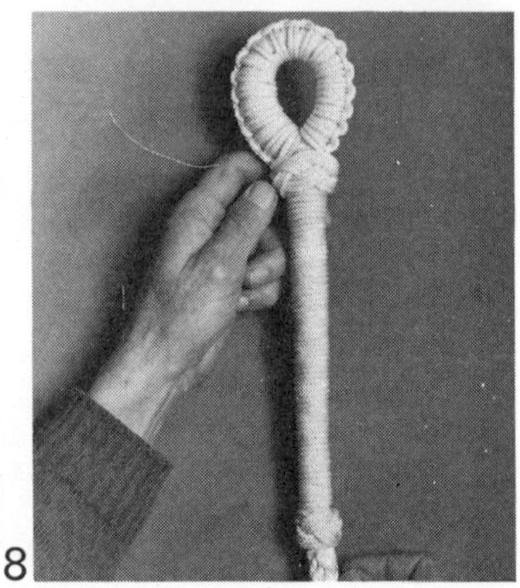
8

A 'former', slightly larger in diameter than the required 'eye' is necessary, along which a number of ties (short lengths of cord) are laid and temporarily secured at both ends. The rope is prepared by applying a whipping, unlaying all strands, halving them and offering the whole up to the 'former', all as in Fig 1.
Each pair of strands is half-hitched over the 'former', care being taken to spread the hitches around the circumference to avoid bunching, Figs 2 and 3. The ends are returned to the standing part where they are tightly whipped, when the ties are released and knotted around the hitched strands, Fig 4.
The ends are tapered and tightly bound and the 'former' removed, Figs 5 and 6, when both 'eye' and taper are served, Fig 7. The finish is a matter of choice, Fig. 8, showing the 'eye' covered with single strand Cockscombing with a Turk's head top and bottom of the taper.

Mats

Although the name 'mats' is given to the following ropeworks, all except one are individually too small to be used as actual mats. The exception is the square mat, which is not 'followed around' and is the only one to increase equally in length and breadth with each additional bight being worked into it. However, there would be little beauty in one large square mat.

The art of mat-making is therefore the combination of a series of small mats conjoined with chosen sennits, all sewn together with sail twine. Those illustrated have been made with manufactured cordage purely for photographic clarity and whilst there are no rules against this, the beauty of any mat will be enhanced if the small mats are themselves made with sennit, the three stranded common sennit (Knot 67) being the most simple for this purpose. Knot 95 shows a suggested multiple mat, in this case made in miniature.

There are several other mats which border on weaving, the sword mat for instance requiring some sort of loom, whilst the wrought mat with its multiplicity of strands needs two pairs of hands. The Russian mat also requires a large number of strands which could become complicated, so a Russian sennit (Knot 76) has been illustrated, the mat being based on the same principle requiring only the additional strands to make up any given width.

81 Ocean Mat, Square

This is one mat which is not 'followed around' and therefore can be made to any predetermined size. Two turned bights are laid down, Fig 1 (the longest and uppermost determining the diagonal size of the mat), the second bight having been dipped under the standing part of the first.

The top part only of this second bight, maintained in an elongated shape is dipped over/under and interlaced with the first bight, Fig 2, once again leaving two standing parts. The next move holds good for all further movements prior to the reeving of the bights.

The left-hand standing part is taken under the right-hand standing part and twisted anti-clockwise, Fig 3, before being reeved up through the mat, Figs 4 and 5, and finally elongated top and bottom, Fig 6. This is continued, the elongations becoming progressively shorter as the mat is infilled from diagonally opposite corners towards the middle (the opposite diagonal), Figs 7, 8 and 9.

Finally, the one end is taken under the remaining standing part, Fig 10, and reeved up to the opposite corner, completing the final diagonal and the finished mat, Fig 11.

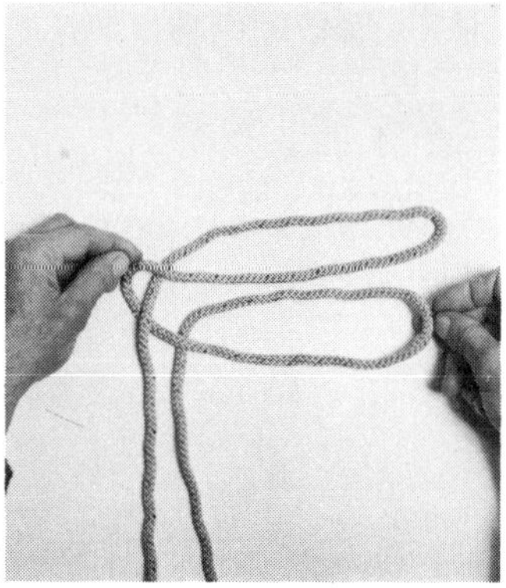
1

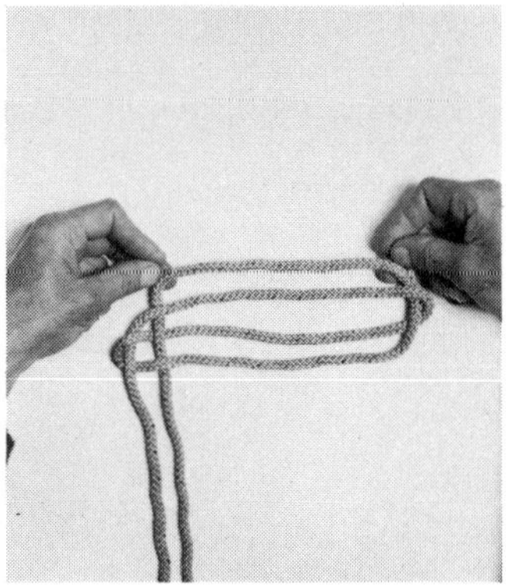
2

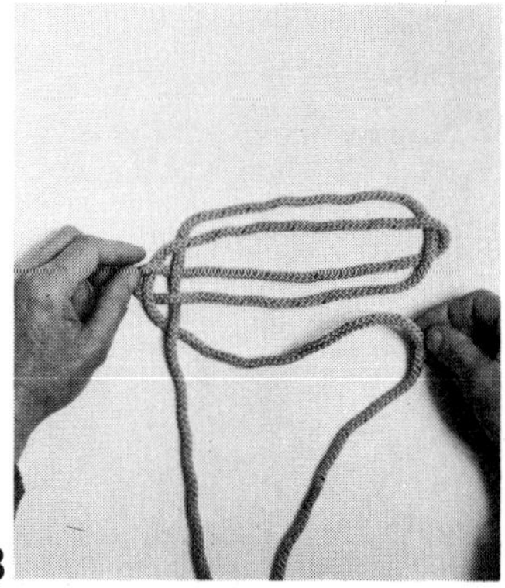
3

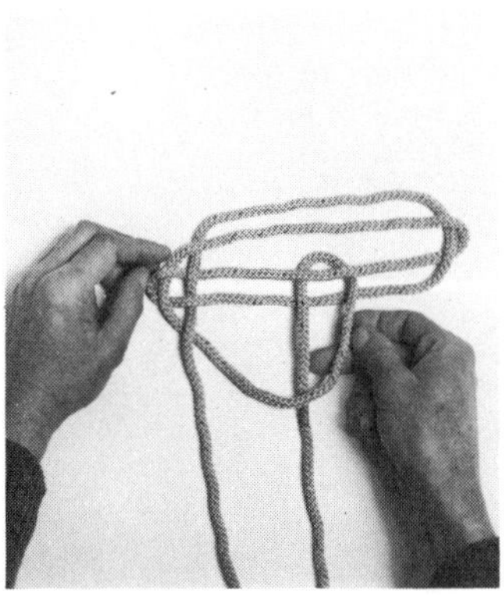
4

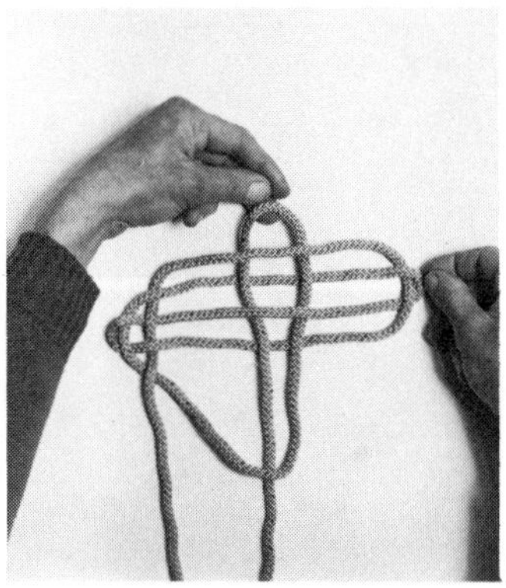
5

6

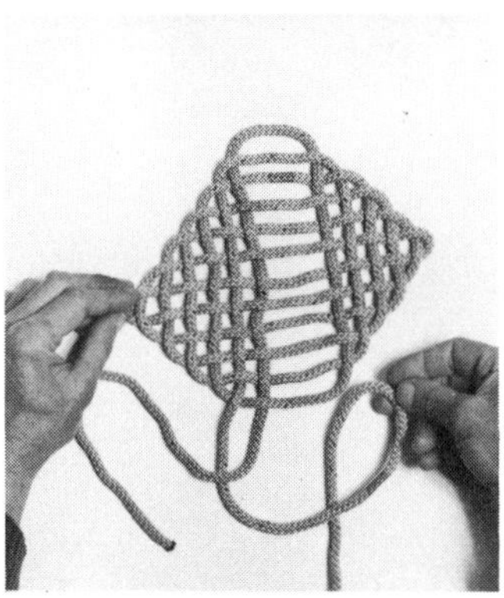
7

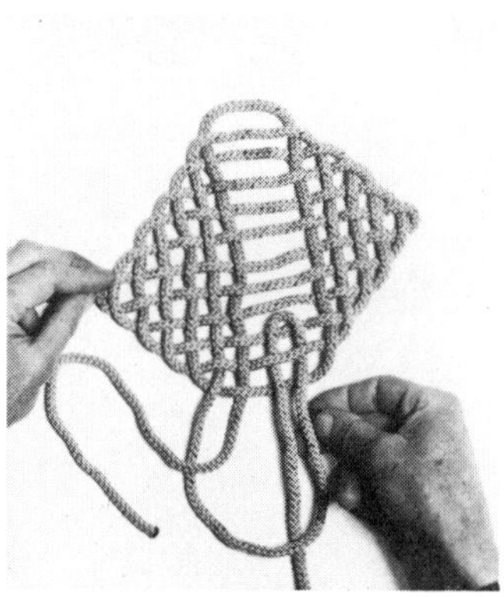
8

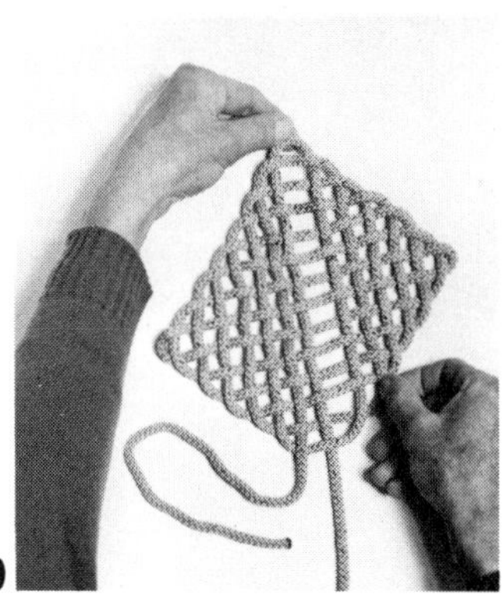
9

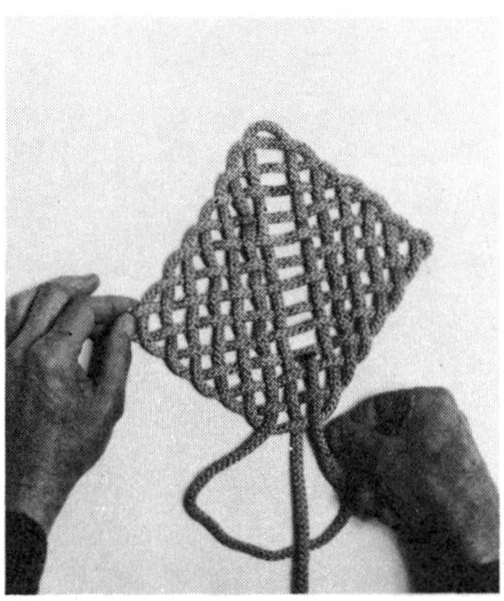
10

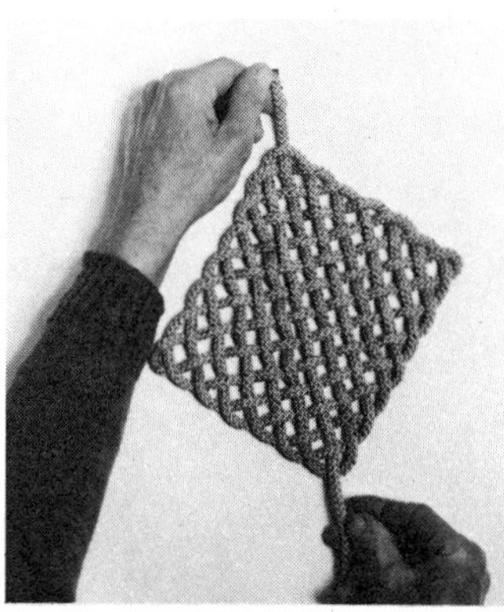
11

82
Carrick Mat

Two bights are laid up as in Fig 1, the left-hand part henceforth remaining static. The right-hand end is brought around, over this part to the top left-hand corner, Fig 2, and reeved through as shown in Fig 3.
Fig 4 returns the end to the start of the mat after which the first 'follow around' is made, Fig 5, and the completed mat, after the second 'follow around', Fig 6.

1

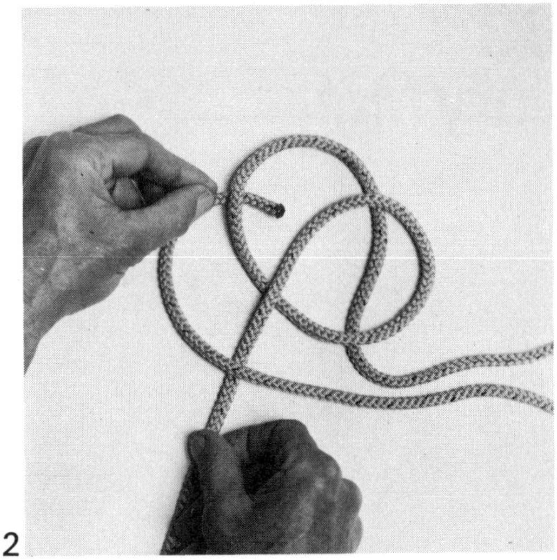

2

3

4

5

6

83 Jury Mat

This mat is based on a jury masthead knot, the bights of which are arranged as Figs 1 and 2, after which the centre bights are drawn out, over one/under one, to the extremities, Figs 3 to 6.
The new central bights, Fig 6, are crossed, the right-hand bight being on top of the left, the working end reeved through the centre of the mat from right to left, Fig 7, and returned to the start, Fig 8. It remains only to 'follow around' twice to complete the mat, Figs 9 to 12. See also Knot 24.

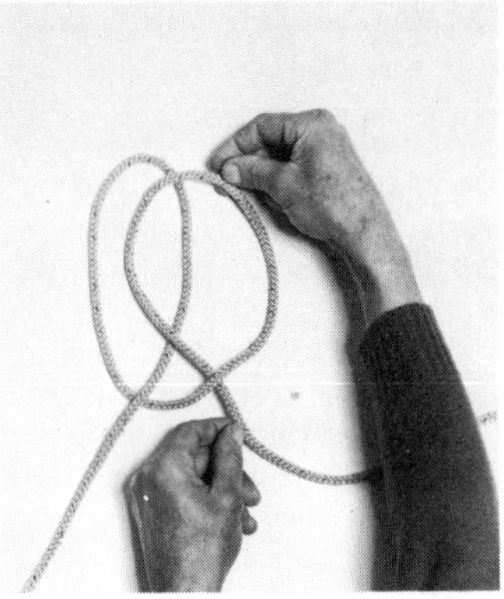
1

2

3

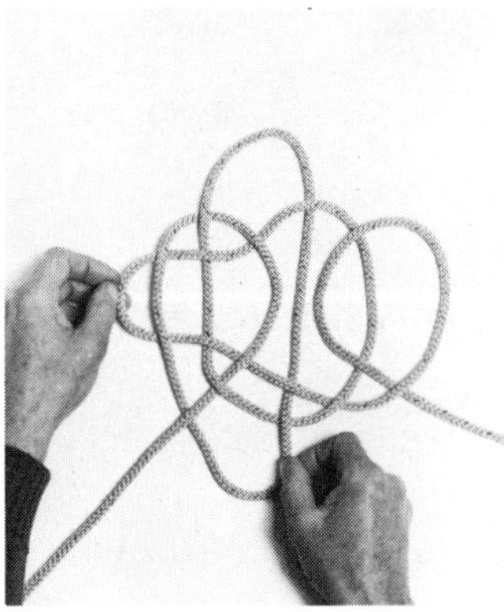
4

5

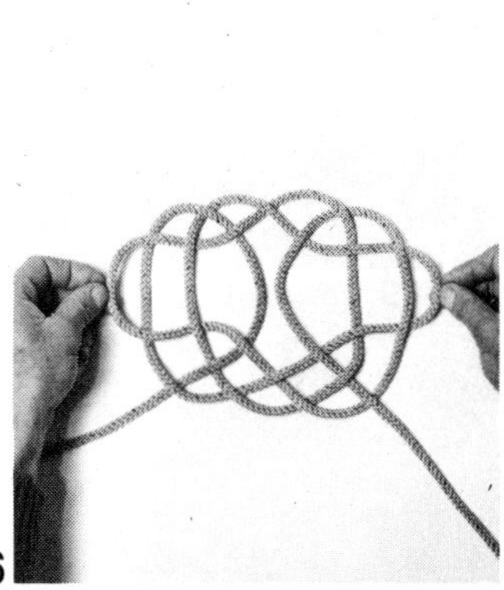
6

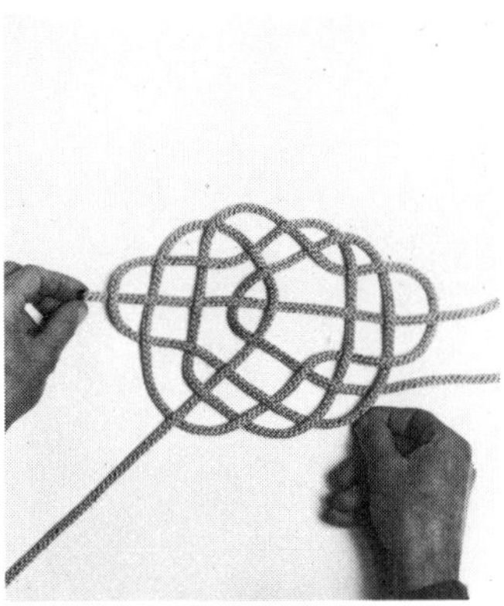
7

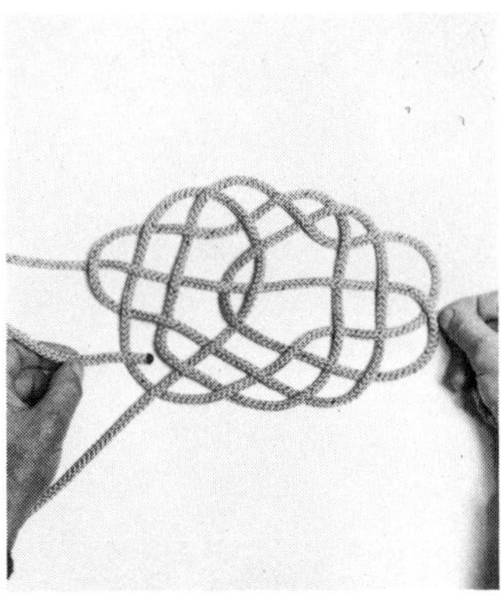
8

9

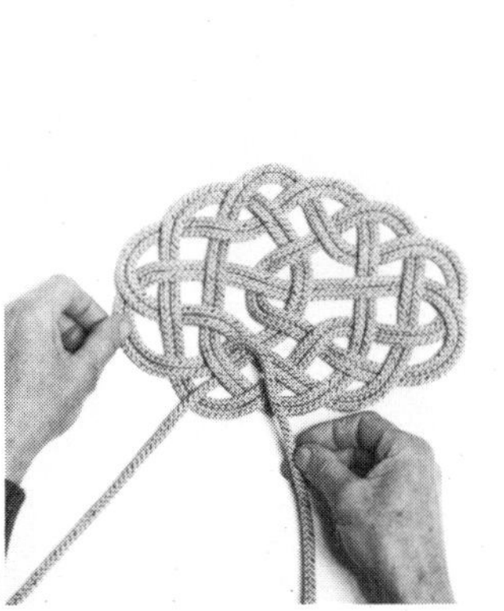
10

11

12

84 To 'Point' a Rope's End

The purpose of pointing a rope, apart from decoration, is to provide a stiff, tapered end to ensure speed and ease when reeving it through a block.

A whipping is applied, the rope unstranded, perimeter strands set aside, with the remainder tapered and bound. The method shown involves a warp (similar to Spanish hitching) which is attached, all as illustrated in Fig 1. In the 'lay' illustrated, strands are worked in pairs, Fig 2, showing their positions ready for commencement. A turn is taken with the warp, all 'up' strands brought down and 'down' strands taken up, prior to a further turn of the warp, Fig 3 showing several turns. This procedure is repeated (dropping odd strands as the taper narrows) until the point is covered, when the ends are either secured with a whipping or half-hitched around the warp, the whole being finished with a Turk's head (Knot 60), Fig 4.

The most elementary lay is one strand up/one down, but various patterns can be obtained. Three down/one up, raising the 'down' strands one at a time, produces a spiral pattern for instance. Alternatively, both types of Spanish hitching can be used or the warp dispensed with and the point covered with continuous crowning (Knot 53) or similar.

To prevent the ends of long, working strands from becoming tangled they are best bundled and secured with a clove hitch, thus allowing only sufficient working length to be drawn out as required.

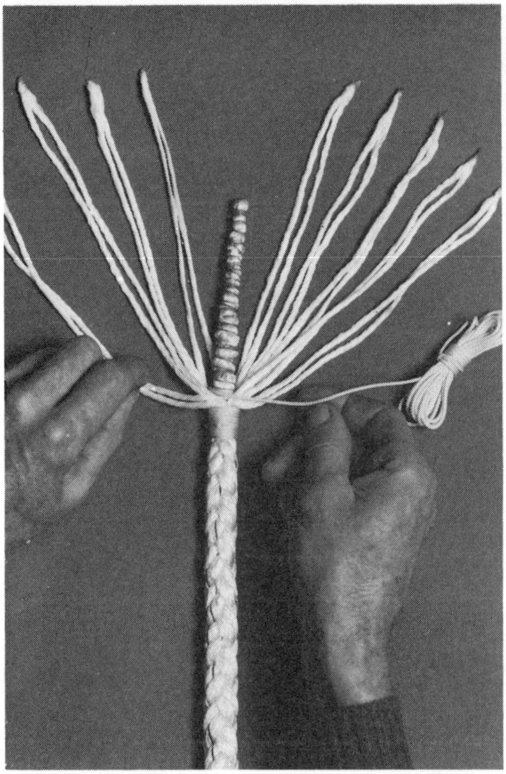
1

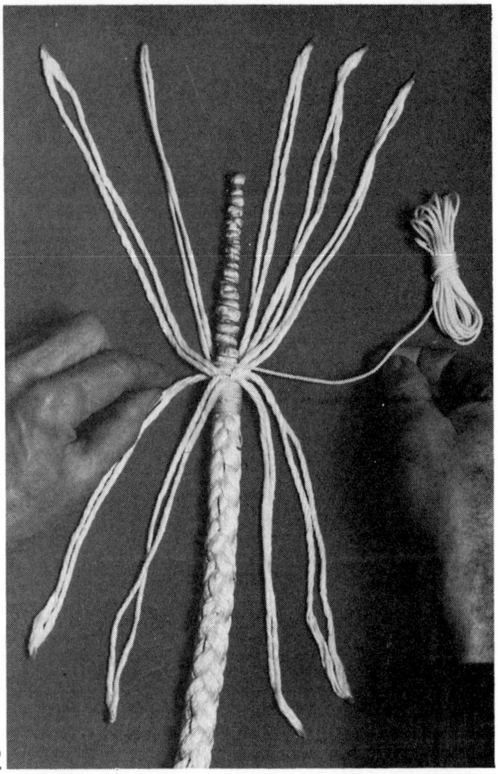
2

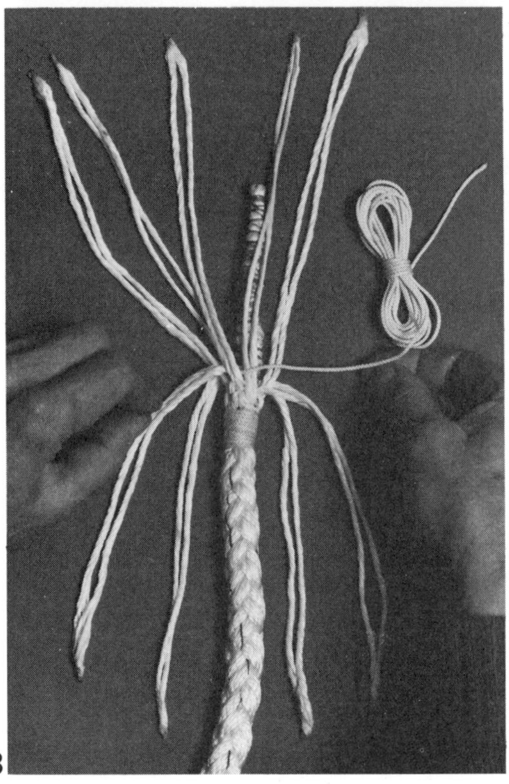
3

4

85 Blood Knot

This knot is usually associated with small cordage, particularly if slippery, making it a favourite amongst fishermen for joining nylon lines etc. The knot illustrated is the most common but there are several variations.
Figs 1 to 3 show the right-hand half of the knot, after which the process is repeated with the other end, working in the opposite direction, Figs 4 and 5.

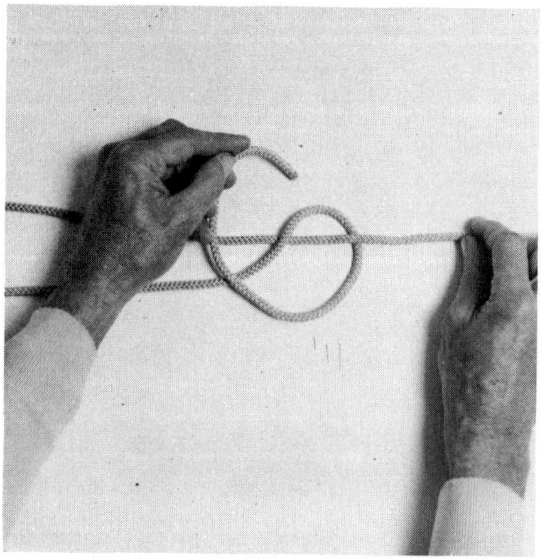

1

2

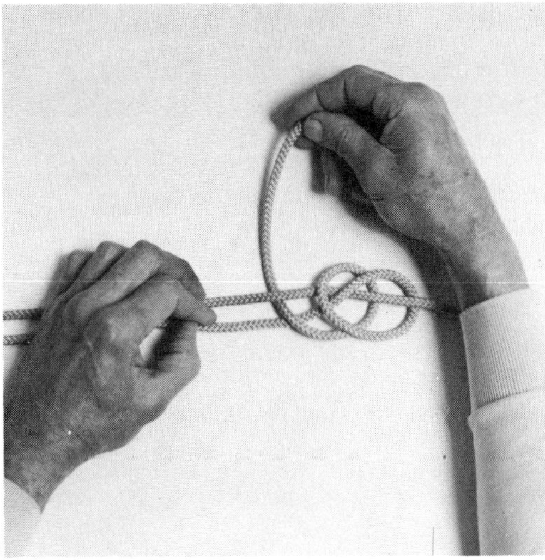
3

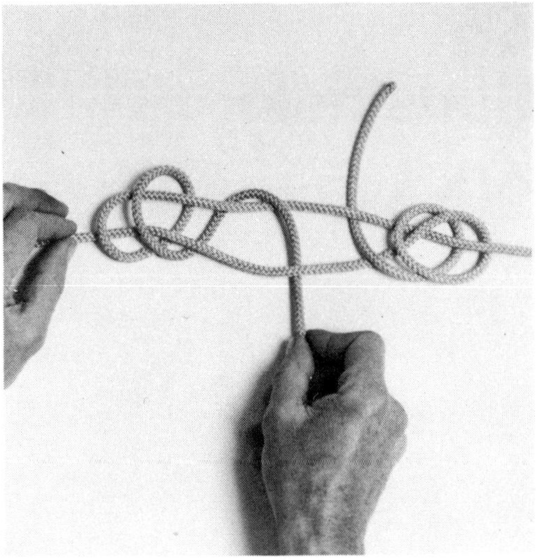
4

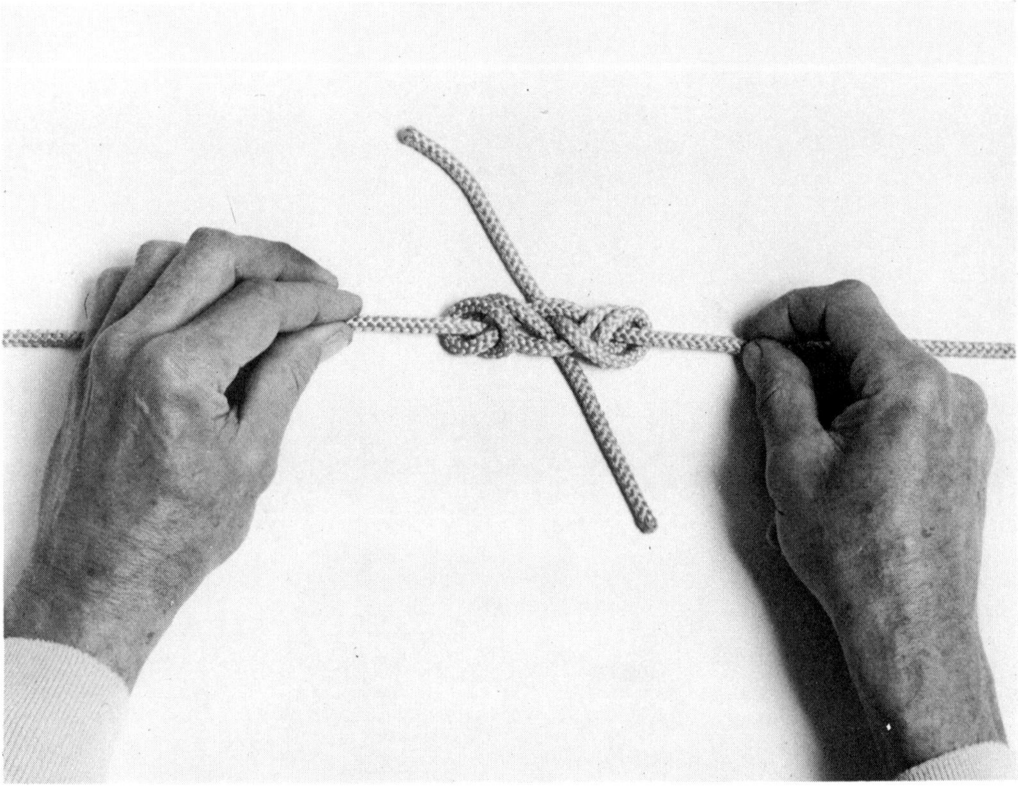
5

86 Constrictor Knot

This is an extremely useful working knot for when hauled tight it will lock solid, making it ideal for a quick lashing around, say, a bundle of rods or something similar. It is shown here as an easily applied temporary whipping, saving time, effort and sail twine.

1 

2

3

87 Waggoners' Hitch

Habitually used by lorry drivers to lash down loads it is the combination of a knot and a purchase which has been in use for many years as its name implies. The purchase is very similar to a Spanish burton (without blocks), giving a mechanical advantage which allows the standing part to be bowsed-down really tightly. The bight held on the left-hand side, Fig 7, would be around a cleat, the right-hand end providing the hauling part. It comprises half a sheep shank, Figs 1 to 3, with the bight twisted several times, Figs 4 and 5, before the bight of the hauling part is passed through, Fig 6, and arranged ready for hauling, Fig 7.

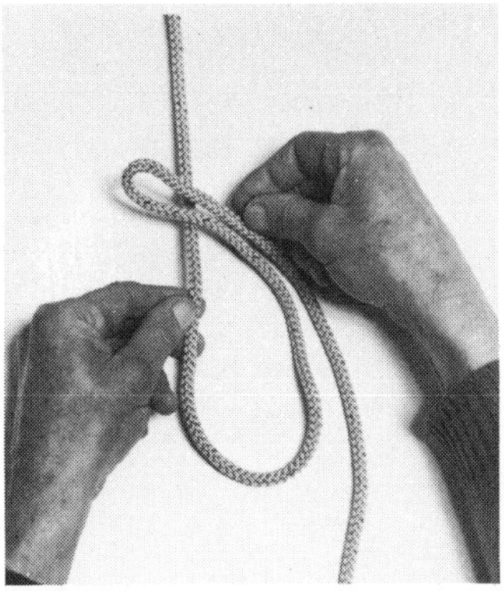
1

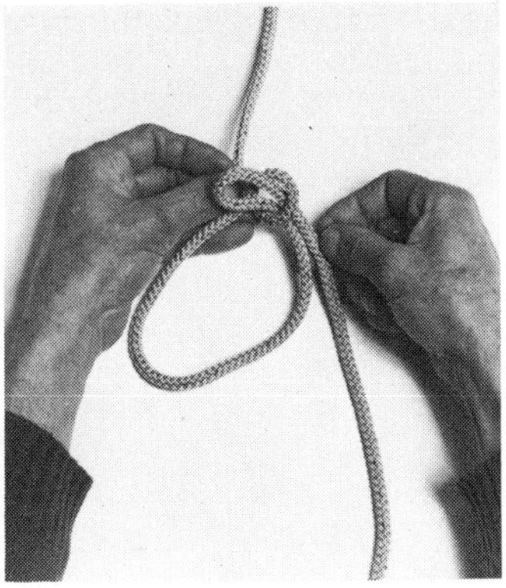
2

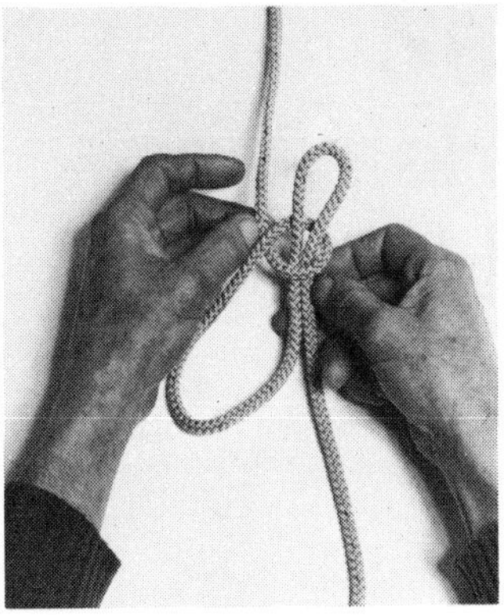
3

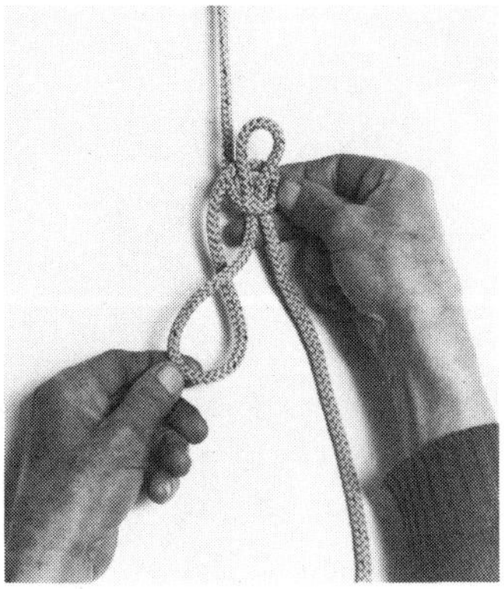
4

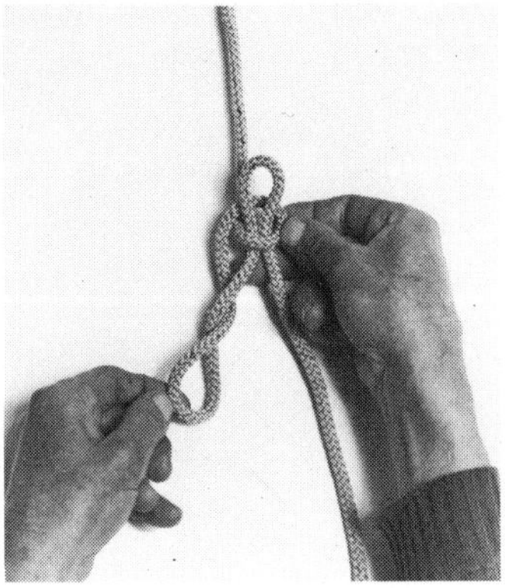
5

6

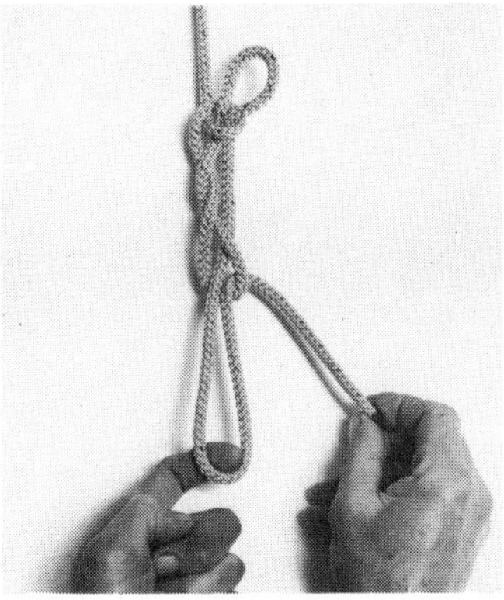
7

88 Heaving Line Bend

As the name implies this bend is used to make a heaving line fast to a hawser. It is quickly and easily applied, will not jam and being almost a slippery hitch can equally quickly be 'let go', particularly if the heaving line has a monkey's fist on its end.

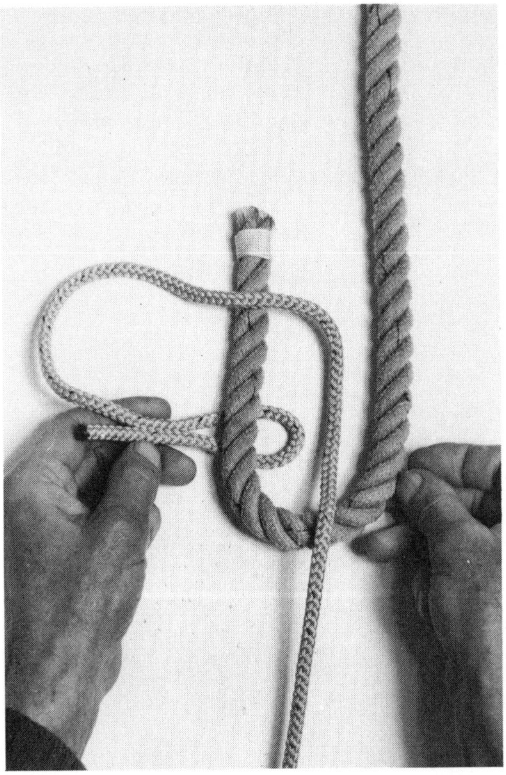
1

2

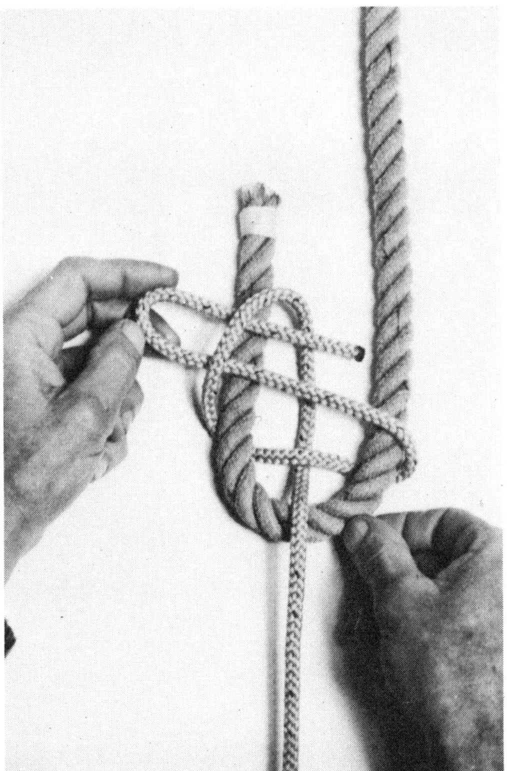
3

89 Decorative Shamrock Knot

This knot is made by working three bights and both ends, tucking each in turn under the previous one in a clockwise direction, Figs 1 to 4, with the completed first stage drawn tight, as shown in Fig 5.
The bights and ends are then crowned in the normal manner, Figs 5 and 6, whilst the finished knot, Fig 7, will be found to have the same appearance, front and back. See also Knot 14.

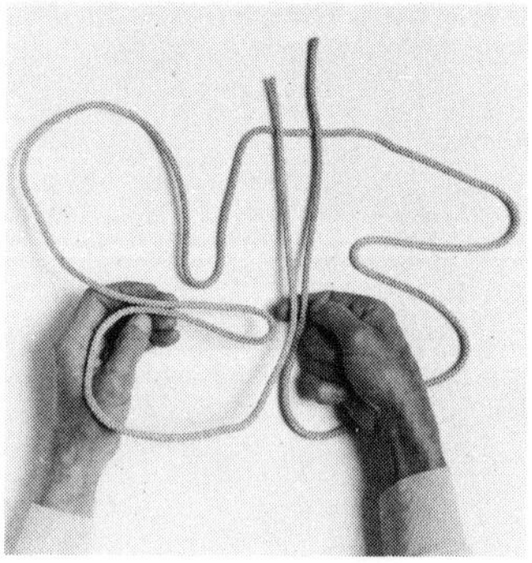
1

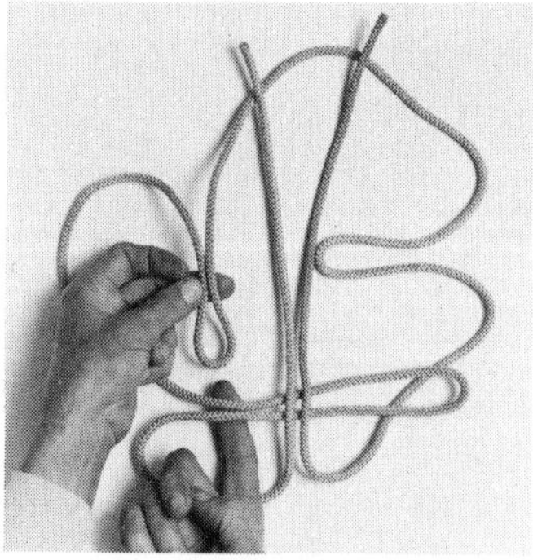
2

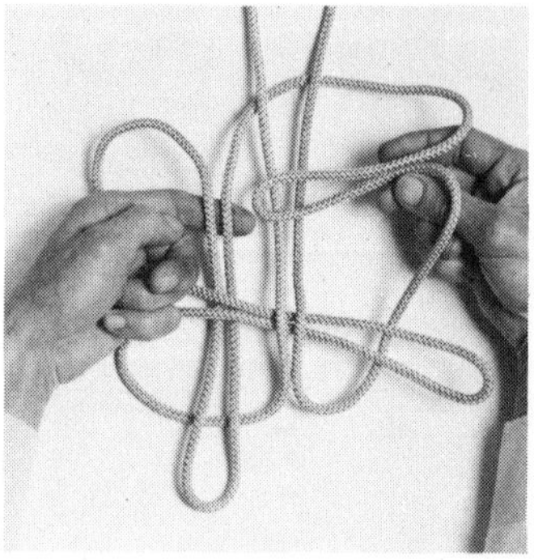
3

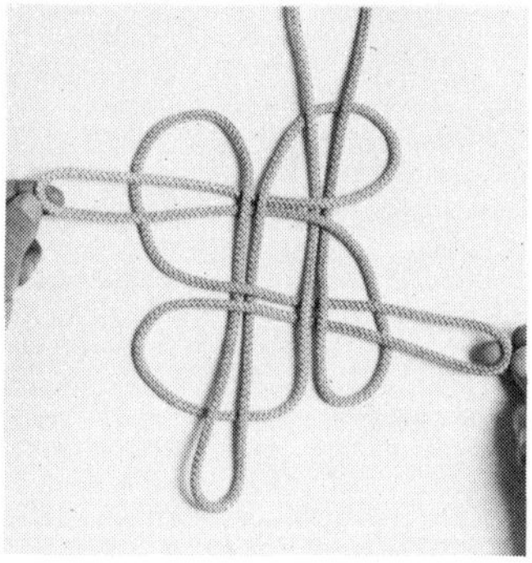
4

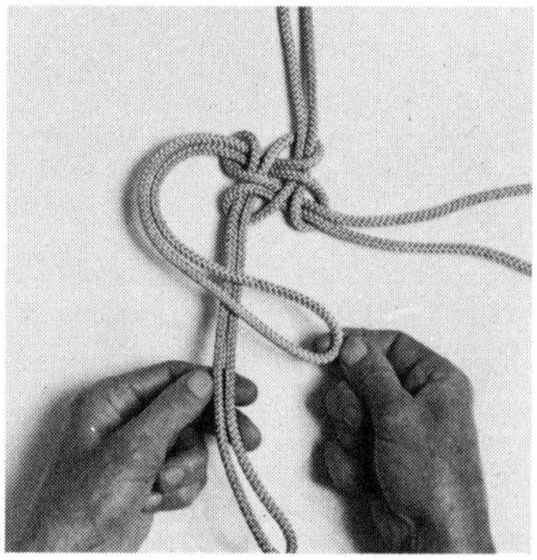
5

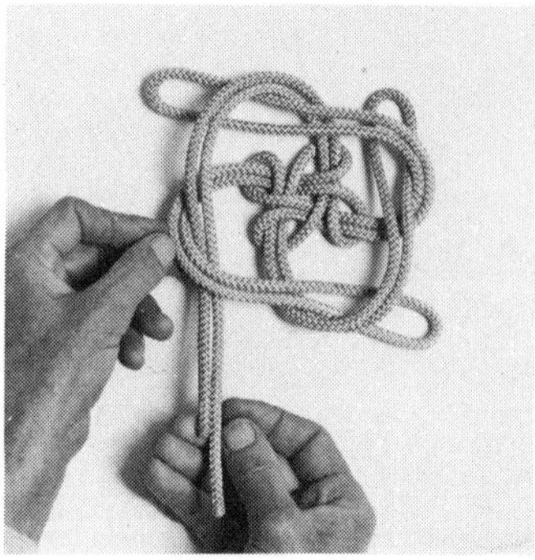
6

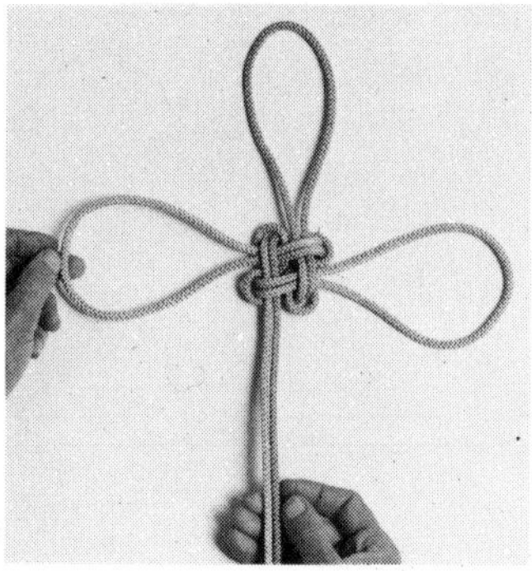
7

90 'Threef' Knot

Consider the two knots shown in Fig 3. Are they both reef knots? The lower has been called a thief knot, but to avoid confusion with the draw hitch (a fire-service term), also sometimes called a thief knot, perhaps a combination of thief and reef is preferable.
It is a 'tell-tale' knot, which if used to tie the neck of a sea-bag for instance, may not catch a thief but will indicate some interference, as the chances are that the intruder will re-tie the bag with a normal reef knot.

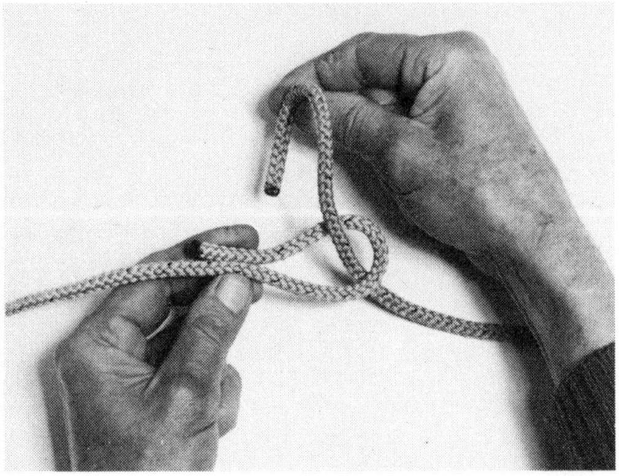

1

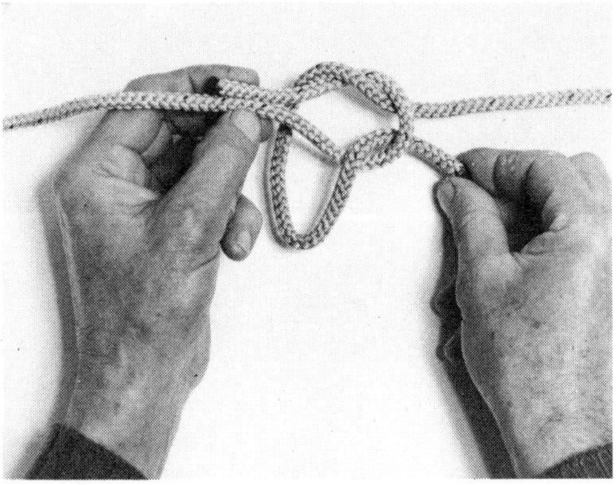

2

3

91
French Bowline

The initial moves in making a French bowline are exactly the same as for an ordinary bowline (Knot 15), the tail being laid across the standing part, Fig 1, which is lifted over to form the bight with the end automatically 'up through', Figs 2 and 3.

In the French bowline the end is taken in a complete full turn, Fig 4, before being returned up through the loop, Fig 5, around the *standing part* and back down through both loop and bight, Fig 6.

This knot, producing two bights on a single end, is particularly useful where chafing of the bight is likely or when working with wire.

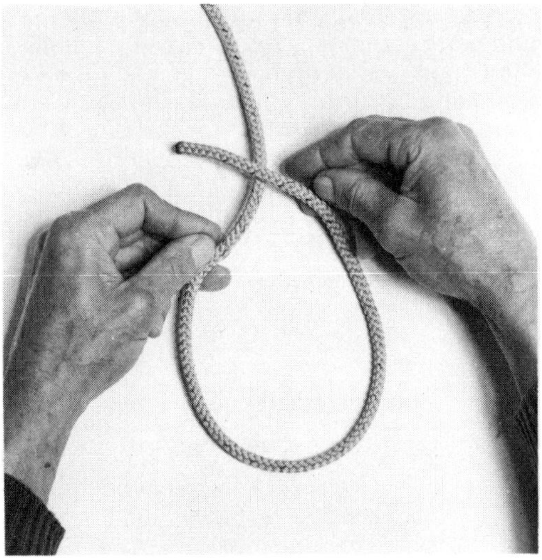
1

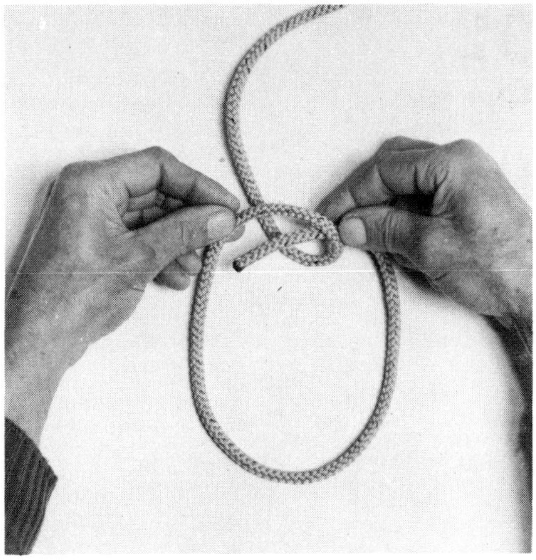
2

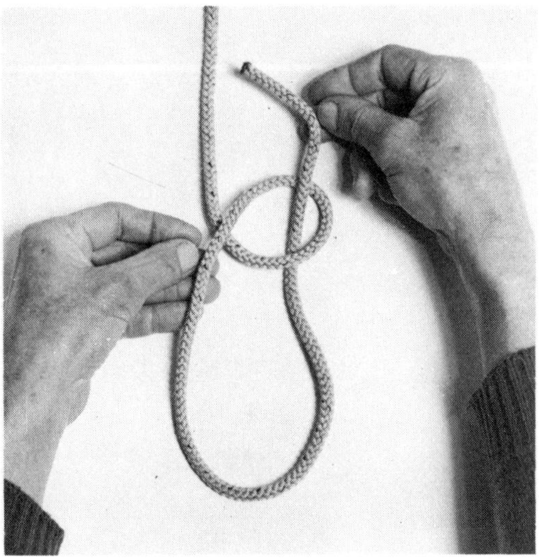
3

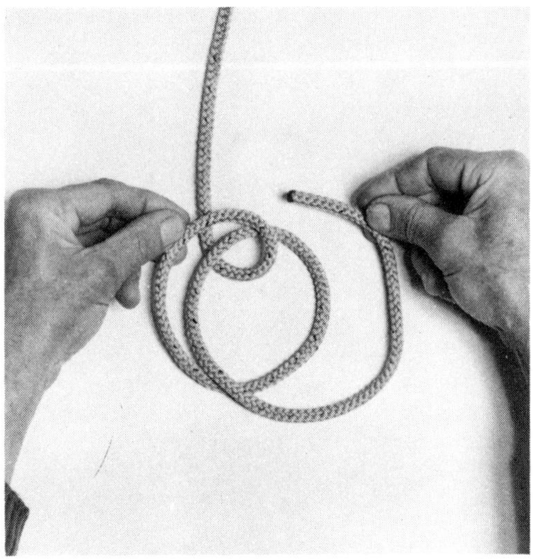
4

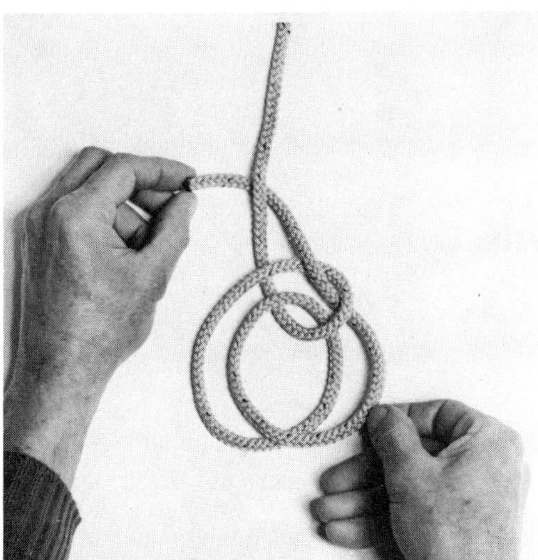
5

6

92 Spanish Bowline

This knot is made on a bight and used under conditions where both standing parts are under load. It would normally be made 'in the hands' but is shown 'flat' to simplify the layout which consists of a series of bights, Fig 1, which becomes Fig 2 by crossing the large bight clockwise. The resulting top bight, Fig 2, is taken down, over the two small bights, Figs 3 and 4, and back up behind the standing part, Fig 5. Each side of this bight is tucked down through its respective small bights below, as shown in Fig 6, then hauled tight, Fig 7.

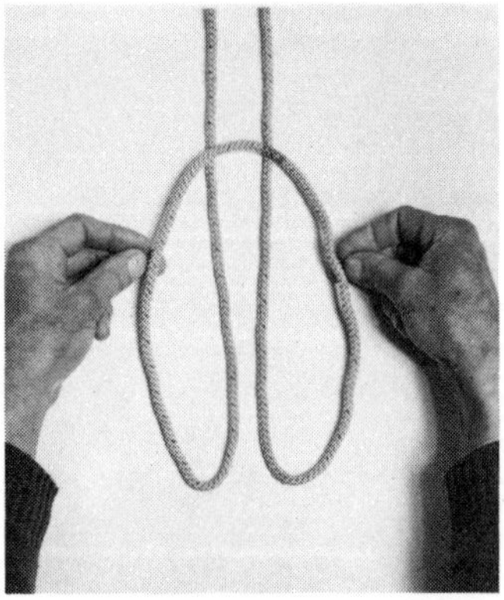
1

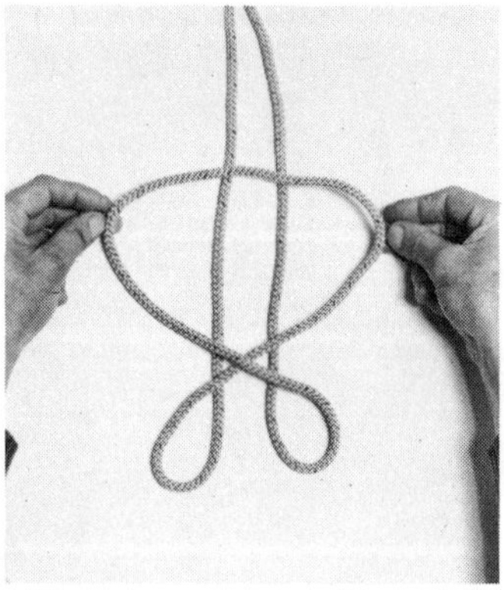
2

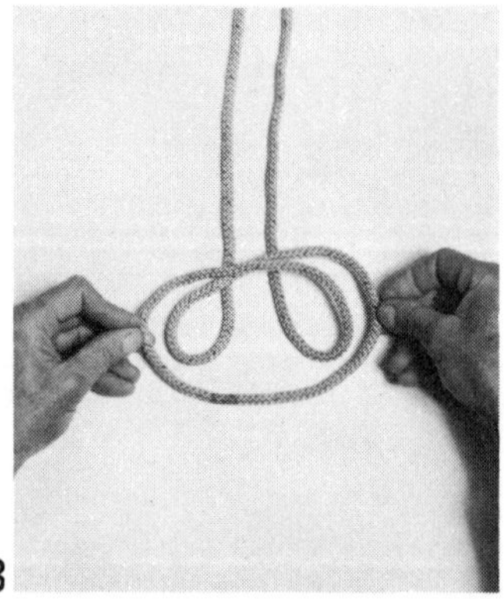
3

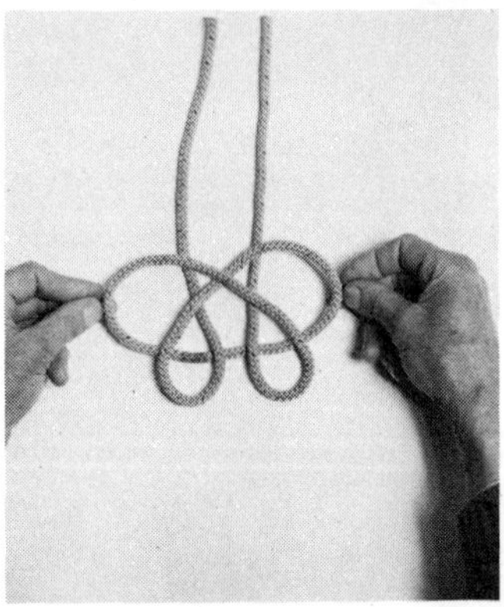
4

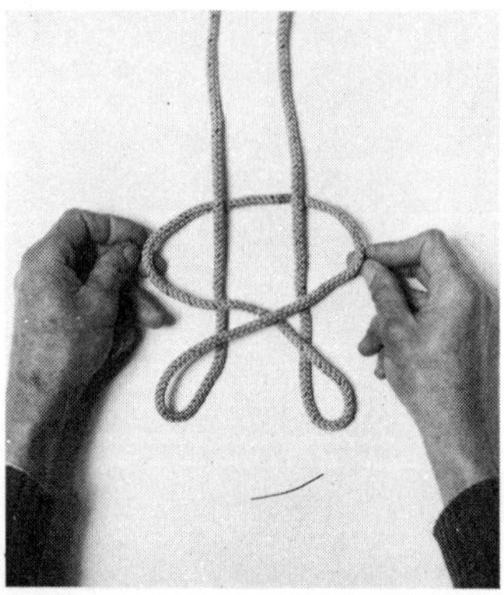
5

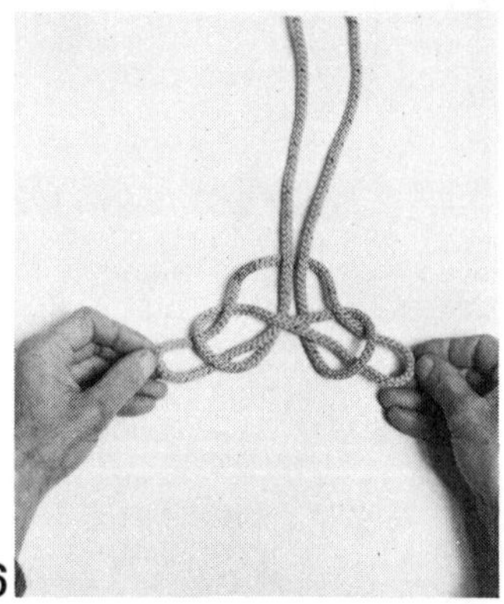
6

7

93 Small Bell Toggle, Single Stranded

Although useful on a small bell, this is something of a novelty to illustrate what can be done on a single strand, one end of which stops at the commencement of the square plait, whilst the other continues through to the tassel.

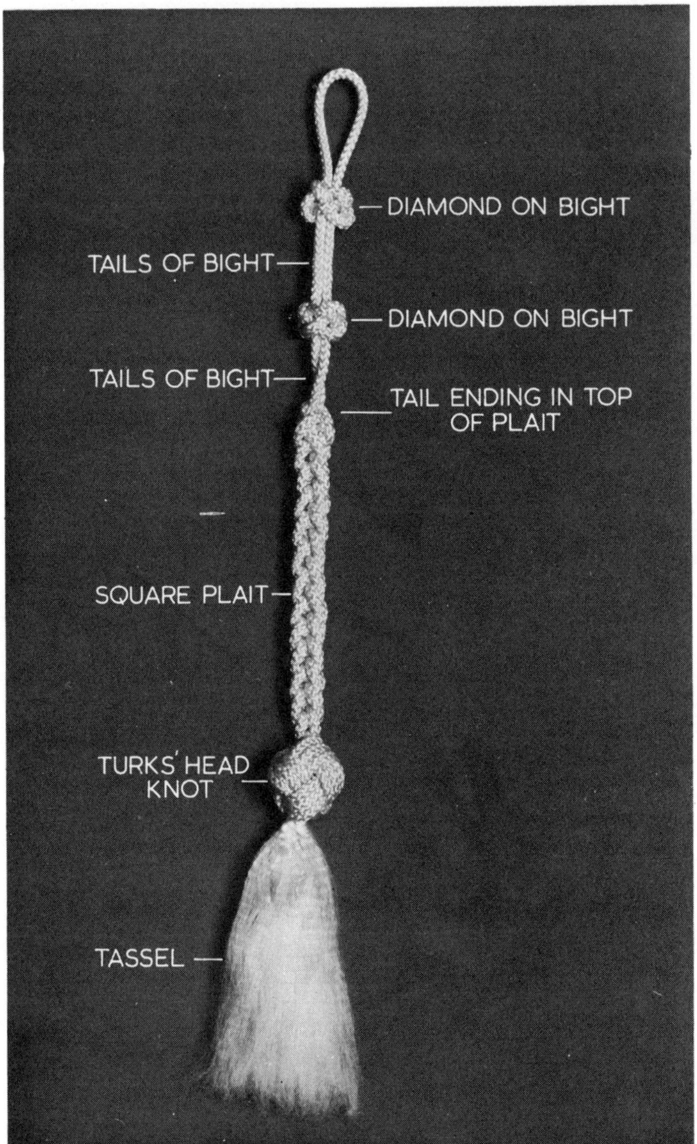

94 Large Bell Toggle, Six Stranded

This example of a typical bell toggle was made from three lengths of 3mm diameter standard eight strand plait. Two strands being 10ft long and one 9ft, all doubled to form six strands, resulting in the finished toggle being 12in long, including a 4in-long tassel.
It was made without a heart, but a wooden meat skewer forced up through on completion not only tightens the lay but also provides a useful stiffness.

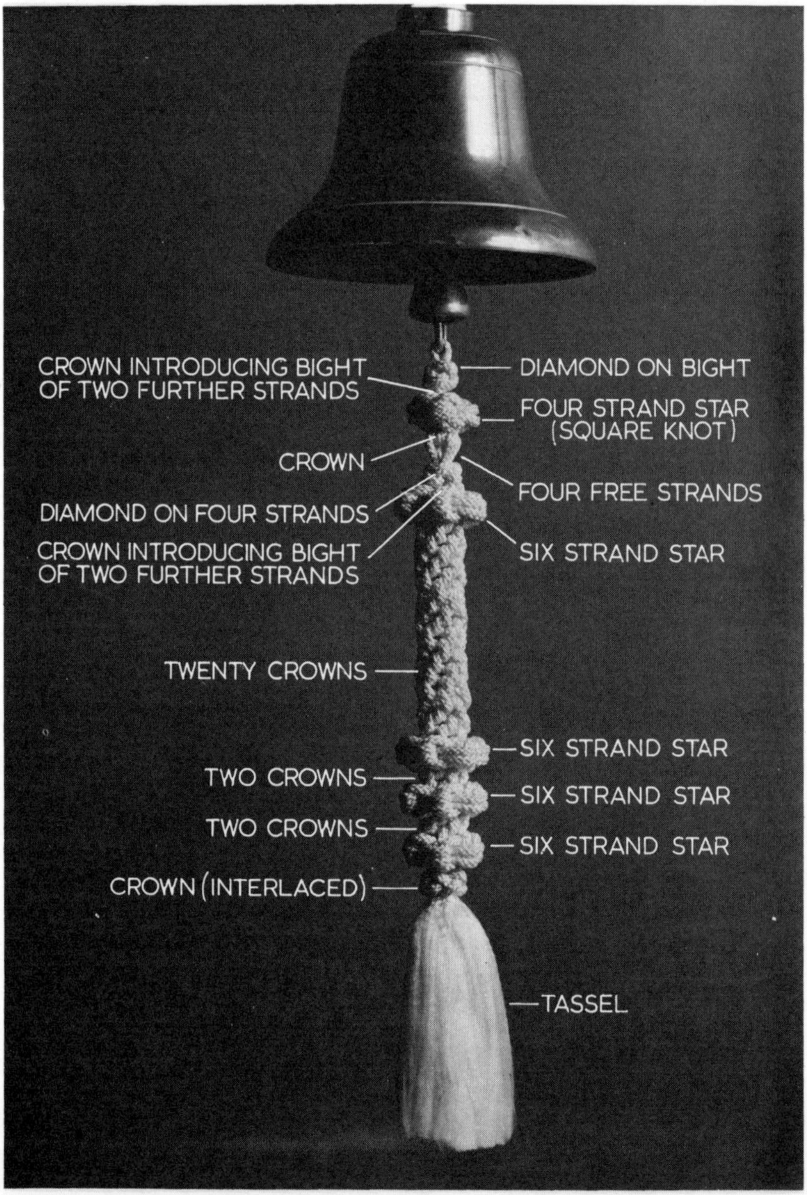

95 Suggested Layout of Multi-Unit Mat

Mats, perhaps more than any other form of decorative ropework, provide the means of creating a multitude of designs, the illustration merely showing a suggested layout comprising a jury mat centrepiece surrounded by an oval of double chain plait.
Eleven individual carrick mats surround the centrepiece followed by four runs of three-strand common sennit, the first scolloped and the remainder forming the border, the whole being sewn together with sail twine or the modern equivalent.

Glossary

Bight The bight is the curvature of a rope when its direction is changed from that of a straight line, to the maximum of a full circle.
Any point within this curvature is said to be in the bight.

Bowse-Down The act of hauling tight by means of a purchase, with or without sheave blocks.

Braided/Plaited rope as distinct from a 'laid' rope, one in which strands are woven, with or without a central core, or when a woven core is enclosed within a woven outer sheath.

Bulldog Grip A metal fitting used to clamp two wires together, side by side. It is never used on rope and consists of a shaped part into which fits a U-shaped bolt. It is tightened with two nuts, both parts of the wire being trapped between the U-bolt and the shaped part.

Cable-Laid A cable-laid rope comprises three hawser-laid ropes, each of three strands, laid up together, left handed.

Fibres The thread-like filament of vegetable or synthetic substance of which the yarns are made.
Main vegetable fibre ropes: coir, Manila, sisal, cotton and Italian hemp.
Synthetic fibre ropes: nylon, polyester, polypropylene.

Hawser A heavy mooring rope.

Hawser-Laid A rope is said to be hawser-laid when it consists of three strands, generally laid up right-handed, ie the strands are laid from left to right.

Heart The strand, impregnated in the case of wire, running through the centre of a shroud-laid rope or a wire, around which all working strands are laid.
The central core of a plaited rope may be said to be a heart, whilst some wire is made with a wire heart. (Not to be confused with the inner rope of the multiple strand, 17 by 7 and 34 by 7 construction.)

Heaving Line A light, throwing line, subsequently used to haul a heavier rope ashore.

Lay The word has two definitions when applied to rope. It can mean the direction in which the strands were twisted during the manufacture of the rope, ie, a right or left-handed lay. Alternatively, it can mean the 'nature' of the rope when, dependent on how tightly the yarns were twisted during manufacture, a rope may have a *soft, medium or hard lay.* In decorative work it means the pattern resulting from the assembled strands.

Marline (Spunyarn) This is an impregnated cordage, available in various sizes and grades of quality, used mainly to bind around a splice (serving) as a protection against wind and weather. A good-quality marline of the correct size might be used for a seizing or even as a whipping on a very large rope.

Monkey's Fist A rope ball formed on the end of a heaving line to give it carrying quality. See Knot 30.

Parcel See **Serving**

Parts, relative to a Turk's Head The number of strands seen on cross-section if the knot was cut across prior to any 'follow around'. The number of parts governs the length of the knot.

Pilot Ladder See Knot 25.

Purchase An arrangement of rope, with or without sheave blocks, whereby a mechanical advantage is obtained.

Rope Ladder See Knot 25.

Seizing A seizing is a lashing used to secure two ropes or two parts of the same rope (or wire) together, usually side by side. The size and type of cordage used to seize the ropes depends on their size and the load to which they will be subjected. There are flat, round, throat and racking seizings.

Serving Serving is normally associated with worming and parcelling and whilst a serving may be put on without either of the latter, the reverse does not apply, worming and parcelling being useless without the serving to complete the job. Worming is done by laying lengths of marline, or similar small cordage, in the valleys between the strands, infilling them and making the rope more nearly cylindrical.
The worming must be done with the lay and it is next parcelled, also with the lay, by being bandaged with a 2 to 3 inch wide strip of canvas or similar material, impregnated with tar or other waterproofing substance.
The whole is finally served by being tightly and continuously bound with marline. This is laid on with a serving mallet, a tool that not only ensures the even lay of the marline, with no gaps between turns, but also by its leverage, provides the required degree of tightness. The serving is put on against the lay and the whole is best remembered by the mnemonic, 'Worm and parcel with the lay, turn and serve the other way' (see Knot 40 for illustration).

Sheaves The grooved wheels or single wheel, set within the framework of a block.

Shrouds The standing rigging from a mast to the sides of a vessel as distinct from the 'fore and aft' standing rigging.

Shroud-Laid A shroud-laid rope consists of four strands, laid right-handed around a central heart.

Stage A plank of timber, when suspended as a working platform, with or without horns (see Knot 26).

Standing Part The remaining part of a rope other than the ends, a bight or that amount used in forming a knot, usually that part which is under load. In a reeved tackle, the standing parts are those parts of rope between the two blocks, the remainder becoming the hauling part.

Stopper (**To stopper off**) See Knot 18.

Strands Laid yarns. The appropriate number of strands being laid together to form the finished rope.

Tack The lower, forward corner of a fore and aft sail.

Tail (**or tail end**) The extreme end of a rope or any of its individual strands.

Topping Lift Part of the running rigging from the mast to the outer end of a boom to relieve the sail from the weight of the latter, usually associated with older vessels. Set in pairs, one each side of the sail.

Tucking *Against the Lay* The action of passing the tail end of a strand over a strand of the standing part and under the next, in the opposite direction to the lay of the rope.
With the Lay The action of passing the tail end of a strand around any strand of the standing part in the same direction as the lay of that strand.

Turns, relative to a Turks' Head The number of 'cross-overs' made before the working end returns to meet the standing part, in parallel, for the first time. The diameter of the cylinder, in relation to the diameter of the cordage used, governs the number of turns required.

Whipping A series of turns of sail twine or similar thread, forming a lashing at the end of a rope or any of its individual strands to prevent fraying.

Worming See serving

Yarns Woven fibres laid up together.

Index of Knot Numbers

(The word 'knot' is not included in the entries. Thus 'Decorative shamrock knot' is listed as 'decorative shamrock' but all other entries are listed as named in text: *eg* 'eye splice', sheet bend' etc.)